The Night Malcolm X Spoke
at the Oxford Union

The Night Malcolm X Spoke at the Oxford Union

A Transatlantic Story of Antiracist Protest

Stephen Tuck

with a foreword by
Henry Louis Gates Jr.

UNIVERSITY OF CALIFORNIA PRESS

The publisher gratefully acknowledges the generous support of the African American Studies Endowment Fund of the University of California Press Foundation, which was established by a major gift from the George Gund Foundation.

University of California Press, one of the most distinguished university presses in the United States, enriches lives around the world by advancing ·scholarship in the humanities, social sciences, and natural sciences. Its activities are supported by the UC Press Foundation and by philanthropic contributions from individuals and institutions. For more information, visit www.ucpress.edu.

University of California Press
Oakland, California

All quoted speeches by Malcolm X are from *Malcolm X: Collected Speeches, Debates and Interviews (1960–1965)*, edited by Sandeep Atwal, and are available online at http://malcolmxfiles.blogspot.co.uk/p/malcolm-x-e-book.html.

CIP data for this title is on file at the Library of Congress.

ISBN 978-0-520-27933-9

Manufactured in the United States of America

23 22 21 20 19 18 17 16 15 14
10 9 8 7 6 5 4 3 2 1

In keeping with a commitment to support environmentally responsible and sustainable printing practices, UC Press has printed this book on Natures Natural, a fiber that contains 30% post-consumer waste and meets the minimum requirements of ANSI/NISO Z39.48–1992 (R 1997) (*Permanence of Paper*).

For my mother, Norah, and in memory of my
father, George (1930–2013)

Yes. One thing . . . travel always broadens one's scope. Travel does.

—Malcolm X, interview with Les Crane, December 27, 1964

Brother Malcolm was our manhood, our living, Black manhood! . . . our own Black shining Prince, who didn't hesitate to die, because he loved us so.

—Magazine of the *Black Eagles,* a British Black Power group, 1965 (quoting eulogy to Malcolm X by Ossie Davis)

CONTENTS

FOREWORD

This year, the American public is commemorating the fiftieth anniversary of the Beatles' "British Invasion," broadcast on CBS's *Ed Sullivan Show,* which delightfully electrified the spirit of a heart-heavy nation, still in shock and mourning over the assassination of John F. Kennedy. But 1964 also witnessed the reverse transatlantic journey of a man once known as Malcolm Little—better known as Malcolm X—in a revolutionary and more substantive performance at the legendary Oxford Union, an Oxbridge staple that has been showcasing another form of entertainment since long before Ed Sullivan hit the air. In fact, the Union, now in its 190th year, has hosted figures as diverse as Gladstone and the Dalai Lama, with Einstein, Churchill, Reagan, and Tutu in between. On the night of December 3, 1964, Malcolm X arrived to debate the topic of "extremism in the defense of liberty," in a world swirling with social struggle in the United States, a nascent war in Vietnam, and the awkward birth of independence in postcolonial Africa. His performance is as iconic as any in the Oxonian pantheon of great debates, and now, thanks to Stephen Tuck, we can revisit that stage and see, hear, and grasp the words exchanged on that historic evening.

These days in our country, we lament that political debates are all too often the pitiful middle course between the hype and spin that precedes and follows each side's carefully crafted talking points. But back then, in the black-and-white days before instant news, social media, 24/7 cable news, and worldwide Internet coverage, speakers on their feet could riff, improvise, and develop positions in the thrust and parry of spontaneous, at times raucous, discourse. Malcolm X was a genius of this medium, and the Oxford Union represented the pinnacle of the tradition dating back to its founding in 1829, when slavery was still legal in the British Empire and expanding ever more deeply in Malcolm X's native United States. Fifteen years after his landmark debate performance, I was humbled to receive a doctorate degree from Oxford's rival, the University of Cambridge, but I always marveled at this venerable tradition "down the road." There is no other marketplace for ideas like it in the world.

In an ironic twist, Malcolm X was invited to the Union to defend the position that former U.S. presidential candidate Barry Goldwater had staked out in his acceptance speech at the 1964 Republican National Convention—an event that, to many, marked the dawn of the conservative movement in America: "I would remind you that extremism in the defense of liberty is no vice. And let me remind you also that moderation in the pursuit of justice is no virtue." But Malcolm surely knew Senator Goldwater had not said anything new in those quickly famous lines, and so he didn't waste any time referring to him during his debate. The truth is, Malcolm's signature sentiment "by any means necessary" hearkened back to the African American abolitionist movement's earliest phase during the founding days of the Oxford Union, none more famously than David Walker's 1829 *Appeal . . . to the Coloured People of the World United States, but in Particular, and Very Expressly, to Those of the United States of America,* in which he urged slaves to rise up against their masters and resist efforts to uproot African Americans from their American homeland. Malcolm X followed in that tradition (interestingly, both men had spent time living in Boston), but for him, the stakes were not about resisting emigration but forging an international alliance among those on the fragile side of the transition from Jim Crow and colonialism to equal rights and independence. As he spoke, the Civil Rights Movement in America was about to make a most dramatic turn toward voting rights in Selma, Alabama, and Malcolm was working out what lay beyond the bridge.

Looking at the video of his performance, one sees mainly white faces in the audience, a tuxedo here and there against wood-paneled chambers. But in this rich volume, Stephen Tuck shows us that Oxford was anything but insulated from the gales of change in 1964 and that, as out of place as he might have appeared to some within the frame, Malcolm X stood tall as an honored, respected guest, invited by the Union's second West Indian student president, Eric Anthony Abrahams. Abrahams, a twenty-four-year-old Rhodes Scholar, went on to become the first black television reporter at the BBC before assuming various leadership roles in the Jamaican government.

As unique a moment as it was, however, Malcolm X's debate performance flowed out of a much longer Anglo-American narrative of slavery to freedom, reaching back to the eighteenth-century black British abolitionist author and lecturer Olaudah Equiano and the American-born abolitionist Frederick Douglass. Douglass in particular successfully leveraged the distance between England and the New World to indict American slavery for twenty eventful months between 1845 and 1847. There, inside the king's realm, Douglass delivered more than three hundred antislavery speeches across England, Ireland, and Scotland. Like Malcolm X, Douglass had cast off his slave master's name, both out of protest and in an attempt to establish a certain protective anonymity to mask his identity as a fugitive slave.

A century after emancipation, Malcolm X was a different kind of fugitive. Not only had he broken with the Nation of Islam and his leader and former mentor, Elijah Muhammad; he was also viewed by many Americans (even those inside the Civil Rights Movement) as a violent extremist, in part based on his appearance in the 1959 CBS television documentary *The Hate That Hate Produced.* After an intensive pilgrimage to Mecca in the spring of 1964, in which he began to turn more fully to an international human rights perspective, Malcolm X seized on the Oxford Union invitation as a chance to correct the record and, in so doing, turn the very brand of extremism that had been fixed on him against his accusers, while exposing a violent hypocrisy in society that had made racism and war seem moderate, prudent, and measured compared with blacks' resistance to their own oppression.

In this way, Malcolm X's connection to Frederick Douglass ran deeper than a change of name. Both men, blessed with a keen instinct for public relations, recognized the unique opportunity of being able to paint a picture of home from an ocean away, of broadcasting a message with the potential to pressure their government from without: Douglass fighting the American slavocracy, Malcolm X fighting the turmoil of American apartheid, terror in the Congo, and other racialized crisis points around the globe. But as often happens, in the process of travel and a most cosmopolitan exchange of ideas, Douglass and Malcolm X were themselves changed.

As Douglass movingly explained in his farewell address to the people of England at London Tavern on March 30, 1847: "I go back to the United States not as I landed here—I came a slave; I go back a free man. I came here a thing—I go back a human being. I came here despised and maligned—I go back with reputation and celebrity; for I am sure that if the Americans were to believe one tithe of all that has been said in this country respecting me, they would certainly admit me to be a little better than they had hitherto supposed I was."

Stephen Tuck's book is about that same journey taken by Malcolm X. While his debate at the Oxford Union is less remembered than, say, the Kennedy-Nixon debates of 1960, it was broadcast on the BBC and thus preserved forever the testimony of where Malcolm was headed as the self-proclaimed leader of Islam in America, as he described himself to Nasser. The change exploding outside the debate hall was dramatic that night: two days earlier, the Johnson Administration had met to discuss the bombing campaign in Vietnam, and early that very morning, at the University of California at Berkeley, eight hundred protesters taking part in the student Free Speech Movement were arrested for a sit-in at an administration building. A week later, the Rev. Dr. Martin Luther King Jr. would receive the Nobel Peace Prize and the Cuban revolutionary Che Guevara would address the United Nations General Assembly while the U.S. Supreme Court weighed the impact of the 1964 Civil Rights Act on public accommodations. To that world, of that moment, Malcolm X was delivering his message of extremism in the name of international human rights. Unlike Dr. King (whom Malcolm X fiercely criticized for being "too soft"), Mal-

colm projected less the prophet's voice than that of the pros-
ecutor exposing crimes few in the media admitted to seeing.
Malcolm X's brand of extremism, he said that night, was "intel-
ligently directed extremism," and he manifested it with his jab-
bing finger, his confident laughter, his trim black suit, his nar-
row tie and starched white shirt, those trademark professorial
glasses. In a sense, Malcolm was the political face of an aesthetic
triumvirate that included Muhammad Ali and Miles Davis, each
in their own ways expounding and improvising upon what they
saw as the "castration of the black man."

Here are some of my favorite lines he tossed off that night:

> Anytime anyone is enslaved or in any way deprived of his liberty,
> that person, as a human being, as far as I'm concerned he is justified
> to resort to whatever methods necessary to bring about his liberty
> again.

> When a black man strikes back he's an extremist, he's supposed to
> sit passively and have no feelings, be nonviolent, and love his enemy
> no matter what kind of attack, verbal or otherwise, he's supposed to
> take it. But if he stands up in any way and tries to defend himself,
> then he's an extremist.

> I have more respect for a man who lets me know where he stands,
> even if he's wrong, than the one comes up like an angel and is noth-
> ing but a devil.

> Out of the thirty-six committees that govern the foreign and
> domestic direction of that [U.S.] government, twenty-three are in
> the hands of southern racialists.

> The racialist never understands a peaceful language, the racialist
> never understands the nonviolent language, the racialist has spoken
> his type of language to us for over four hundred years. We have
> been the victim of his brutality, we are the ones who face his dogs

who tear the flesh from our limbs, only because we want to enforce the Supreme Court decision. We are the ones who have our skulls crushed, not by the Ku Klux Klan, but by policemen, all because we want to enforce what they call the Supreme Court decision. We are the ones upon whom water hoses are turned on, practically so hard that it rips the clothes from our backs—not men, but the clothes from the backs of women and children, you've seen it yourself. All because we want to enforce what they call the law. Well, any time you live in a society supposedly and it doesn't enforce its own laws, because the color of a man's skin happens to be wrong, then I say those people are justified to resort to any means necessary to bring about justice where the government can't give them justice.

I read once, passingly, about a man named Shakespeare. I only read about him passingly, but I remember one thing he wrote that kind of moved me. He put it in the mouth of Hamlet, I think it was, who said "to be or not to be." He was in doubt about something. Whether it was nobler, in the mind of man, to suffer the slings and arrows of outrageous fortune—moderation—or to take up arms against the sea of troubles and, by opposing, end them. And I go for that; if you take up arms you'll end it, but if you sit around and wait for the one who is in power to make up his mind that he should end it, you'll be waiting a long time. And in my opinion, the young generation of whites, blacks, browns, whatever else there is, you're living at a time of extremism, a time of revolution, a time when there's got to be a change, people in power have misused it, and now there has to be a change. And a better world has to be built, and the only way it's going to be built is with extreme methods. And I, for one, will join in with anyone—don't care what color you are—as long as you want to change this miserable condition that exists on this earth.

Technically, Malcolm X may have lost the debate on points, but listening to him turn Shakespeare and Patrick Henry to his advantage is all the more poignant because, shortly after this hour of apotheosis, he exited the world stage—gunned down in his home city of New York by Black Muslim assassins on February 21, 1965. Tragically, the Oxford Union debate was one of the last gospels Malcolm X was able to preach to the world.

It is especially powerful for me to listen to this debate half a century later, since I was just fourteen at the time, a middle school student in eastern West Virginia with scant traces of teaching in my school about African or African American history and absolutely no idea that, just a decade later, I would move to England to study English literature as a graduate student. At the Oxford Union, Malcolm X helped articulate the new struggle that was unfolding for both Africans and African Americans at a time of revolution—which, by the time I arrived in Cambridge in 1973, was in full bloom. There I met two men who would become close and dear lifetime friends and mentors, the philosopher Kwame Anthony Appiah and the playwright and activist Wole Soyinka. Tuck's splendid book connects me to the energy of the racial climate at Oxbridge in those men's generation.

Of course, the only thing better than listening to this debate would have been the chance to watch it unfolding live, and then to interview Malcolm X myself. But in these pages, Stephen Tuck gives us more than his words; he delivers up the "hidden transcript" of a debate held when debating mattered, the meaning and weight behind each *rat-a-tat-tat* of Malcolm's verbal machine gun. He shows us the man who hustled his way through youth and learned to debate in prison, a prisoner and Muslim convert who read incessantly and developed his rhetorical skills with the cold walls of confinement against his back.

Following Malcolm's assassination, Dr. King issued a statement: "We must face the tragic fact that Malcolm X was murdered by a morally inclement climate. It reveals that our society is still sick enough to express dissent through murder. We have not learned to disagree without being violently disagreeable."

However one might score Malcolm X's performance that December evening in 1964, or his legacy of struggle, I hope we can all agree that at the Oxford Union, Malcolm admirably demonstrated how one meets the highest standard of verbal exchange, using his uncommonly resonant voice to defend the black pursuit of liberty and equality in the extreme.

Henry Louis Gates Jr.
Alphonse Fletcher University Professor,
Harvard University
Cambridge, Massachusetts
Spring 2014

ACKNOWLEDGMENTS

This book was a great pleasure to research and write, and there are many people I would like to thank for making it so.

Dozens of participants in the story shared their time and memories. There are too many to list here, but it was a privilege, and a treat, to talk with former students from Britain and around the world, members of Malcolm X's circle, and activists in the British and American civil rights movements. I was taken aback by how open people were about these events. Three moments stand out: when Eric Abrahams's daughter, Tara, in Jamaica, shared her father's answers to questions when he was too frail to write himself; when Louis Nthenda, a Zambian now in a writer's club in Japan, retold the story of meeting Malcolm X in Kenya; and when I spoke on this topic in Washington, D.C., only to have Malcolm X's former publicist, A. Peter Bailey, come and introduce himself and share his thoughts and materials.

Numerous colleagues have given advice along the way. Again, there are far too many to name, but particular thanks go to Anne-Marie Angelo, Tony Badger, Dan Brockington,

Shakina Chinedu, John Davis, Jed Fazakarley, Kevin Gaines, Joshua Guild, Robin Kelley, Martin Klimke, Brian Kwoba, Kennetta Perry, Joe Street, Imaobong Umoren, and Clive Webb for helpful comments at just the right moments. My thanks, too, to colleagues at the Hutchins Center, Harvard, and at Pembroke College, in the history faculty and in the Race and Resistance network at Oxford, for their support. I am also grateful for the many comments from panelists, commentators, and members of the audiences at talks I have given, and for suggestions from my students at Oxford and those who have attended the UNIQ Widening Participation race and protest summer school.

Without exception, the librarians at the Schomburg Library in Harlem, the Widener Library at Harvard University, the Library of Congress in Washington, D.C., the Ralph Bunche Library at UCLA, the Bodleian Library and various college libraries at the University of Oxford, the County Records Office in Oxford, the Sivanandan Collection at Warwick University, the Public Records Office in London, and the Institute of Race Relations in London were helpful beyond the call of duty. Many suggested materials that I hadn't known about, and that proved to be invaluable. All quotations from speeches are taken from Sandeep Atwal, ed., *Malcolm X: Collected Speeches, Debates and Interviews (1960–1965)*. My thanks to Sandeep Atwal for making these speeches available to me.

Niels Hooper at University of California Press had the idea to turn this story into a short book in time for the fiftieth anniversary of Malcolm X's visit. Niels and his team have given great encouragement and advice along the way, and managed a tight timetable with good grace. In Oxford, Laura-Jayne Cannell has been a terrific research assistant. I am also grateful to Anna and

Adam Fowler for helping to get this story onto the radio, and to Anne Canwright for translating the manuscript into American.

Pembroke College, Oxford, kindly agreed to fund a symposium to commemorate these events of fifty years ago. It was a generous and important thing to do. I read recently of a comment overheard by students in Oxford—"It is Malcolm X, right, not Malcolm the tenth?" To be sure, historical memory fades fast, but in this case we should remember some uncomfortable truths about Oxford and about British and American history, even as we celebrate the triumphs.

Above all, I wish to thank my family. Finishing this manuscript used up a fair few late nights and weekends. Katie took it all in her stride, as ever, which meant that Amy, Sam, Anna, and Molly seemed to find the fact that Dad was busy writing a story somewhat interesting rather than too much of a problem—even if the best bit was when it was over. I hope one day they enjoy reading it and learn from it. Best of all, because it is short and sounds intriguing, Katie said—in contrast to my previous books—she just might read this one too.

Prologue

A Black Revolutionary Meets Historic Oxford

On the evening of December 3, 1964, a most unlikely figure was invited to speak at the University of Oxford Union's end-of-term "Queen and Country" debate: Mr. Malcolm X. The Oxford Union was the most prestigious student debating organization in the world, regularly welcoming heads of state and stars of screen.[1] It was also, by tradition, the student arm of the British establishment—the training ground for the politically ambitious offspring of Britain's "better classes." Malcolm X, by contrast, had a reputation for revolution and danger. As the *Sun,* a widely read British tabloid, explained to readers in a large-font caption under a photograph of the American visitor: "He wants a separate Negro state in which coloured people could live undisturbed. And many Americans believe he would use violence to get it."[2] Certainly the FBI did. Its file on Malcolm X, opened in 1953, expanded by the week as he toured Africa during the second half of 1964, giving a series of uncompromising speeches and meeting with heads of state to seek their support in calling for the United Nations to intervene in U.S. race relations.[3]

The peculiarity of his presence in Oxford was not lost on Malcolm X. "I remember clearly that the minute I stepped off the train, I felt I'd suddenly backpedaled into Mayflower-time," he told a friend later. Fresh from visiting newly independent nations in Africa, Malcolm X sensed that in Oxford "age was just seeping out of the pores of every stone. The students were wearing caps and gowns as if they graduated the first day they arrived . . . and they were riding bicycles that should've been dumped long ago." Initially, he wondered whether he had made a mistake accepting the invitation.[4]

At times, Malcolm X's visit proved to be comically awkward. He was met at the rail station by, among others, the (white) Union secretary, Henry Brownrigg, who fell somewhat silent in the presence of an African American revolutionary. Brownrigg accompanied Malcolm X, self-consciously, to Oxford's preeminent hotel, the Randolph, a Victorian Gothic building with a quaint, old-fashioned ambience. Malcolm X, however, seemed to interpret the choice of a hotel somewhat in need of internal refurbishment as a racist insult, a view reinforced by the receptionist's insistence that he sign his surname in full, rather than just with an "X," in the hotel guest book.[5] The dress code at the silver-service dinner, held in the Union's wooden paneled dining room before the debate, did not suit him either. By tradition, speakers wore black bowties, which was also the uniform of the Nation of Islam, the religious movement that he had served for more than a decade. But having left the Nation acrimoniously earlier in the year (and now living under a death threat as a result), Malcolm X wore a straight tie instead, the only speaker or committee member to do so. Wearing a straight tie was a mark of inferior rank at the dinner: the only other person who wore a straight tie was the steward, who served the food and wine.

Ironically, the motion Malcolm X was called on to support in the debate was embodied in a quotation from Senator Barry Goldwater, of all people, the outspoken conservative Republican nominee in the previous month's presidential election, who had opposed the recent passage of the American Civil Rights Act.[6] During his acceptance speech at the Republican National Convention that summer, Goldwater had defended the John Birch Society, saying, "Extremism in the defense of liberty is no vice, and . . . moderation in the pursuit of vice is no virtue." Even before he rose to speak in support of that argument, Malcolm X's debating opponents mocked the notion of a black radical defending "the Goldwater standard." Malcolm X countered that he preferred Goldwater to the winner of that presidential election, Lyndon Johnson, since at least Goldwater was open about his racism.

Malcolm X's friend the black arts poet and filmmaker Lebert Bethune, who was in London in late 1964, could not resist the chance "to see the sacrosanct image of Oxford shattered by the fist of revolutionary logic. So I took a train to Oxford just to be there for the blow."[7] That blow was aimed most directly at Humphrey Berkeley, a conservative MP and Malcolm X's main debating opponent. Berkeley charged Malcolm X with being every bit as racist as apologists for South African apartheid, and joked about his "pseudonym" surname, X.

Perhaps it was the intimacy of the debate, with speakers facing each other at a distance of barely two meters in a chamber modeled on the House of Commons, that caused Malcolm X to come as close as he could remember to losing his temper. He gathered his thoughts, however, regained his composure, then returned Berkeley's insult. "The speaker that preceded me is one of the best excuses that I know to prove our point," he said, and then threw Berkeley's argument back at him: "He is right. X is not my real name." His real name, in fact, had been taken by Berkeley's forefathers, who raped and pillaged their way through Africa. "I just put X up there to keep from wearing his name." The students laughed when Malcolm X suggested that Shakespeare's Hamlet, "I think it was, who said, 'to be or not to be,'" was "in doubt about something." They listened attentively to his assault on the American media, loudly applauded his condemnation of racism, and some booed when he justified the recent murder of white missionaries by freedom fighters in the Congo as an act of war.[8] Malcolm X lost the debate, but he won plenty of admirers.[9] Bethune judged it "one of the most stirring speeches I have ever heard delivered by Malcolm X."[10]

On the face of it, the fact that Malcolm X chose to spend an evening at a fusty old English university seems something of a puzzle.[11] But given the lengths to which Malcolm went in order to make the trip, it was clearly important to him: he accepted the invitation even though he was too busy in late 1964 even to respond to similar invitations from leading American universities; he agreed to speak for no fee even though his finances were in a parlous state; and he accommodated Oxford's fixed schedule even though the debate could hardly have come at a more inconvenient time.[12] Having been abroad during the spring and then again through the second half of 1964, he was eager to be home. "I miss you and the children very much," he wrote to his wife, Betty, in August from Africa, "but it looks like another month at least may pass before I see you."[13] In fact, it would be another three. He returned home to New York on November 24. By that time, Betty was heavily pregnant,[14] his mother was seriously ill, and the Nation of Islam was seeking to evict his family from their home.[15] Meanwhile, his new organizations, Muslim Mosque Inc.

and the Organization of Afro-American Unity, were in a state of organizational shambles owing to his absence.[16] Yet he still felt, as he put it to one of his closest colleagues, Charles 37X Kenyatta, that "the long-run gains [of the trip to England] outweigh the risks."[17] Within a week of his homecoming from Africa, he was back on a plane across the Atlantic to London.

Why coming to Oxford was so important to Malcolm X, why Oxford students chose to invite him, and what effect the visit had on the man and the institution were the starting questions for this book. Far from being a chance or unlikely combination, it turns out there was an unerring logic about the coming together of an outspoken black revolutionary and this historic center of Western learning. By late 1964, black students at Oxford needed Malcolm X to come, and he felt it was urgent to go. Why that was so reveals much about both Malcolm X's life and thought and the university's engagement with race and rights. And more broadly, it has much to tell about Britain at the end of its empire, America during the civil rights era, and the global currents of the black freedom struggle.

From his childhood, Malcolm X had been on the move, eager to learn and in search of a better life—first for himself, then for others. In 1964, his journey took him abroad, to the Middle East, then Africa, and finally Europe. His international travels were a response to changes in his outlook, but they also caused his outlook to change in turn. Thus the debate at Oxford marked the latest stage in Malcolm's transformation from a small-time hustler to the world's most famous black nationalist, from a dogmatic black supremacist to a proponent of human rights, and from an American-based controversialist to a seasoned traveler with a global vision (who remained an irascible critic of America). Ending up at Oxford happened somewhat by chance. But only somewhat. The details of his life—his enjoyment of travel, his fascination with (or rather contempt for) the British Empire, his love of debate, his ease among white students, his desire to connect with the coming generation of postcolonial leaders, his frustration at being dismissed by the media as too extreme, his readiness for a confrontation, and his penchant for associating with famous people and places, even his love of Shakespeare—had prepared him for a debate on extremism and moderation at the Oxford Union.

As for the students of Oxford, they had grappled with the issue of race ever since the Victorian era, first in support of the empire, then to challenge it. In 1964, the issue had come to a head. Malcolm X arrived to speak at the very moment when some two thousand students were demanding an end to the exclusion of black students from university housing, when Britain was beset by the racial politics of immigration, and when global freedom struggles were headline news in Britain. That the Oxford Union issued an invitation to Malcolm X was by no means inevitable. But it made perfect sense. The Union was a high-profile forum for debate with a tradition of outspoken colonial student leaders, heated engagement with gender, race, and colonial issues, and a rising influence of left-leaning students. And in late 1964, a radical Jamaican student—whose hero was Malcolm X—had been elected as president of the Union.

Malcolm X's visit to the Union, in short, was a story with much longer roots, and more far-reaching implications, than the content of the speech alone might suggest. It was a story that interwove the global, national, local, and university politics of race. It was a story that involved a wide cast of characters from four continents. And it was a story that touched on many of the major themes of the era, of empire and nationalism, Black Power and citizenship, immigration and segregation, student rights and human rights, Commonwealth and the Cold War, Islam and Christianity, sexism and class conflict, media and the cult of celebrity, the so-called Black Atlantic and the British-American special relationship, and even cricket. It was precisely because of the broader context of Malcolm X's visit that the content of the speech is so important. It stands as the clearest and most eloquent articulation of his critique of racism and his vision for a remedy after a year of travel and shortly before the end of his life.

The night of the speech was not the end of Malcolm X's connection with Britain. Oxford was the first stop for Malcolm X in a short tour of four English cities, followed by a return trip in February 1965, a week before he died. His visit was but one of many by high-profile U.S. civil rights activists to Britain during this period. Just three days after the Oxford debate, for example, Rev. Dr. Martin Luther King Jr. preached to an overflowing congregation at St. Paul's Cathedral in London. Civil rights travelers, including Malcolm X, sought to use these visits, and the international dimensions of the struggle for equality, for their own purposes. But none of those involved, not even Malcolm X, had complete control over how the story turned out or how the visit changed their outlook or circumstances. Thus the full story of the Union debate also reveals the transformative, and often unexpected, impact of transatlantic connections on issues of race and equality—in this case, an impact not just on the course of British activism, but even on such a renowned global figure as Malcolm X.

The first two chapters of this book tell the stories, in turn, of how Malcolm X's and Oxford's engagement with race and racism over many years eventually brought the man and the institution together. Chapter one shows how Malcolm's life was one of travel and discovery, eventually leading him abroad—to the Middle East, Africa and Europe, and finally to Oxford and the very belly of the English establishment. Chapter two explores Oxford's long association with race and empire, and the impact of immigration on mid–twentieth century Britain. The drama of Malcolm X's visit and the significance of his speech are at the center of this book. Chapter three traces the escalating protests in Oxford and racial tensions in Britain in late 1964 that led to his being invited. Chapter four examines the debate itself, showing how Malcolm X's thought had developed dramatically since his days in the Nation of Islam and following his travels in Africa and the Middle East. By the time he spoke at Oxford, Malcolm X had developed a sophisticated critique of the media and white power structure, a global perspective on Islam and black progress, and an inspiring vision of human rights. The book closes, in chapter five, by tracing the consequences of his visit: the influence of British-American connections on civil rights and Black Power in both countries, the ways in which Malcolm X's thought continued to evolve in response to his time in Britain and Europe, and the impact of his visit on British activism, and on student life at Oxford.

CHAPTER ONE

A Life of Travel and Discovery: Malcolm X, 1925-1964

MALCOLM X IN CAIRO

I felt like I stepped out of prison.
—Travel diary, Cairo, April 1964

On the evening of Tuesday, April 14, 1964, Malcolm X—going by his new Muslim name, Malik El-Shabazz—flew into Cairo, capital of the United Arabic Republic (present-day Egypt), en route from New York to Mecca. He stayed in Cairo for three days.[1]

Malcolm X thrilled to the experience. Exhausted by a hectic schedule of domestic travel, bruised by a bitter public split with his religious mentor, and reeling from vicious threats by former colleagues in the Nation of Islam, he was in need of a break. Most of all, he was just glad to be away from America. Before leaving, he had given a stump speech to a group of students in Connecticut, reiterating his contempt for a country that treated twenty-two million "unwanted" and "repulsive" "Negroes" as "second-class citizens."[2] To his mind it was actually Christian America, the leader of the democratic West, that was the depraved "Babylon, Sodom" of scripture. And on first impression, Cairo, the largest city in the Arab world, seemed to be the heavenly opposite.

For Malcolm X, the so-called city of a thousand minarets was overwhelmingly, intoxicatingly Islamic. "So many mosques," he noted in his diary. "Between a Mosque and a Mosque there is a Mosque." Better still, the people he met shared his anger toward the United States. The "very intelligent, informed, excellent" wife of a prize-winning scientist who had invited him to dinner asked him "why the people of [the] world starve, when America has so much surplus food?"

To Malcolm X's delight, the president of Egypt, Gamal Abdel Nasser, represented a rising challenge to the United States. Nasser was the hero of the Suez Crisis, in which he had faced down Britain, France, and Israel by nationalizing the strategic canal. He would soon be president of the international Non-Aligned Movement. Nasser seemed poised to unify and lead the Arab world as an independent, Islamic power bloc. Malcolm X certainly hoped so. The day after his arrival, Malcolm X visited the Presidential Palace at Qubba in order to "pay respect and honor to His Excellency, our president and leader of Islam, GAN, whom I greatly admire." In a nod to his own ambition, he signed the visitors' book as "M.E.S, Leader of Islam in USA."

Under Nasser's leadership, Egypt had become a symbol of the potential of postcolonial nations to grow from freedom to power. As a Russian woman pointed out to Malcolm X in a chance meeting, "One African country that rises from colonialism to true *economic* independence will serve as a 'dangerous' incentive to the others." Impressed by what he saw, Malcolm X was delighted that there were so many other sightseers in Cairo who would spread the message of Egypt's rise around the globe. "No wonder the industrialization (modernization) by Nasser of today's Egypt is so greatly feared by the former Colonial powers," he noted in his diary with pleasure.

Islam, Intellect, Independence, Anti-Americanism, postimperial promise. This was a heady cocktail for a weary black nationalist Muslim visitor from New York. What struck Malcolm X most about Cairo, though, was the absence of racism. In the bustling streets and markets and cafes, he wrote to his sister, there were people of "all complexions, but . . . no 'color' problem—one family, yet all shades. . . . I met thousands of people of different races and colors who treated me as a human being."[3] In an era of bitter fights about minority rights in America, South Africa, and elsewhere, he noted in his journal, Cairo was an "example for [the] world." For Malcolm X, Cairo was at once a place of rest and freedom. At long last, "I felt at home. . . . I felt like I had stepped out of prison."

Malcolm X knew a lot about prisons, having spent almost seven years behind bars in the United States. His happiness at feeling at home at last was understandable. His family home had been burned down by white supremacists when he was four; he had spent much of his adolescence in foster homes; and just before he flew to Cairo, former colleagues had filed suit to evict his family from their current home. But for Malcolm X, prison and home stood for something more than mere bricks and mortar. American racism was his prison, and a unified, free, black, ideally Muslim global community was the home he dreamed of.

It was these freedom dreams that compelled Malcolm X to travel abroad for much of 1964. Starting in Cairo, he journeyed to the Middle East, to Africa, and at the end of the year, to Europe. "Stepping out of prison" marked a pivotal moment in Malcolm X's life and thought. It reflected his international vision and, as his name change to Malik El-Shabazz signified, his embrace of what he called Old World Islam. But in turn his travels would change his views on race as a concept and his commitment to human rights, such that by the end of the year Malcolm X was eager to speak at a celebrated university that had served as the intellectual hub of the British Empire. At Oxford, taking full advantage of such a prominent platform, he would give the clearest summary of his new position on race, religion, and human rights to date. Coming to Oxford was not the end of his journey. From Oxford, he would travel to several of England's major cities, meeting more black students and immigrants. In the process, his views on racism as a global system, and how that system might be challenged, would further evolve.

In this sense, Malcolm X's trip to Cairo, under a new name and following his departure from the Nation of Islam, was the beginning of the rest of his life—albeit a life that would last barely a year more. But his enjoyment of travel, eagerness to learn, keenness of observation, and willingness to have his views challenged were nothing new. Indeed, from his childhood Malcolm X's life had been a story of travel and learning, as he sought to break out of prison and create a new home. It was a life that would unerringly lead him, through many twists and turns, from a poor black community in the midwestern United States to the Union debating chamber at the University of Oxford.

LEARNING

> When he opened the Harlem bookshop in the morning, the store owner discovered Malcolm, reading. He had been reading the whole night.
> —A. Peter Bailey, Malcolm X's publicist, September 21, 2013

Born Malcolm Little in Omaha, Nebraska, on May 19, 1925, Malcolm X seemed destined from the very start for a life of travel and to be a black nationalist with a global vision. Not only was

Malcolm heir to an international lineage, learning about the glories of Africa from his parents, but he also suffered a childhood in which he was forced to move frequently—first to leave his home, and then his family.

Malcolm's mother, Louise, a fair-skinned, well-educated Grenadian, and his father, Earl, a rough-hewn carpenter and occasional preacher from Georgia, had met in Montreal, Canada, while working for the black nationalist and pan-Africanist Marcus Garvey and his United Negro Improvement Association (UNIA) at the end of World War I. By that time, the charismatic Jamaican was taking the United States by storm. Garvey's call for race pride, economic self-sufficiency, and international black brotherhood was a product of the so-called New Negro zeitgeist of the World War I years. That zeitgeist was born of an era that saw black soldiers fight in a war overseas, black men fight against white mobs at home, and black men and women move into bustling black urban communities across the United States. It was also an era that witnessed a much-heralded cultural and artistic renaissance in Harlem and other black communities. The New Negroes, wrote the Jamaican-born, Harlem-based poet Claude McKay in 1919, at the end of his famous poem "If We Must Die," would face the worst that white supremacy had to throw at them and live "like men."

> Like men we'll face the murderous, cowardly pack,
> Pressed to the wall, dying, but fighting back![4]

Garvey was the man of that moment. At least, *he* certainly thought so. "We meet," Garvey declared in August 1920 at the founding mass meeting of his International Convention of Negroes in Harlem, "not as cringing sycophants, but as men and women standing erect and demanding our rights."[5] Some called Garvey a "Negro Moses," a messianic image that he was only too pleased to promote with a showman's flair for the grand gesture and an appeal to divine support. We should view God "through our own spectacles," he told supporters. His 1924 convention canonized the Virgin Mary as a Black Madonna and Jesus Christ as a "Black Man of Sorrows." There was nothing sorrowful about Garvey at his peak, though. His conventions in Harlem claimed thousands of delegates, and his military-style parades, in which he wore a dress uniform complete with a red and gold silk sash across his chest and a helmet with extravagant plumage on top, were cheered by many more. Garvey's audacious plan to build the Black Star Line, a transatlantic steamship corporation, attracted some thirty thousand stockholders. And his outspoken belligerence attracted the attention of the federal government's fledgling Bureau of Information, which judged him "the cause of the greater portion of the negro agitation in this country."[6] Four decades later the bureau's successor, the Federal Bureau of Investigation (FBI), would say similar things about another popular pan-Africanist spokesman with a flair for publicity who invoked divine support: Malcolm X.

As it turned out, Garvey was the proverbial comet who lit up the sky before crashing to earth. He was quick to make enemies, his shipping company collapsed, and in 1922 the Justice Department arrested him for mail fraud. He would be deported in 1927 and die, penniless and isolated, in London in 1940.

But for a few exhilarating, fleeting years, anything seemed possible. In 1920, to much fanfare and with no little hubris, the UNIA's first International Convention of Negroes issued a global Declaration of Rights—the "Magna Carta of the Negroes of the World"—and elected Garvey as the provisional president of Africa.[7] Recalling the "hungry days" of 1921, one follower later remembered: "When Garvey rode by in his plumed hat, I got an emotional lift, which swept me above the poverty and prejudice by which my life was limited."[8] The UNIA expanded fast. Soon it would boast hundreds of branches in the United States and abroad, in West Africa, southern Africa, and the Caribbean.[9] When Malcolm X later claimed in his inscription in Nasser's guestbook to be the leader of Islam in America, he was displaying some of Garvey's chutzpah.

Louise and Earl Little eagerly volunteered for Garvey's campaign. Soon after their wedding in 1919, they agreed to leave Montreal to establish a UNIA chapter in the American midwest, some thousand miles away.[10] Traveling was a feature of African American life during the World War I era as hundreds of thousands of people left the rural south in search of work and freedom. But 1919 gave warning of the perils awaiting African American travelers and agitators, even in, or perhaps especially in, the heady era of the New Negro. There were eighty-three lynchings of black men that year, the most in a decade, and at least twenty-five antiblack race riots, in which hundreds were killed and thousands injured. African Americans called the summer of Louise and Earl's marriage a "red summer" on account of the blood that flowed. In the south, the so-called Jim Crow era of legally enforced segregation and disfranchisement, backed up by a white supremacist policing and prison system, seemed entrenched. But migrants did not find much of a better life in the northern and western states—not when white unions kept black workers from decent jobs, white gangs kept black families from buying homes in white neighborhoods, and some "sundown" towns refused to allow black migrants to stay after dark.

The Littles moved to the town of Omaha, Nebraska, in 1921. This was hardly an auspicious place or time to launch a militant black nationalist movement. That year the Ku Klux Klan was reborn in the state as part of a national revival of the hooded hate organization. Within two years, Klan membership had reached forty-five thousand in the Cornhusker State. The outspoken Earl soon became a marked man. When Louise became pregnant with Malcolm late in 1924, no doubt she feared the child—her fourth—would witness a run-in with the Klan in his or her first years. In fact, the first confrontation came before Malcolm was even born. One night that winter, a posse turned up at the Littles' home demanding to see Earl. Louise stepped onto the porch and explained that Earl was away (he was in fact off preaching) and insisted that they leave. They did so, but only after smashing all the windows and warning Earl not to cause any more trouble.

The Littles were not intimidated, but Omaha's black community was. Unable to establish a UNIA branch, the Littles moved away. The pattern of protest and reprisals followed them, so they moved across the midwest, all the while drilling their children in the promise of black nationalism. They eventually settled on the outskirts of Lansing, Michigan. In 1929, their home was burned down. Two years later, Earl was killed in a supposed streetcar accident. The family was convinced that he had been murdered by white supremacists. Worn down by poverty, intimidation, and an unwanted pregnancy, Louise had a breakdown in 1939 and was committed to the state asylum. Her eight children were split up and sent to foster homes. Malcolm was thirteen years old.

Angry at the persecution his family had endured, ashamed of his mother's illness, increasingly alienated from his peers, and presumably traumatized by the violence he had witnessed, Malcolm spent his teenage years on the move, shifting between foster homes in Michigan. Although he was popular with classmates, he soon learned of the most powerful of all interracial taboos: sex across the color line. While he "wasn't supposed to dance with any white girls," he later recalled that some white friends urged him to get intimate with white girls; breaking the interracial taboo would give the boys the "hammer over the girls' heads" and allow them to blackmail the girls into having intimate relations with them. He also learned of the suffocating restrictions for African Americans in terms of education and opportunities. Although he was academically gifted, one teacher told him to become a carpenter, since Malcolm's dream of becoming a lawyer was "no realistic goal for a nigger."[11]

In 1940, in an attempt to escape the racism he was fast becoming aware of, Malcolm went to Boston to visit his half-sister Ella, his father's eldest daughter from his first marriage. Staying with Ella meant living with someone who was proud and free. Malcolm was entranced. Ella "wasn't just black," he later wrote, "but like our father, she was jet black." The way she sat, moved, talked—did everything—bespoke someone who did and got exactly what she wanted. "I had never been so impressed with anybody." Malcolm wanted to find out more. And so, the following year, he moved to Boston.

HOME TO HARLEM

I have already traveled through twenty-three different states.

—Letter from Malcolm Little to Zolma Holman of Jackson, Michigan, November 18, 1941

Moving to Boston was also the way to seek out a better, black world. When first catching the bus to Boston, Malcolm later recalled, "If someone had hung a sign, 'HICK,' around my neck,

I couldn't have looked much more obvious." In Boston, he took a job working as a dishwasher on the railway, giving him a chance to travel along the East Coast and to visit some of the northeast's bigger black communities. None, however, was bigger, or more intoxicating, than Harlem. Malcolm had long hoped to visit what had become the capital of black America, having heard stories from his father of Garvey's parades and the boxer Joe Louis's victories there. Malcolm's first impressions fulfilled his lofty expectations. "New York was heaven to me. And Harlem was Seventh Heaven!"

Malcolm explored and embraced Harlem with the enthusiasm of a first-time tourist. "I was mesmerized," he wrote later. Harlem was like some "technicolor bazaar." Every layover night in Harlem, "I ran and explored new places." He was thrilled to walk the streets of a bustling black city community, one that, following street fights between white and black soldiers, was "officially off limits to white servicemen." And he was excited to visit the various dance and music halls, such as Small's Paradise. "No Negro place of business had ever impressed me so much." In Harlem's nightspots he saw "such famous stars as Dizzy Gillespie, Billie Holiday, Ella Fitzgerald, and Dinah Washington." As he would in his travels abroad, Malcolm sought out, and took great pride in meeting, influential figures—which for a young man in Harlem meant anyone with access to the famous musical stars. As Malcolm noted with no little satisfaction, "My friends now included musicians like Duke Ellington's great drummer, Sonny Greer, and that great personality with the violin, Ray Nance. He's the one . . . [with] that wild 'scat' style: 'Blip-blip-de-blop-de-blam-blam.'"

Yet even when chasing Harlem's high life, Malcolm observed its people and ways with the studied detachment of an ethnographer. "I combed not only the bright-light areas, but Harlem's residential areas from best to worst, from Sugar Hill up near the Polo Grounds, where many famous celebrities lived, down to the slum blocks of old rat-trap apartment houses, just crawling with everything you could mention that was illegal and immoral." Such a thorough investigation of society, from the most privileged to the warts-and-all of everyday life, would become a hallmark of his travels.

Although pleasure and profit were on his mind at this stage of his life, Malcolm learned the history of Harlem—a history, in his understanding, of "immigrant musical chairs," when each national group from Europe would leave Harlem when a new group arrived, and where "today, all these same immigrants' descendants are running as hard as they can to escape the descendants of the Negroes who helped to unload the immigrant ships." He learned of Harlem's many generations of protest, including recent black boycotts—inspired by a Housewives League—of white merchants for "refusing to hire a Negro even as their stores raked in Harlem's money." He gained a sense of Harlem's strategic place in international black politics, too, overhearing a salesman explain that the "Negro and white canvassers" who sold copies of the Communist Party newspaper, the *Daily Worker*, and called for justice for the Scottsboro boys (nine wrongly accused black youths in a widely publicized trial for the rape of two white women in Alabama) were "somehow . . . tied in with the Russians."

The lessons he learned in Harlem would frame his understanding of white people. He was appalled by the rich "white men—in their sixties, I know, some maybe in their seventies—" who snuck up to a Harlem brothel "to cringe on their knees and beg and cry out for mercy under" the whip of a black prostitute.

News from abroad seemed to confirm his views. A decade or so later, now going by the name Malcolm X, he would compare the sexual antics of rich white New Yorkers to those of the British establishment during the Profumo scandal of 1963, in which a cabinet minister had an affair with a woman who was the lover of a Russian spy. He also commented on American and British white women's lust, "particularly 'taboo' lust" across the color line: "After England's leaders [in the Profumo scandal] had been with those white girls, those girls, for their satisfaction, went to Negroes, to smoke reefers and make fun of some of England's greatest peers as cuckolds and fools."

To his mind, then, British and American race relations were both absurd, cruel systems. As Malcolm X, traveling to Britain would thus provide an opportunity to tackle the same enemy that he despised at home. But he was quite clear about which of the two countries was most to blame: "America is subsidizing what is left of the prestige and strength of the once mighty Britain," he wrote in his autobiography. "The sun has set forever on that monocled, pith-helmeted resident colonialist, sipping tea with his delicate lady in the non-white colonies being systematically robbed of every valuable resource. Britain's superfluous royalty and nobility now exist by charging tourists to inspect the once baronial castles, and by selling memoirs, perfumes, autographs, titles, and even themselves."

For Malcolm Little in postwar New York, though, it was particularly the poverty and despair he encountered on so many Harlem streets, in sight of Manhattan's skyscrapers, that fueled his anger against white America. There may have been exciting "blam-blam" by night, but by day there was "dirt, garbage cans overflowing or kicked over; drunks, dope addicts, beggars." In later life he thought often about those friends of his who tried, and so often failed, to eke out a living. "All of us—who might have probed space, or cured cancer, or built industries—were, instead, black victims of the white man's American social system."

DESTINY

> Out there in the streets, hustling, pushing dope, and robbing, I could have had the dreams from a pound of hashish and I'd never have dreamed anything so wild as that one day I would speak in coliseums and arenas, at the greatest American universities, and on radio and television programs, not to mention speaking all over Egypt and Africa and in England.
> —Malcolm X, *Autobiography*

Harlem may have seemed a Seventh Heaven when he first arrived, but it quickly transformed into a personal hell. As Malcolm put it in his autobiography, he became "one of the most depraved parasitical hustlers among New York's eight million people."

In Malcolm's breathless and sensational telling, he got into trouble for putting a soldier—who turned out to be an undercover detective—in touch with a prostitute. He started dealing marijuana and "sold reefers like a wild man. I scarcely slept." After running foul of the narcotics squad and being placed under surveillance, he began to carry a gun. When he was summoned to an army draft interview, he told the military psychiatrist that he couldn't wait to be conscripted so he could turn his gun on white racist American soldiers. He wasn't called up. To pay for his drug habit and flashy clothes, he started stealing; he also brought white clients to a brothel and supplied drugs to a woman he described as "the white lesbian who lived downtown." He got involved in fights—with gamblers and with his best friend's lover. The problems escalated. He became hooked on hard drugs and took other risks that he thought would leave him dead. Within a couple of years he found himself on the run from the police, a hustler, Italian mobsters, and a West Indian man called Archie. He was not yet twenty-one.

"Recalling all of this," he wrote in his autobiography, "I don't know, to tell the truth, how I am alive to tell it today." Now as Malcolm X, he attributed his seemingly superhuman turn of fortune to Allah's care. In fact, though, the reason for his survival was rather less epic: according to a recent biographer, his underworld life was most likely not the dramatic one that he later described so colorfully, but rather a fairly common one of petty crime.[12] Without a doubt Malcolm's version made for a much more gripping narrative than the actual facts would have, and perhaps more important, his grand tale sought to achieve a higher purpose. As Malcolm put it in his autobiography, he hoped the stories of his life would show just how low "the American white man's society" would allow the black man to fall.

Still, minor crime was enough to get him into major trouble. At the end of 1945, he was part of a team that went on a stealing spree in the smarter white areas of Boston. Not long thereafter, he was arrested for burgling a house in the wealthy suburb of Newton. To make matters worse, in a time when adultery and interracial relationships were taboo, one of his team was a married white woman who was also his lover. He was sentenced to jail for eight to ten years.

For a man who needed to be on the move and liked to keep his own company as and when he chose, jail was harsh punishment. So initially, he caused trouble in order to be sent to solitary confinement, where "I would pace for hours like a caged leopard, viciously cursing aloud to myself." At that point in his life, it seemed inconceivable that the small-time thief and long-term jailbird Malcolm Little would end up an American leader, global traveler, and sought-after speaker.

Yet his time of confinement proved to be a time of learning, even transformation—for in the rage of jail, he gained spiritual peace. "I found Allah and the religion of Islam," he wrote later, "and it completely transformed my life." It was in the confines of prison that he developed his world vision and learned to debate; it was also where he first read about Britain and, most likely, first heard about the Oxford Union.

PRISON

Debating was a weekly event there at the Norfolk Prison Colony. My reading had my mind like steam under pressure. Some way, I had to start telling the white man about himself to his face. I decided I could do this by putting my name down to debate.

—Malcolm X, *Autobiography*

During a visit from his brother Reginald, who had recently joined the Nation of Islam, prisoner Malcolm learned of the religious movement, and he soon struck up a correspondence with its leader, Elijah Muhammad. The Nation of Islam had started during the Great Depression as one of many religious sects that particularly appealed to confused or impoverished Americans (both white and black Americans, though in this case black). The Nation's early theology was somewhat confused and impoverished too. As far as Malcolm Little understood it, Allah had created the first human beings, who were black. But an evil scientist, Yacub, had bred white people on the Island of Patmos. This devil race had then lived as savages in European caves for two thousand years, before Moses civilized them. Allah then sanctioned white domination for six thousand years, as punishment and to cleanse the black race through suffering, until a mighty representative should lead black people to restored spiritual purity, and then to freedom and dominion. That mighty man was Wallace Fard, who founded the Nation in Detroit in the 1930s. Fard disappeared almost as quickly as he appeared, leaving a successor, Elijah Muhammad, whom Malcolm came to know and serve and, for a time, adore.

Malcolm had long rejected Christianity, dismissing it as "the white man's religion." As he would later often say, "All it's done for black men is help keep them slaves."[13] He had entered prison an atheist. Joining the Nation would be the start of a religious journey that within a decade would lead him to Mecca in search of true Islam and eventually to England to meet with other Muslims. But at Concord Reformatory and then Norfolk County Prison, both in Massachusetts, he took his first steps into his new faith—and he did so with gusto. Like other members of the Nation, Malcolm dropped his surname, because it was a white man's name inherited from slaveowners, replacing it with an X to underline the point. He enthusiastically followed the Nation's strict moral code on matters of sex (only within heterosexual marriage, which should only be to other members of the Nation), diet (one main meal a day, no pork), lifestyle (regular fasting and no tobacco, alcohol, or gambling), prayer (five times daily, facing toward Mecca), self-reliance (no acceptance of state benefits), and, on leaving prison, dress code (suit and bow tie). And he embraced the Nation's theology of black supremacy. Reflecting on his encounters with white people, he found that the Nation's teaching that "the white man is the devil" rang true.

Being stuck in prison proved to be a blessing for the new convert, who had previously always been on the move. "Where else but in a prison could I have attacked my ignorance by being able to study intensely sometimes as much as fifteen hours a day?" Having learned from Muhammad that history had been "bleached" (an issue that nonwhite colonial students would raise a few year's later in England), Malcolm X set about finding out the truth. He virtually set up residence in what was, fortuitously, an extensive prison library, and when library hours were over he continued to read into the night in his poorly lit cell. Through the written word, he discovered the world. Rather than losing his wanderlust in prison, then, Malcolm X found that reading whetted his appetite for more travel. But he also gained focus, and after his release he would journey with purpose rather than drift from place to place, as if to make up for the lost, wandering years of youth.

Malcolm X's time in prison set the scene for his 1964 world travels. His conversion led to a yearning to visit Mecca. He was also fascinated by the history of Africa. Malcolm X delighted in discovering how many famous historical figures, though portrayed as white in movies, were in fact African. "Jesus grew up in Africa . . . Mary's people were Africans," he wrote, exultantly. "The great Carthaginian general, Hannibal himself, was a full-blooded African . . . *A BLACK MAN.*" Even "the face on the Sphinx is that of a full-blooded African . . . A BLACK MAN . . . it drove Napoleon almost insane" (and so Napoleon struck off the Sphinx's nose). Little wonder that Malcolm X would travel to Mecca and then Africa at the first opportunity, or that he would start his journey in Egypt. Or that when he visited Britain, he would spend his time with African and Muslim groups.[14]

What is perhaps surprising is that prison also stimulated his interest in Britain, and even prepared him for his Oxford speech.

In his travels through literature, Malcolm X paid close attention to Europe, and especially—with repulsion—to the British Empire. "The cannibalistic white powers of Europe," he noted, had first "murdered or enslaved . . . over 115 million African blacks," then "carved up, as their colonies, the richest areas of the black continent." In the Far East, meanwhile, the Treaty of Nanking, among other terrible things, "had fixed China's import tariffs so low that cheap British articles soon flooded in, maiming China's industrial development." Little wonder that the Chinese had cried, "Kill the foreign white devils!" in the Boxer Rebellion of 1901. When Britain won, "the vicious, arrogant white man put up the famous signs, 'Chinese and dogs not allowed' in prestigious areas of Peking." Coming not just to England, but to Oxford specifically, would allow him to challenge this evil empire at its intellectual heart—an irresistible challenge for a pugnacious man of such intelligence. And when he got there, he was no doubt struck by the irony of finding himself in a city where students were challenging "No blacks or dogs" signs in landladies' windows.

Prison even prepared him for the Oxford Union parley itself. The Norfolk County inmates engaged in weekly debates, and Malcolm X soon became fond of the activity. Topics included race but ranged far and wide. "[One] hot debate I remember I was in had to do with the identity of Shakespeare," he wrote in his autobiography. "No color was involved there; I just got intrigued over the Shakespearean dilemma." During his Oxford debate, one of his best-received moments was when, feigning ignorance, he remarked, "I read once, passingly, about a man named Shakespeare," and proceeded to quote from *Hamlet*. Little did the students know that he was calling on a trick that he had honed in prison, or that he had learned the art of debate behind bars. It is possible that Malcolm X heard, or at least heard about, visiting Oxford Union debaters who challenged inmates in Massachusetts prisons during a tour of America in the 1950s.[15]

TRAVEL

> [Straight after leaving prison in 1952] I bought a
> suitcase.... I have thought since that, without fully
> knowing it, I was preparing for what my life was
> about to become.
> —Malcolm X, *Autobiography*

Upon his release from prison, Malcolm X traveled extensively through the United States in service of Elijah Muhammad, helping to build temples in Detroit, Boston, Philadelphia, Atlanta, New York, and Los Angeles and, with Muhammad's blessing, becoming the Nation's most prominent spokesman. In 1959, a sensational television documentary on the Nation of Islam, *The Hate That Hate Produced*, shot Malcolm X to fame (or rather to infamy for many people), and his public engagements around the country grew even more numerous. Eager to record his journeys, he picked up a secondhand camera. "I don't know how many rolls of film I shot until I could take usable pictures," he later remarked. The hobby would remain a passion. When he came to Oxford, Malcolm X spent the afternoon before his debate taking photos of students.[16]

On the face of it, becoming the public face of a religious organization that called all white people "devils" might not seem a likely step toward the Oxford Union. But even at this stage, there were indications that an invitation to an elite white student venue might be attractive. "Except for all-black audiences," he reflected in his autobiography, "I liked the college audiences best." Because student minds were "alive and searching ... the college sessions never failed to be exhilarating." Muhammad had assured him "that I never need fear any man's intellect who tries to defend or to justify the white man's criminal record against the non-white man"; Malcolm X therefore embraced debates with the best and brightest students, calling them "exciting battling with ideas." His frequent trips to campuses allowed him to master techniques for speaking to white, young, learned audiences. "As a doctor, with his finger against a pulse, is able to feel the heart rate, when I am up there speaking, I can feel the reaction to what I am saying."

In the summer of 1959, Malcolm X traveled briefly to the Middle East and Africa on behalf of the Nation. It proved to be a tantalizing but frustrating visit, and he reflected on the trip with "regret." His journey was delayed, he suffered from diarrhea, he was embarrassed by his lack of understanding of Islam, and he felt compelled to decline an invitation to meet with the president of Egypt because "he was just the forerunner and humble servant of Elijah Muhammad." Also, because Elijah Muhammad had yet to visit Mecca, Malcolm X felt, out of deference, that he shouldn't go himself. Forgoing a visit to Mecca was "an experience which would break the average Moslem's heart" and clearly broke his.

Nevertheless, his journey stimulated his desire for more international travel, and it challenged his thinking as well. For one thing, he began to question the Nation's dogmatic racial separatism. As he noted in a 1961 article for the widely read African American newspaper the *Pittsburgh Courier,* "There is no color prejudice among Moslems."[17] He also began to be excited about prospects for a global alliance of nonwhite peoples. "As I discovered among the Arabs, the Africans are . . . more concerned about the condition of our U.S. people of pigmentation than with their own status," he told readers of the *Courier*. During his trip, writing for the New York *Amsterdam News,* he wrote: "Here in Africa, the all-seeing eye of the African masses is upon America."[18] He longed to return.

In the meantime, he followed world events carefully. And from his base in New York, where he had moved in 1958 with his wife, Betty Shabazz (née Sanders), the world came to him. Harlem had long been a global community—a place of meetings and news, of cultural exchange and pan-African organizing. In September 1960, Fidel Castro visited New York to speak at the United Nations, and Malcolm X helped to persuade the Cuban leader to stay in Harlem. He was also the first person to meet with Castro there, in front of photographers. A month later, Malcolm X met with Ghanaian president Kwame Nkrumah and sat behind him at a Harlem rally at which Nkrumah declared that the twenty million Americans of African descent constituted "the strongest link between the people of North American and the people of Africa."[19]

Such high-profile, well-publicized meetings occurred against the backdrop of heady though violent days of nationalism and repression in Africa. The United Nations declared 1960, a year in which thirty countries were expected to gain independence, the Year of Africa. That March, South African police killed sixty-nine black demonstrators protesting the pass laws in the township of Sharpeville—many shot in the back as they turned to flee. The following February, the first prime minister of newly independent Congo, Patrice Lumumba, was assassinated. Black nationalists in Harlem believed (rightly) that the United States had wanted him dead, although he was in fact killed by political rivals funded by the former Congolese power, Belgium, rather than the poisoned toothpaste that the CIA had shipped out. When demonstrators angry at Lumumba's murder and U.S. interference broke into the United Nations and a media storm erupted, Malcolm's position in the Nation precluded him from speaking out in support. He did, however, say publicly—and pointedly: "I refuse to condemn the demonstrations."[20] The Nation would not be able to constrain him much longer.

BLACK NATIONALISM AND ISLAM

> Our success in America will involve two circles. Black Nationalism and Islam—it will take Black Nationalism to make our own people conscious of doing for self and then Islam will provide the spiritual guidance.
>
> —Malcolm X, speech notes for Africa trip in 1964

The Nation of Islam introduced Malcolm X to the two issues to which he would devote the rest of his life: black nationalism and Islam. His passion for both would lead him to travel abroad in order to understand and promote them better. In turn, his embrace of global race alliances and of mainstream Islam would also force him, in 1964, to leave his religious family because of its narrower focus on the (American) Nation of Islam.

Until that point, however, he served Elijah Muhammad with the utmost loyalty. Although Malcolm X became known—and feared and followed by the FBI—as a black nationalist fire-brand, his speeches always started with spiritual matters. A 1961 speech at Harvard Law School was a case in point. "To understand" about the topic at hand, "The American Negro, Problems and Solutions," he told the audience, "you must first realize that we [the Nation of Islam] are a religious group."[21] True religion started with devotion to "Mr. Elijah Muhammad [who] is teaching and working among our people to fulfill God's Divine Purpose today." That purpose was to free the twenty million ex-slaves in America, and black nationalism flowed out of this theology. "Mr. Muhammad declares that the only solution to America's serious race problem is complete separation of the two races." White America must comply immediately, he concluded, otherwise "your entire race will be destroyed and removed from this earth by Almighty God, Allah."

Even at this early point in his speaking career, Malcolm was aware that the Nation of Islam was not in sync with what he called "the Old World of Islam," but he insisted at Harvard and elsewhere that "the basic principles and practices are the same." Any differences were because the Nation had adapted Islam to the "uniquely pitiful" state of black Americans, former slaves. "Thus our acceptance of Islam affects us uniquely ... differently than all other Muslim 'converts' anywhere else on this earth." When he traveled abroad in 1964, however, he would reverse the argument and align himself squarely with the Old World of Islam.

Malcolm X's rise through the Nation's ranks coincided with the rise of the civil rights movement in America. Starting with a bus boycott in Montgomery, Alabama, in 1955, which propelled Rev. Martin Luther King Jr. to prominence, African Americans in the southern states launched a decade-long series of public demonstrations and mass marches, freedom rides and boycotts, to force the American government to guarantee their civil and voting rights. Malcolm X's separatist ideology, (quasi-)Islamic theology, global perspectives, and outspoken personality made a public falling-out with southern civil rights leaders something of a certainty. He criticized the movement's goal of integration, charging that "the white man is not going to share his wealth with his ex-slaves." He condemned the movement's philosophy of nonviolence, calling it "criminal." He lampooned the movement's tactics: "I don't believe that we're going to overcome by singing. If you're going to get yourself a .45 and start singing 'We shall overcome,' I'm with you." And he condemned the movement's religion: "'Now I'm letting you bow to my god, a white god,' says the white man. 'Now you can act just like a white man . . . and you should be thankful.'"[22]

Martin Luther King Jr. came in for particularly harsh criticism. Malcolm X derided the celebrated civil rights leader for preaching that blacks should "love the white man" and called him a "chump not a champ" for allowing women and children to walk at the front of a 1963 march in Birmingham, Alabama, which was met by violent policing. Malcolm X also dismissed King's close colleague Bayard Rustin as "nothing but a homosexual." The March on Washington for Jobs and Freedom of August 28, 1963, when King delivered his famous "I have a dream" speech, was nothing but "a farce on Washington." Contra King, Malcolm X declared that "the black masses in America were—and still are—having a nightmare." In a speech to an African Asian Unity Bazaar in Harlem soon afterward, Malcolm X likened the march to a Hollywood production and awarded various Oscars: President Kennedy was best producer, the white speakers were best actors, and the six black speakers (including Martin Luther King Jr.) were the supporting cast. A few weeks later in Los Angeles, he switched the analogy to the big top: "Nothing but a circus, with clowns and all."[23]

Civil rights leaders shot back. The baseball legend Jackie Robinson (whom Malcolm X had called a "white man's hero") chided Malcolm X for "being militant on Harlem street corners, where militancy is not dangerous."[24] James Farmer, who had led the Freedom Rides, in which black volunteers rode at the front of buses into the Deep South while white volunteers sat at the back—both groups at great risk to their safety—complained that "Malcolm had done nothing but verbalize."[25] It was true that Malcolm X worked within black communities rather than confronting segregationists and that his chief contribution was his words rather than organizing protest organizations (though he had made a formidable contribution to the Nation of Islam). But to dismiss him as a mere sniper on the sidelines missed the point, as Farmer, who had deep respect for Malcolm X, well knew. From his base in Harlem, Malcolm X was fast developing a positive, albeit innovative and controversial, world vision for human rights. And verbalizing was his best way of making it into reality.

In 1964, Elijah Muhammad threw Malcolm X out of the Nation of Islam with more than a hint of a death threat. Tensions began, according to Malcolm X, when Muhammad became "insanely jealous" of his popularity. They increased when Malcolm X began to comment on American politics (which was not allowed under the Nation's code) and to be drawn to mainstream Islam. Tensions came to a head when Malcolm X discovered that Muhammad had seduced, and made pregnant, at least two teenage secretaries. When President Kennedy was assassinated on November 22, 1963, Muhammad instructed all his ministers to refrain from commenting. Malcolm X famously spoke out at a rally soon afterward, saying unsympathetically that Kennedy "never foresaw that the chickens would come home to roost so soon." The insubordination provided Muhammad with the pretext he needed. He suspended Malcolm X for ninety days.

A bitter parting of the ways followed. On March 12, 1964, Malcolm announced his formal split from the Nation—though he remained publicly respectful of Muhammad, at least initially. (In private he was convinced Muhammad wanted him dead because "I know where the bodies are buried.")[26] The split, though, allowed Malcolm X to become involved in political protest—and he made an immediate impact. One week later, at a gathering of militant black leaders and celebrities in Pennsylvania, Malcolm X received the loudest applause. The following week, in New York, local leaders asked him to support a boycott that led to a quarter of a million children staying home from school. The chief of police credited, or rather blamed, Malcolm X for the huge response.[27] The split also allowed him to speak more frankly, and more frequently, with white reporters. In a lengthy piece, one journalist with the *Herald Tribune* found Malcolm X's enthusiasm for guerrilla warfare unnerving, his skill at masking his true feelings frustrating, but his personality "above all else, utterly charming."[28]

Increasingly confident of his standing, Malcolm X told supporters that he would "plunge headlong into politics at 'the proper moment.'" He was also confident that his human rights vision would catch on. In a letter to a correspondent in Sudan on March 21, 1964, he promised that "the Civil Rights Struggle of the past will shift gears this year and become a Human Rights Struggle with international implications."[29] Travel abroad was very much in the cards.

First, though, Malcolm X wanted to learn more about Islam. In mid-March he started a new religious organization, Muslim Mosque Inc. (MMI). Unlike the Nation of Islam, this new creed embraced the politics of black America. As he explained in an interview in March 1964, "the political philosophy of the Muslim Mosque will be black nationalism, the economic philosophy will be black nationalism, and the social philosophy will be black nationalism." But the "religious base" will be "the religion of Islam."[30] Learning about and promoting that religion would prompt his lengthy travels abroad during 1964. Within a month of leaving the Nation, he was on a plane to Egypt—his ultimate goal: Mecca.

HAJJ

> I just returned from Mecca! This is indeed an
> eventful day.
> —Malcolm X, travel diary, April 18, 1964

When Malcolm X headed to Cairo airport on April 16, 1964, to fly to Jeddah under the name of Malik El-Shabazz, his feeling of expectation was matched by one of gratitude. Five years before, he had been unable to go to Mecca for the Hajj, out of deference to Elijah Muhammad. Now he was his own man, head of his own Muslim organization, free to join Muslims from around the world on the annual pilgrimage and thus fulfill the religious duty of every able-bodied Muslim who could afford to do so. His main purpose for making the Hajj, though, as he explained to a fellow pilgrim, "was to get an understanding of true Islam."

For Malcolm X, the very details of his departure pointed to the presence of a divine hand guiding him and to the promise of a new global role for him to play. At the airport there were "Muslims from everywhere, hugging, embracing, warm friendly spirit." He was convinced that "Allah placed me in the best hands, everywhere I've turned, someone was offering to help me, to guide me, American Muslim." In the airplane the Egyptian pilots invited him into the cockpit, which no American pilot had ever done. At the end of that heady first day, he recorded in his notebook: "Never in America had I received such respect and honor as here in the Muslim world, just upon their learning I was a Muslim."[31]

His sense of divine oversight increased at every turn. On arrival at Jeddah airport, feeling "blue ... alone, lonely," he called a contact, Dr. Omar Aygam. "Out of the thick darkness comes sudden light," he exulted. "My, how fortune can change." Aygam helped him past passport control and took him home, where he introduced Malcolm X to his father, the secretary of the Arab League—"one of the most powerful men in the Muslim world"—who in turn gave up his bed at the Jeddah Palace so that Malcolm X could have a place to sleep. "Such hospitality! Never so honored!" Malcolm X met Prince Muhammed ibn Faisal of the UAR, too, "a tall, handsome man, educated in America," who had a "humble dignity." Ever alert to his own public profile, Malcolm X was flattered that Faisal had seen him on television. The prince told Malcolm X of the wonders of the annual pilgrimage, marveling over "the power of religion" and the pilgrim's "belief in the *Oneness of God: Allah*."[32]

On Saturday morning, Malcolm X recorded that "my excitement, sitting here in the hotel waiting to go before the Hajj Committee, is indescribable." Looking out at the gathering pilgrims, he had never "seen such a beautiful sight, witnessed such a scene, nor felt such an atmosphere. . . . I must thank God for this blessing." There were more blessings to come. The Hajj Committee in Jeddah recognized Malcolm X as a "true Muslim" and recorded him as such in the register. Prince Faisal graciously lent him a car for the journey to Mecca. "I must admit I was thrilled," he wrote that night, exhausted, "feeling . . . important, humble and thankful all at the same time."[33]

Malcolm X pondered the gravitas of joining a pilgrimage that had existed "at least since the days of Abraham," while "Mecca is as ancient as time itself, and looks it," with sections of the city "no different than when the prophet Abraham was here over 4,000 years ago." Together with many thousands of pilgrims, he walked counterclockwise seven times around the Ka'aba, the cuboid building in the sacred mosque that is the most holy site of Islam. "It was a sight to witness." On Monday he began the ritual visits to the desert around Mecca. On Tuesday he climbed Mount Arafat to pray for the removal of past sins, and then collected nine pebbles on the plain of Muzdalifah, which he threw at the devil (a *white* monument, he noted with satisfaction) in Mina on Wednesday before walking around the Ka'aba a further three times. On Saturday he flew to the "peaceful and serene city" of Medinah to visit the mosque that holds the tomb of Muhammad. "Never have I felt more relaxed, more at peace, or nearer to God," he wrote. "This feeling that I have right now is *in itself* worth my entire pilgrimage."[34]

Yet despite noting approvingly that "people of every rank, from King to beggar, are all ... the Hajj equalizes all," in fact Malcolm X felt less than equal. He had "difficulty praying" in the traditional "form of the prostration. . . . My big toe is not used to it." He found it hard at mealtimes, "as one raised in Western culture[,] to squat as easily as those here in the Orient." A case of constipation and a fever didn't help. Above all, he felt that "not being able to speak the language is like being in a fish bowl: everyone looking at me, talking about me and to me, and me not able to understand or to answer back." He resolved to learn Arabic, but still, his humbling made him loath to judge others. Even one haughty, anglicized Pakistani general could be forgiven, "because his country was colonized by the English for some time."[35] It was good preparation for Oxford, where he would meet—and treat with courtesy—plenty of haughty students, including some from former colonies.

Yet even as he was humbled, he also felt special. As an American Muslim, he was "always the object of extreme curiosity and attention." At every turn—especially in his hotel, which "seems to be the focal point for all VIP activity"—people asked him about the state of American segregation. And when they didn't ask, he took every "opening to preach to them a quick 'sermon' on American racism and its evils."[36] He was proud of the fact that "I have not bitten my tongue once, nor passed a single opportunity in my travels, to tell the truth about the *real plight* of our people in America. It shocks these people. They knew it was 'bad' but never dreamt it was as inhuman (psychologically castrating) as my uncompromising projection of it pictures it to them."[37] As he increasingly saw things, his destiny was to become the representative of black Americans abroad and to tell the wider world the truth about American racism. That message would be at the heart of his speech at Oxford.

He also let his travel experience test his existing views, particularly his views on race. What impressed him most about the Hajj, he told a fellow pilgrim, was "the *brotherhood,* people of all races, colors, from all over the world coming together *as one* which proved to me the power of the One God." From this moment on, through to the end of his life, Malcolm X adopted—and advocated—a color-blind view of human potential and human rights. "It is only being a Muslim which keeps me from seeing people by the colour of their skin," he told a British audience a week before he died. "This religion teaches brotherhood."[38] During the Hajj he became convinced that this brotherhood of equality under Allah, rather than a belief in black superiority, would best challenge racism, the "earth's most explosive evil . . . the inability of God's creatures to live as *One,* especially in the West."[39]

By the end of the week, Malcolm X had moved from wide-eyed praise to more sanguine, keen-eyed observation. Mecca might be ancient, but cars changed things, and some of the newer sections "look like a Miami suburb." For all the interracialism on show, he noticed that different color groups tended to stay together. He was critical of one sheikh's bigamous commitment to interracialism—in the form of one "real dark" and one "real white" wife. He was angered by the hypocrisy of those who gave money to win the praise of others. He disapproved of the Arab penchant for cigarettes: "It's one of the evils that the Prophet Muhammad didn't put a taboo on, but only because smoking hadn't yet been discovered in his day. If he were alive, he'd ban it." He was also frustrated that "the Arabs are poor at public relations. They say *insha Allah* and then wait, and while they are waiting the world passes them by."[40] The American in him reckoned they needed to up their marketing game. And in that regard, he might have much to teach—though he also knew he still had a lot to learn.

Not only did he feel special in Arabia, but he was sure that he was being prepared for a unique role upon his return home. The head of the Hajj Committee "told me he hoped I would become a great preacher of Islam in America." Just as Martin Luther King Jr. was convinced he had a calling from God to lead the American civil rights movement, Malcolm X felt that divine selection was propelling him to return to the West to talk about Islam. "America needs to understand Islam because it is the one religion that erases the race problem from society," he said, with the potential to "remove the 'cancer of racism' from the heart of white America."[41] In Oxford, he would extend that analysis to Britain.

He continued to talk about black nationalism, too—though to be sure, after his time in Cairo he "no longer subscribe[d] to sweeping indictments of any one race." In a letter to an Egyptian newspaper, he insisted that "the spirit of unity and true brotherhood displayed" in Mecca, "from blue-eyed blonds to black–skinned Africans … served to convince me that *perhaps* some American whites can also be cured of the rampant racism which is consuming them."[42] Some, but not all. "I have to be a realist," he told a London audience the following February. "I live in America, a society that does not believe in brotherhood in any sense of the term."[43] Thus even as he recognized the brotherhood of man under Allah and adopted a human rights agenda, black advancement remained his priority. "I must leave here by Sat so I won't miss my African trip," he noted in his diary after his royal host suggested he stay a little longer. If he was to fulfill his duties as both a black man and a Muslim he needed to spend time in Africa every bit as much as in the Middle East. "Black Nationalism will link us to Africa and Islam will link us spiritually to Africa, Arabia and Asia."[44]

AFRICA

I am writing these things so that you will know for a fact the tremendous sympathy and support we have among the African States for our Human Rights struggle.

—Letter from Malcolm X to actor and social activist Ossie Davis, May 19, 1964

Exposing American deceit and oppression was at the heart of Malcolm X's agenda when he visited Sudan, Lebanon, Nigeria, and Ghana in late April and early May. "You who think the black man has been emancipated in America," he told a group of five hundred students in Ibadan, Nigeria, "just go there and visit without your national costume and you will be subject to unheard of indignities.... The government of the United States is a government of the white people, by the white people, and for the benefit of the white people."[45] To students in Accra, Ghana, he spoke of the dogs and bayonets, cattle prods and water hoses, that American police used against civil rights activists. As for members of the American Peace Corps, supposedly working for health and education in the poorer parts of Africa, they were "paving the way for neo-colonialism" by extending American influence over African life.[46]

The reaction was mixed. One South African lecturer walked out at Ibadan, complaining that Malcolm X was worse than the South African leader Hendrik Verwoerd.[47] (His main debating opponent in Oxford would level the same charge of reverse apartheid.) But according to the press coverage back in America, the tour was a great success. This was not simply good fortune. Eager to promote his cause and status, Malcolm X communicated regularly with American journalists, trumpeting his meetings with dignitaries and celebrating the size of his audiences. His final press release in Ghana told of "seven days of overwhelming success building bridges of goodwill and better understanding at all levels of Ghanaian government." (He overlooked the fact that he hadn't met with the president.)[48] It may well have been on this 1964 tour of Africa that Malcolm X grasped the value of generating prestige abroad to build status at home.

True to character, Malcolm X learned other lessons as he mingled in the markets and on the campuses, his trusty camera in hand. He was "impressed with the wealth and beauty of the people and the geographic area" in Ghana. The people, he noted, "are by far the most progressive and independent minded." Indeed, "all Africa is seething with serious awareness of itself, its potential wealth and power, and the roles it seems destined to play."[49] Africa had its challenges, to be sure, especially a need to unite. But he enthusiastically embraced the sense of the continent's destiny. Or as he put it during a radio interview back in America in June, Africa was "the greatest place on earth."[50] He had arrived a pan-Africanist—that was why he made the trip. However, he returned convinced that American progress depended on African support.

"African feeling, this is the key," Malcolm X noted in his journal. "We must identify with (migrate to) Africa culturally, philosophically, psychologically and the 'life' or new spirit will then give us the inspiration to do the things necessary (ourselves) to better our political and economic and social 'life' here in America."[51] Even more important was how Africans felt about America. He may have overemphasized the point for propaganda purposes in his public statements, but his private travel diaries reveal genuine delight about African interest in the plight of African Americans.

UNITED NATIONS

> How is the black man going to get "civil rights"
> before first he wins his human rights? If the American
> black man will start thinking about his human rights,
> and then start thinking of himself as part of one of
> the world's great peoples, he will see he has a case for
> the United Nations.
> —Malcolm X, *Autobiography*

Malcolm X returned to America on May 21 already planning a longer trip to Africa later in the summer, to persuade heads of newly independent states to call on the United Nations to intervene on behalf of African Americans. This was an old tactic. African Americans had appealed to the League of Nations after World War I and the United Nations after World War II. But the civil rights movement of the 1960s was a game changer. The famous boycotts, protests, and marches had aimed at persuading the U.S. government to intervene in southern race relations in support of American ideals. Martin Luther King's dream was born in the American dream. Malcolm X now wanted the UN to challenge what he called the American nightmare by making American racism an international issue, much as had been done with South African apartheid.

In Harlem in June, Malcolm X founded the Organization of Afro-American Unity (OAAU), based within his Muslim Mosque Inc. and modeled on the Organization of African Unity (OAU), which had recently been established to help newly independent African states forge shared agendas. The OAAU's role was to promote his global vision for all black Americans, regardless of religion, and to provide a platform for African leaders to take up African Americans' cause. Malcolm X's two organizations, the OAAU and the MMI, housed in the same building but focusing on different issues, embodied his twin, intertwined priorities. "As a new convert," he explained to supporters, "I feel obligated to fight for the spread of Islam until all the world bows before Allah, but as an Afro-American I can never overlook the miserable plight of my people in America, so I have two fights, two struggles."[52]

In practice, the OAAU was a tiny organization, little more than a name, a shared office, and a few score ardent supporters. But his trip to Africa, and especially the attendant publicity, earned Malcolm X a seat at the table with top American civil rights leaders. His softening of criticism of those leaders helped. He had praised Martin Luther King in Africa, and said the main difference between him and King was that King didn't mind getting beaten up—and he did. On June 13, Ossie Davis invited Malcolm X to join a conference of the "big six" leaders of the main protest organizations. King couldn't make it, but his speechwriter Clarence Jones attended as his representative. Jones was persuaded by Malcolm X's argument about the United Nations. He called Davis at 9:25 that evening (the precise time and transcript of the conversation are courtesy of an FBI phone tap) and said, "Reflecting on today's conference, the most important thing discussed was that we internationalize the question of civil rights and bring it before the United Nations." Davis agreed. It was time to bring the problem of American race "before the whole world."[53]

Malcolm X returned to his favorite city, Cairo, on July 9, ahead of the second Organization of African Unity meeting, which he attended. A fortnight later he sent a memo to OAU delegates "on behalf of 22 million African Americans." His actions unnerved officials at home, especially since they came at a time of well-publicized violence in some black communities in America. The *New York Times* reported, "The State Department and the Justice Department have begun to take an interest.... Officials said that if Malcolm succeeded in convincing just one African Government to bring up the charge at the United Nations the United States Government would be faced with a touchy problem.... [The situation would] contribute to the undermining of the position the United States has asserted for itself as the leader of West in the advocacy of human rights."[54] FBI head J. Edgar Hoover, in a memo to his team, was more succinct: "Do something about Malcolm X. ENOUGH OF THIS BLACK VIOLENCE."[55]

In his memo, Malcolm X urged African heads of state to realize that "your problems will never be fully solved until and unless ours are solved. . . . We pray that our African brothers have not freed themselves of European colonialism only to be overcome and held in check by American dollarism."[56] Malcolm X's prayers were not answered: to the relief of the State Department, not one African government petitioned the UN In a letter to his wife at the end of July, Malcolm X wrote: "The enemy has successfully alienated most African governments from wanting to get directly involved in the problem." He concluded, ruefully: "the science (art) of diplomacy and political 'maneuvering' at the international level is much different and more delicately difficult than getting on the soap-box there in Harlem."[57]

A quick learner, Malcolm X proceeded to entice governments to his cause by doing what he did best—reaching out to the grass-roots. Seeking to win the hearts and minds of students, he toured campuses in North, West, and East Africa. One American journalist in Nigeria, Victor Reisel, worried that the "good people, friendly people," of Ibadan "now shudder when they think of us—for Malcolm X was here, brutalizing us, charging us with being a vast national torture chamber."[58] John Lewis, leader of the Student Nonviolent Coordinating Committee (SNCC), the main American student civil rights group, traveled to Africa in 1964. He was astonished at Malcolm X's popularity across the continent. "All of Africa was for Malcolm," he wrote later.[59] Malcolm X was delighted by the attention his African trip brought him at home. He told Betty that there was set to be a "top article on me in the *Saturday Evening Post* and I will get back just in time to capitalize upon the publicity."[60]

As his popularity soared, Malcolm X gained access to eleven heads of state and their parliaments. After speaking to the Kenyan

National Assembly, Malcolm X was thrilled that the body proposed, and passed, "a resolution of support for our human rights struggle."[61] (The American ambassador to Kenya was not so thrilled—he met with Malcolm within hours and accused him of being a racist.) Nonetheless, in a speech in New York after his return, Malcolm X reckoned that the meetings had made more of an impact on him than vice versa. "The understanding that I got broadened my scope so much that I felt I could see the problems and complaints of Black people in America and the Western Hemisphere with much greater clarity."[62]

EUROPE

> Many of our people in Paris, as well as from the
> African continent, are organizing. They are just as
> concerned with what is going on over here as you and
> I are.
>
> —Malcolm X, speaking to a rally in Harlem,
>   November 29, 1964

Paul Robeson, the great African American actor, singer, and anti-imperialist activist, who petitioned the United Nations to condemn lynching in America in 1951, famously said that he discovered Africa in London, thanks to all the Africans he met there. For Malcolm X a decade or so later, somewhat the reverse was true: he discovered London in Africa. During his travels, he jotted down the names and addresses of dozens of Arab and African students who were studying in Britain, mostly in London, and in Paris, and he received invitations to both cities. By quite early in the summer, then, it was clearly on his mind to go there and meet with black immigrants and students. "If this [trip goes] as planned," he wrote to his wife, "I shall visit Kuwait, Arabia,

Sudan, Ethiopia, Kenya, Tanganyika, Morocco, Algeria, Paris, London—and then into New York."[63]

The plans changed slightly—London became Oxford—following a chance meeting in Kenya. Malcolm X flew into Nairobi on October 5 and checked into the luxurious Victorian-era New Stanley Hotel, where he intended to stay for a couple of weeks. That same day, Zambian student Louis Nthenda also checked in for the night. Nthenda was en route to Oxford to take up a graduate research scholarship at St. Antony's College. He was looking forward to riding in the world's only supersonic plane, the VC10, the next day. That evening in the hotel dining room, Nthenda recognized Malcolm X immediately, having followed his Middle Eastern and African travels on television. "We were the only blacks in the dining room," Nthenda recalled later, "and I asked if I could move over to his table. By the end of the evening, he had accepted my suggestion of the Oxford Union inviting him to a debate before year end."[64] Nthenda hadn't even started at Oxford, let alone joined the Union. As chance would have it, the president of the Union proved eager to follow up on the suggestion.

Malcolm X decided to return to New York before flying to England to spend a few days in Oxford and other British cities. Malcolm X did, though, spend a week in Paris on his way home from Africa—stopping in Geneva en route to meet with Islamic leaders there. He had been invited to Paris by Alioune Diop, the Senegalese-born writer and founder of the pan-African cultural magazine *Présence Africaine,* to speak at the Salle de Mutualité. Paris enjoyed a long tradition of hosting black militant writers, some of whom found a home, or even their voice, there. Just a few weeks before Malcolm X's visit, Diop had organized an appearance by the poet Langston Hughes. In Malcolm X's case, thanks to his popularity with African students and European leftists, not to mention his notoriety in the French media as a "hater of white men," the venue was packed with hundreds of supporters and journalists.[65] As one reporter noted, Malcolm X could "barely push into the room over the assorted legs of those" who were sitting on the floor.[66]

The trip to Paris was a classic Malcolm X visit. He spent much of the time meeting with local people, asking them questions and testing his views. As Lebert Bethune recalled later, "Brother Malcolm wanted to hit the streets and to visit every nook and cranny of Paris where Afro-American brothers hung out."[67] By day he met with African students in cafes, and one evening he got together with show business performers. He was excited by what he learned and made plans to return. At the Salle de Mutualité, he also took the opportunity to teach. In what became a question-and-answer session rather than a speech, Malcolm X denounced America, "the number one racist society on the face of the earth"; called for global black brotherhood between the West and Africa; urged revolutionary rather than nonviolent protest; and warned his listeners to beware of liberals offering reform.[68] With a nod to his audience, he extolled the powerful example of the Haitian revolution, where "black slaves had the soldiers of Napoleon tied down."[69]

By all accounts, the crowd was impressed. Bethune credited his success to the "charming and irresistible but uncompromising style of his manner" as much as to the "moral and ideological truth which his demands for freedom at all cost drove home to the audience. The French, regarding even the truth as credible only when it is stylishly presented, succumbed to Malcolm's presence and power."[70]

As chance had it, given the topic of his forthcoming Oxford

debate, Malcolm X was also asked about his extremism. He replied that he was proud of that identity. "The conditions that our people suffer are extreme," he explained briefly, and an extreme illness "cannot be cured with a moderate medicine."[71] Just over a week later, across the channel, he would be able to address the illness, and suggest an extreme cure, at greater length.

CHAPTER TWO

Oxford, Britain, and Race, 1870-1964

OXFORD AND THE WHITE MAN'S BURDEN

> I read how, entering India—half a billion deeply religious brown people—the British white man, by 1759, through promises, trickery and manipulations, controlled much of India through Great Britain's East India Company. The parasitical British administration kept tentacling out to half of the subcontinent.
>
> —Malcolm X, *Autobiography*

"The duty of the University of Oxford," declared the prominent Victorian intellectual John Ruskin, was "to educate English gentlemen."[1] And the duty of "the most energetic and worthiest" of these gentlemen, Ruskin further explained in his inaugural lecture as Oxford's Professor of Art in 1870, was to be "seizing every piece of fruitful waste ground" that England "can set her foot on" and to make the "sceptered isle for all the world a source of light."[2]

In those bold imperial days when, to quote Ruskin again, Britain was "mistress of half the earth," the University of Oxford did its duty. As Britain scrambled for Africa, consolidated its administration of the Caribbean, and named Queen Victoria the Empress of India, Oxford established something of a monopoly on the training of Britain's "most energetic and worthiest" gentlemen who sought to take the light of the sceptered isle to the ends of the earth. During the period of British rule in India, fifteen viceroys and governors general were Oxford men (compared with only five from Cambridge).[3]

The ambitious master of Oxford's Balliol College from 1870 to 1893, Benjamin Jowett, spotted an opportunity to govern the world through his pupils. A clergyman and professor of Greek who sought to make Balliol Oxford's academic powerhouse, Jowett used his influence to shape new regulations that enabled candidates who passed the Indian Civil Service examination to attend Oxford or Cambridge University for two years. Jowett ensured that most of these men went to Balliol. One in six Balliol men who matriculated between 1874 and 1914 "spent a substantial part of their working lives in India."[4] Balliol even provided three viceroys of India in succession between 1888 and 1905.[5] The last of these, Lord Curzon, returned to Oxford to become chancellor in 1907. At the dawn of the twentieth century, then, nonwhite nations and peoples loomed large in the outlook and experience of Oxford gentlemen.

Of course, Britain already had a domestic nonwhite population of its own. Small communities, mostly segregated and almost always squalid, developed near the seaports of London, Liverpool, and Cardiff, where colonial seaman in the merchant navy stopped and stayed while on shore leave, often with local white women. By 1910, such communities were home to some ten thousand people. Although the workers came from countries and cultures as diverse as India, Arabia, Kenya, and the Caribbean, they were lumped together as one racial group—in this period, as "negroes" or "coloured people." Meanwhile, a few score students, clergymen, traders, entertainers, domestic workers, and descendants of African Americans who had fought for Britain in the American Revolutionary War lived in Britain's largest cities. As the motherland of the empire, Britain also attracted visitors from the colonies who came to the metropolis to speak out for the indigenous people's rights. In 1900, Henry Sylvester Williams, a Trinidadian who had lived in North America, trained for the law in London, and would later settle in South Africa, organized the First Pan-African Conference. Thirty-seven delegates from the United States, United Kingdom, Africa, and the West Indies met in London's Westminster Hall to "promote and protect the interests of all subjects claiming African descent."[6]

In his closing speech at the conference, "Address to the Nations of the World," the towering African American intellectual and activist W.E.B. Du Bois warned: "The problem of the twentieth century is the problem of the color line, the question as to how far differences of race . . . will hereafter be made the basis of denying to over half the world the right of sharing to utmost ability the opportunities and privileges of modern civilization."[7] Du Bois's words would prove prophetic for British and imperial history (and indeed, much of global history). As opportunities and rights were increasingly denied to Britain's domestic black communities and colonial subjects based on racial difference, anti-imperial sentiment became a staple of black political life in both Britain and its colonies. Six more pan-African conferences were convened to discuss issues of racism, self-government, and political and civil rights.

Yet in the late Victorian era, Ruskin's "worthiest gentlemen" knew nothing of such anti-imperial visitors or of Britain's black population. For them, nonwhite peoples were to be found in the colonies, and the question of a color line was to be addressed across the seas. This had important implications for how the idea of race was understood in Victorian Britain. In the southern United States and in South Africa, those in power asserted that black men, who formed a large proportion of the domestic population, needed to be segregated and on occasion lynched because they were prone to violence against white men and rape of white women. In imperial Britain, in contrast, academic and political elites celebrated the potential of the nonwhite colonial subjects. Frustrated by just how widespread the idealized view of native peoples' potential was in the imperial imagination, the supposedly worldly-wise editor of the *Sunday Chronicle*, in 1919, blamed the fact that "the average Englishman rarely comes into contact with a black man at home." As a result, "he has never realised, as every white man who has lived a few years in South Africa has realised, that there can never be any question of equality between the blacks and whites."[8]

This is not to say that racialism was absent from the imperial mind. Quite the opposite. As former Oxford student and mining magnate Cecil Rhodes put it in 1877, "I contend that we are the finest race in the world and that the more of the world we inhabit the better it is for the human race." Nor did he presume that relations with nonwhite nations would or should be peaceful. "You cannot have omelets without breaking eggs," Rhodes noted; "you cannot destroy the practices of barbarism, of slavery, of superstition, which for centuries have desolated the interior of Africa, without the use of force." However, under British influence, the darker peoples of the imperial world could be uplifted. "Just fancy those parts that are at present inhabited by the most despicable specimens of human beings," the Oxford alumnus continued. "What an alteration there would be if they were brought under Anglo-Saxon influence."[9]

That was the theory, at least. The hope of empire lay in inculcating colonial subjects in the culture, religion, and character of the Anglo-Saxon colonizers. Or as the celebrated Victorian writer Thomas Macaulay put it in a discussion of Indian education, what was needed was to turn the best colonial subjects into "brown Englishmen."[10] Sending Oxford-trained missionaries, educators, and administrators (along with soldiers and businessmen) abroad was part of this project. But the best way to train up "brown Englishmen" for a career of imperial service was to bring colonial subjects to British universities.

Where better than the University of Oxford? After 1871, when religious tests were no longer required for admission, Indian students were able to apply. Not surprisingly, Jowett's Balliol College quickly took advantage. In 1873, a Balliol undergraduate recorded in his diary that "the whole world in miniature" could be found inside the college walls, with "Hindoos and Frenchmen, Americans, Englishmen, Brahmins and Catholics" all in attendance.[11] By 1893, forty-nine Indian students had matriculated at Oxford in preparation for careers in the colonial civil service. Almost half of them attended Balliol.[12]

Unfortunately for Rhodes, Macauley, Ruskin, and their ilk, the theory of making patriotic "brown Englishmen" did not seem to work in practice. Abroad, what made the so-called Indian Mutiny of 1857 so troubling to imperial presumptions was that many of the leaders of the rebellion were those with the closest connections to the British administration. A British "Army of Retribution" executed many hundreds of the rebels. Some were tied to the front of cannon that were then fired. Reading of the retribution nearly a century later in the library of his jail, a horrified Malcolm X thought that this was hardly cracking eggs to make an omelet. "Some of the desperate people of India finally mutinied," Malcolm X wrote later, "and, excepting the African slave trade, nowhere has history recorded any more unnecessary bestial and ruthless human carnage than the British suppression of the non-white Indian people."[13]

Back home, many of England's worthiest gentlemen students did not want to associate with visiting students from the colonies, let alone help to help transform them into brown Englishmen. At the University of Oxford, the romantic view of the overseas native with potential frequently turned to concern when that native turned up in the college quad wearing an academic gown. When in 1902, a year after his death, Cecil Rhodes's will provided funds for twenty colonial scholars, some talked of an impending reverse colonial invasion. Students from nearby Magdalen College referred to Balliol as "Basutoland," while students at Trinity College, next door to Balliol, taunted their neighbors by calling out "Basutos" across the dividing wall.[14] The real Basutoland—modern-day Lesotho—had become a crown colony in 1884 after decades of skirmishes between Africans and British forces.

When other colleges followed Balliol's lead by taking overseas students, concerns spread. The anonymous "Lament of an Old Oxonian," which warned of the threat that nonwhite students posed to historic colleges such as Oriel, Magdalen, St. Johns, and Christ Church, revealed the savagery of cultural stereotypes at the turn of the century:

The married mussalman arrives
With 37 moon-eyed wives
And fills a quad at Oriel

While Magdalen's classic avenues
Are occupied by shy Yahoos
Whose habits are arboreal.
The Afghan hillsmen, knives in hands
Pursue the Proctor in his bands
From Folly Bridge to Johns
And Dyak head collectors stalk
Behind the elms of Christ Church walk
Decapitating Dons.
O—that such things should come to be
In my old University
But if some folk prefer 'em
And like a Barnum-Bailey show
Then Oxford's where they ought to go
My son shall go to Durham [University].[15]

Concern about colonial students in Britain turned to out-right alarm in 1909, when violent Indian nationalism spread from the colony to the metropole. At the annual party of the National Indian Association in London—set up to encourage genteel social interaction between Indian visitors and British residents—engineering student Madan Lal Dhingra shot dead Sir Curzon Wylie, the political aide-de-camp to the secretary of state for India. Lal argued further that only those resisting white violence, not the white perpetrators themselves, were called murderers—the very argument Malcolm X would use half a century later. In court, Lal claimed that the murder of one British official was a reasonable response to the British murder of eighty million Indian civilians during the previous fifty years and to the British removal of one hundred million pounds from India year after year. Lal was sentenced to death. His executioner adjusted the rope to ensure Lal's final breaths were particularly painful.

The turmoil of World War I added to the climate of fear. So, too, did a government inquiry reporting friction between British and Indian students at Oxford. Several colleges expelled Indian students. In 1915, even Balliol College declined to admit a greater number of Indian students. This was more than just a momentary backlash. Two decades later, the president of Magdalen College informed a schoolmaster writing in support of an Indian applicant that Magdalen "is very English [and] seems unable to absorb anything quite so foreign." Soon after, in the face of mounting rumors of Indian unrest, the vice chancellor summoned all Indian students to a meeting and admonished them to behave.[16]

Resistance to the presence of nonwhite colonial students was part of a wider turn against colonial subjects coming to Britain. During World War I, colonial sailors moved to Britain in unprecedented numbers to fill the employment gaps in the docks and shipping industry. In Liverpool, the nonwhite population more than doubled, from 2,000 to 5,000. Following the war, though, unemployment soared, with more than a million men out of work by April 1919. The first- and worst-hit industry was the merchant navy. Seafarers' unions introduced a "color bar" to prevent colonial sailors from competing for jobs—the first of many such restrictions in British industries. Tensions rose. Violence followed. In Liverpool, mobs ranging in size between 2,000 and 10,000 people roamed the streets and, according to a confidential police report to the Colonial Office, began "savagely attacking, beating, and stabbing every negro they could find."[17] There were antiblack riots in at least ten other towns.[18] The Cardiff *Argus* reported in May 1919 that during the funeral procession of a West Indian man in Glamorgan a mob stopped the hearse, smashed the coffin, severed the head from the body, and then kicked it around like a football.[19]

In the back alleys of these seaport towns, there was no talk of the cultural potential of brown Englishmen in the colonies. There was only outrage that brown colonial subjects were coming to Britain at all. Mainstream union leaders endorsed the anti-immigrant sentiment. Indeed, they often fueled it. Seeking to draw white sailors into a general strike for a forty-hour week, union leaders strategically conflated the issues of working conditions and black competition. Their willingness to sacrifice black workers' rights for the sake of their main priorities remained a characteristic of British labor activism for at least half a century. One of the most vocal supporters of the color bar in Glasgow, Emmanuel Shinwell, would go on to become the city's Labour Party MP and serve in Clement Attlee's cabinet.[20]

It is striking just how quickly the British justification for backlash came to resemble white supremacist rhetoric in the American south and South Africa. The Manchester *Guardian*, a newspaper with a reputation for liberalism, attributed white violence to the increasing size of the colored community and the "low moral standard of the blacks" who "are taking the bread out of the mouths of the discharged soldiers."[21] Above all, there was the sex question—"consorting with white women." Local newspapers went even further. As one put it, the "popular anger" was an understandable response to "the fact that the average negro is nearer the animal than is the average white man," and these "low types . . . insult and threaten respectable women in the street."[22]

The government responded to this first wave of violence by introducing an Aliens Restriction Act in 1919, which it extended the following year, and then passing a Special Restriction of

Special Restriction (Coloured Alien Seamen) Order in 1925. Black seamen and settlers may have been the victims of the violence, but they were also to blame. The government's instinct to bar "coloured immigrants" in order to curb racial tensions would be seen again at mid-century during the next, much larger, wave of immigration—shortly before Malcolm X's visit to Oxford.[23]

"COLOURED" STUDENTS, 1879 TO WORLD WAR II

How does it feel to be a problem?
—W. E. B. Du Bois, *The Souls of Black Folk*, 1903

The logic of empire, together with the provision of scholarships, meant that nonwhite students from British colonies continued to come to Oxford during the early twentieth century. By World War II, some 6 percent of Oxford's matriculating students were from the colonies, many of them "coloured." Pixley ka Isaka Seme, the first black South African to study at Columbia University in New York—where he won first prize in a speaking competition for an oration on the "regeneration of Africa" in which he celebrated "awakened race consciousness"—came to Jesus College in 1906.[24] The cadre of African students that he met in Oxford exhilarated Seme. "Here are to be found the future leaders of African nations," Seme told the African American educator Booker T. Washington. "These men will, in due season, return each to a community that eagerly awaits him and perhaps influence its public opinion."[25] Seme, a Zulu, organized an African students' club in Oxford, and on return to South Africa became one of the founders of the African National Congress.[26]

Seme was correct about the leadership potential of Oxford's

colonial students—and not just sub-Saharan Africans. His circle included Hamid El Alaily, future president of the Egyptian Society of England; Lala Har Dayal, the future Indian nationalist leader; and Alain LeRoy Locke, the first African American Rhodes Scholar and future writer, philosopher, and leader of the Harlem renaissance.[27] Five years after Seme graduated, Norman Manley, the future chief minister of Jamaica, arrived at Jesus College on a Rhodes Scholarship to read law. The gradual increase of colonial students at the University of Oxford was part of a wider British and imperial story. The University of London was home to India House and a slightly larger cohort of African students than Oxford, with some seventy students during the World War I years. Little more than an hour away by bus or train, many of Oxford's colonial students were integrated into London networks. It was colonial (or rather postcolonial) students who would bring Malcolm X to Oxford.

Some colonial students thrilled to their time at Oxford and reveled in all that it stood for. None more so than Kuruvila Zachariah, from Calicut in southern India, who came to Merton College in 1914 on an Indian government scholarship. He wrote home: "What Oxford stands for is not really the actual work done but the spirit, the tone, the atmosphere. It has taught me more than one can measure or write down, and I can never cease to be thankful that I had this chance of coming to Oxford." A committed Christian, Zachariah became the college's Christian Union representative. Eager to fit in with Oxford life, he bought a bicycle and tried out rowing. He also toured Europe with other visiting scholars. Far from feeling insulted, he found it hard not to laugh when a German Rhodes Scholar asked him "whether I had shot elephants in India"; in fact, he'd never "even shot a pigeon."[28]

Other students, while they enjoyed Oxford life, developed a sense of race consciousness through the company of colonial students. Alain Locke, already an advocate of racial integration at home in the United States, was delighted to find the university to be free from the formal segregation of American society—even though several colleges turned him down on account of race. (Although white American Rhodes Scholars failed to bar Locke's scholarship, they did manage to exclude him from Thanksgiving dinner.) A natty dresser, cultural elitist, and aspiring academic, Locke embraced Oxford culture. Together with Pixley Seme, Locke rode horses, took afternoon tea, and dined in a dinner jacket and bow tie. Associating with Seme also meant spending time with a man who celebrated "the ancestral greatness, the unimpaired genius, and the recuperative power of the [African] race."[29] Locke left Oxford a committed pan-Africanist, professing a dislike of the lack "of racial curiosity" in white British "cultured circles," which threatened "one's own humanity."[30]

Meanwhile, a few colonial students arrived—and departed—feeling only disdain for the empire. Indian nationalism flourished in Oxford and London. Shyamaji Krishnavarma, who had come to Balliol to read Sanskrit in 1879, advocated "complete non-co-operation with the foreigner in maintaining his domination over India."[31] After organizing against the empire in India, Krishnavarma returned to Britain in 1897 to support what he hoped would be the next generation of nationalist leaders. It was Krishnavarma who set up India House and an Indian Home Rule Society in 1905, which sought to "enlighten the British public with regard to the grievances, demands and aspirations of the people of India." India House was home for Madan Lal Dhingra, who shot Sir Curzon Wylie. Twenty years later, Nigerian law student Lapido Solanke formed the West African

Students Union and founded Africa House as a hostel for nationalist students.

Overall, then, there was no single nonwhite colonial student experience in Britain. There was not even a united "coloured" or "negro" community. Indians, West Indians, and Africans tended to move in different circles. Indeed, even students from the same country had widely different experiences. Kuruvila Zachariah was astonished to learn in March 1913 that Oxford was home to eighty-four Indian students, since he knew only about a dozen.

What is striking—and ironic—is how often nonwhite colonial students came to Oxford as imperial loyalists and aspiring "brown Englishman," yet returned home as nationalists. Cecil Rhodes established his scholarships to promote the empire by bringing the brightest colonial students to Oxford and letting them soak up Anglo-Saxon influence. As it turned out though, these and similar awards actually served to make Oxford a training ground for the anti-imperial cause.

Sometimes colonial students changed their views as a result of exposure to nationalist circles in Oxford and London. Lala Har Dayal, for example, had excelled in colonial schools in Delhi, won a government scholarship to read Sanskrit, and looked forward to a successful career with the Indian Civil Service (ICS) after attending St. John's College. But at Oxford he fell in with the Cosmopolitan Club, with its discussions of race, nationalism, and empire. He also regularly visited India House, where he met with Krishnavarma, who funded Har Dayal's wife's student fees at Oxford. Har Dayal eventually resigned his scholarship in 1907, believing that "no Indian who really loves his country ought to compromise his principle ... for any favour whatever at the hands of alien oppressive rulers of India."[32] Or as he put it more succinctly, "To Hell with the ICS." After Oxford, Har

Dayal inspired the Ghadar Movement, which sought to provoke a mutiny in the British Indian Army.[33]

The altered outlook of Oxford's colonial students was also a reaction to the cold shoulder offered by England's "worthiest gentlemen." The future Jamaican leader Norman Manley wrote to his wife soon after his arrival in Oxford that he felt alone, like "a speck floating about or swimming in a liquid mass—in it but not of it." Manley's feeling of isolation only grew. "I have not made a single friend here.... I have been an alien first and last.... I cannot get behind the barrier that is always there, I feel chained."[34]

Manley's comments were typical of the complaints of many Indian, Caribbean, and African students. Such feelings of isolation were in fact similar to those reported by white British students who came from lower-class backgrounds. Visiting colonial students, by contrast, tended to be from more privileged classes (and were lighter skinned) than many of their countrymen, whom they had kept at a distance back home. But in England they found themselves racially and socially downgraded, at the bottom rather than the top of the shifting racial ladder. Lumped into the category of "negro" or "coloured," many now chose to identify as such for the first time.

Very occasionally, racial discrimination took the form of explicit segregation. Oxford's Carlton Club, for example, a politically conservative dining club, was notoriously, exclusively white. For the most part, however, racial discrimination was not overt; rather, it seemed to be hidden behind a mask of politeness and gentility—and for that, colonial students resented it all the more. Eric Williams, who came to Christ Church in 1932 to read history and later became the first prime minister of Trinidad and Tobago, sensed it in an encounter on the streets of Oxford. One day while out walking, he passed a don, one of Britain's leading progressive author-politicians, who had been on Williams's examination panel. "He eyed me so curiously when he passed, without speaking, that I glanced back," Williams later wrote. When he did so, Williams found the don gaping at him. Embarrassed, the don hurried on. A few moments later, Williams turned around—and caught the man's gaze on him again. This racially tinged version of the childhood game that the English call grandmother's footsteps (and Americans call red light, green light) carried on until the don turned into his college. "No doubt," Williams concluded caustically, the don went on "to continue his championship of liberalism."[35]

The brightest and best colonial students did not invoke racism in response to academic struggles. Far from it. The academically brilliant Har Dayal went on to earn a doctorate from the University of London. Manley won a prize at Oxford for his essay on the Victorian philosopher and writer Samuel Butler. Eric Williams was top of his year. ("I had come, seen, and conquered—at Oxford!" he exulted.)[36] On paper, growing up in the colonies was not a hindrance to outstanding academic performance. Williams's best exam marks came in his colonial history module.[37] Still, Williams was convinced that he failed to win a prestigious fellowship at Oxford's All Souls College because of the color of his skin. When the forty members of Williams's fellowship examination panel roared with laughter when he made a mistake in his French translation, he had the "distinct impression that the roar was aimed at me and not at the mistake. . . . This is one of those difficulties that whites can never understand."[38]

Williams concluded that even the brightest colonial subject had to stay in his place—and that place was at home in the colonies, not in Oxford. With a paternal tone, Williams's college advisor encouraged him to give up his academic dreams and return to Trinidad, where he could "render the greatest service to his people."[39] Instead Williams applied to the all-black Howard University, in Washington, D.C., where he wrote *Slavery and Capitalism,* a book which argued provocatively that profit, not humanitarianism, was the reason Britain had ended slavery. When he did return home, the service he rendered would be to form the People's National Movement, which would lead Trinidad and Tobago to independence.

During the early twentieth century, then, Oxford inadvertently seemed to do its duty to the anti-imperial cause every bit as much as to the imperial one. Educating the very best Indian, Caribbean, and African student leaders and unwittingly transforming them into race-conscious nationalists become a new tradition for the ancient university, one that would grow as student numbers from the colonies increased in the era of independence. Connecting with the future leaders of Britain's colonial nations was a powerful motivator in Malcolm X's acceptance of the invitation to come to Oxford.

OXFORD AND IMMIGRATION, 1948–1962

Similarly, just let some mayor or some city council somewhere boast of having "no Negro problem." . . . I'd say they didn't need to tell me where this was, because I knew that all it meant was that relatively very few Negroes were living there. That's true the world over, you know. Take "democratic" England— when 100,000 black West Indians got there, England stopped the black migration.

—Malcolm X, *Autobiography*

On August 28, 1951, the once-a-decade World Methodist Conference convened at the University of Oxford's historic Sheldonian Theatre, in the heart of the city.[40] King George VI and the archbishop of Canterbury welcomed 450 delegates from around the world. The American delegation included Bishops William J. Walls, Sherman L. Greene, and Bertram Doyle, representing the three largest African American Methodist denominations. Following Nazi racism during World War II, Indian Independence in 1947, and the United Nation's adoption of the Universal Charter of Human Rights in 1948, the time seemed apt for a forthright challenge to both empire and racial discrimination. Where better than at a global ecumenical Methodist gathering—a denomination founded by an abolitionist, with a long history of African American and black African membership—at Oxford University, with its reputation for enlightened thinking?

Freedom and equality were certainly on the black bishops' agenda. William Walls in particular was an outspoken opponent of racial discrimination. The story was often told by fellow clergy about Walls, in 1934, refusing to leave a whites-only restaurant at Union Station in Washington, D.C., until he was served—and sat there for seven hours when he wasn't. Two of the other African American Methodist representatives in Oxford had served on President Truman's ground-breaking Committee on Civil Rights. Meanwhile, back in the United States, black Methodists were taking part in the assault on Jim Crow. One minister in Kansas, Oliver Brown, had already filed a lawsuit that in 1954 would lead to the famous *Brown vs. Board of Education* ruling that outlawed school segregation. The following year the actions of Rosa Parks, a committed member of a black Methodist church in Montgomery, Alabama, would prompt a bus boycott that helped launch the civil rights movement.

The Oxford conference got down to business, and things looked promising. Following morning worship and opening sessions that affirmed the authority of the Bible, the sufficiency of the gospel, and the necessity of the church, the delegates turned to the subject of "Christian responsibility in a divided world." One of the world's divisions was the color line. In a special resolution, the conference vowed "to oppose racial discrimination wherever it is found, at home or overseas; in particular to support and apply the principle of partnership in all relationships, official and personal, with other members of the multi-racial Commonwealth to which we all belong."[41]

The African American bishops, however, were anything but delighted. The conference's resolution on race may have been correct on paper, and black clergy may have been invited to lead the prayers at the morning worship, but, complained Walls, the white Methodist leadership "completely ignored representatives of Negro churches" during all the "social, historical, theological and political" debates. Walls stormed out in protest at what he called "the most segregated program that the Methodist Ecumenical Conference ever had,"[42] and later he, along with Doyle and Greene, held a public protest prayer meeting in Wesley Chapel in central Oxford. On their return to the United States they released a damning statement to the press, noting that "the Black world was silent in the World Conference."[43]

In many ways, the story of postwar Britain regarding matters of race was the story of the Methodist Conference in Oxford writ large. The war years had offered promise. Some 130,000 black American GIs came to Britain, and most received a warm welcome. In 1942, the British government removed the Aliens Restriction Order to allow the immigration of colonial workers who could bolster the war effort. Some 7,000 West Indians served in the Royal Air Force, others were recruited from the Caribbean to work in defense factories, and seamen from across the colonies came to work in British ports. While most returned home when the war was over, those who remained in Britain encountered no American Jim Crow or South African apartheid-style system of segregation. Meanwhile, the government voiced support for human rights, not least as Britain prepared for its imperial territories to become Commonwealth partners.

In practice, though, black Britons often suffered discrimination or exclusion from housing and jobs. "It is important that it should be recognised that a 'colour bar' exists in various forms in this country," the Welfare Department of the Colonial Office stated in 1946. "At present there seems to be a tendency to try and ignore the existence of such a state of affairs, particularly as it is not recognised by any provision for or against in the Statute book such as is the case in the Union of South Africa and in the U.S.A."[44]

Following an antiblack riot in Liverpool in 1948, that state of affairs became harder to ignore. As in 1919, violence followed a campaign by white seamen to force out black wartime workers. And once again, mainstream media blamed the black workers, with stories of roving gangs of "Negroes . . . armed with bottles, swords, daggers, iron bars, 'coshers' and axes."[45] Some fifty black men were arrested. In court, the defendants accused the police of unprovoked assaults and raids on black clubs. Witnesses testified to police violence, doctors reported on the arrested men's injuries, and one policeman admitted that he "laid about" one black man "with a baton" (he was acquitted).[46] The Liverpool riot was one of many antiblack fights across the country. Around the London docklands the following summer, a month of intermittent fighting followed reports that "a Negro put his arm around a white girl."[47]

An unofficial color bar, antiblack violence, and police harassment set a disturbing scene for the first substantial group of nonwhite immigrants to Britain in mid-century. On June 22, 1948, the *Empire Windrush*—described by the *Evening Standard* as "a dirty white ship"—arrived in London with five hundred Caribbean passengers looking for work.[48] The following month, the British Nationality Act, passed under a Labour government with Conservative support, confirmed that all colonial citizens had the status of a British subject—and thus the right to live and work in Britain. The framers of the act were interested in securing the British Commonwealth, not in promoting immigration, at a moment when former (white) colonies such as Canada were passing their own citizenship legislation. No one expected more than a handful of the 600 million people living in Britain's colonies and former colonies to actually come to Britain. (In fact, colonial officials planned for 100,000 people in poorer British West Indies colonies to move to other parts of Caribbean).[49]

Following the arrival of the *Windrush*, the perturbed minister of labour, George Isaacs, told Parliament that he hoped "no encouragement will be given to others to follow their example."[50] It wasn't. Successive Labour and Conservative cabinets established a series of working parties to find ways to restrict immigration.[51] But in the decade following passage of the act, with unemployment at an all-time low, some 200,000 Caribbean, Indian, and Pakistani immigrants moved to Britain.

The lived experience of nonwhite immigrants varied from place to place and depended greatly on country of origin. But more often than not, the journey to Britain, to quote the title of a survey by Jamaican bus conductor and journalist Donald Hinds, who immigrated in 1955, became a "journey to an illusion." For Hinds, who had been brought up reading classic British literature and watching movies about upper-class British culture, arriving in a country where poor white women wore hair rollers in public and white men did "black men's" work and menial jobs had left him "struck dumb." The greatest illusion, however, was Britain's reputation for civility and equality. "In all sections of society," one ex-serviceman, Kevin Webb, complained to Hinds, "the theme was 'The bloody war you came to fight is over so why the hell don't you go back to your own country.' We therefore found ourselves in the ridiculous position of having fought for a civilization which turned out to be a 'whites only' civilization."[52]

The city of Oxford was very much a part of this mid-century story of discrimination and squalor. The city had seen a few Indian and Pakistani immigrants before the 1950s, including former seamen from the Mirpur district of Pakistan. Some were employed in Indian restaurants, others had come to Oxford as peddlers. But in 1955, the bus service in some parts of Oxford came almost to a standstill due to staff shortages. Bus conductors and cleaners had taken up better-paid jobs at the new Morris Motors company in the Cowley district of East Oxford. Unable to replace them with locals, the bus company hired a dozen West Indian ex-servicemen. The hospitals, British Rail, and some building firms followed suit: on losing their lowest-paid employees to the car industry, they offered jobs to "coloured workers." Meanwhile, Oxford's Mirpuri ex-seamen passed word to their kin that jobs were available. When an economic recession hit the north of England in 1958, unemployed West Indians, Indians, and Pakistanis looked south for jobs. Soon, immigration had taken off. Between 1955 and 1965, Oxford had the fourth fastest-growing immigrant community in the country.[53]

Hundreds of low-paid jobs were indeed available, but in the late 1950s decent jobs were not. The Morris Motors workforce remained stubbornly white, and immigrant workers on the buses remained stuck in unskilled jobs. At a Worker's Educational Association weekend in South Oxfordshire in 1956, a union lecturer insisted that white busmen would not allow colored workers to become drivers. The chairman of the Oxford branch of the main Transport and General Workers Union denied the claim, saying that we "don't care whether they are black, blue or yellow"—a denial undermined by the fact that there *were no* black, or blue or yellow, drivers.[54]

Decent low-rent housing was not available either. Accommodation for immigrants in Oxford was overcrowded and overpriced. One Sikh-owned house in Oxford's central Jericho district had between forty and sixty Indian and Pakistani residents at any one time. A generation later, one former resident refused to talk to an interviewer about just how horrible it had been.[55] Recalling his time in a different Oxford house in the late 1950s, a Pakistani immigrant named Amjad remembered, "It was terrible living there. We slept two or three men to a bed and each bedroom had two or three double beds in it. People also slept on the stairs and even outside.... During the week, for three months, we ate nothing but baked beans." Amjad concluded: "No wonder our English neighbours disliked us."[56] He was right. Being restricted to poor housing and menial work led to the self-perpetuating stereotype that immigrants created bad conditions and were unable to do better jobs.

Stereotypes having to do with black criminality quickly developed, too. One white female Oxford student from this period still remembers her first sight of Caribbean men —hanging around the rail station selling drugs.[57] Many moral panics about immigrant life resulted from cultural misunderstandings. Amjad remembered one newspaper headline that read, "Pakistanis eat cats," a rumor that he presumed was started by garbage collectors who found the skeletons of chickens that had been bought live from farms and were slaughtered in "the *halal* way."[58]

Caribbean immigrants even received criticism for holding parties, especially in London. "I do not object to people enjoying themselves," one Brixton resident complained to his MP in 1959, but "when your rest is broken practically every night of the week ... I begin to appreciate how racial hatred starts. My wife, a very very tolerant woman, now tends to talk of these people as 'ignorant niggers.'"[59]

Misunderstandings, fears, and stereotypes had practical consequences. The British commissioner for Caribbean migrants promised government ministers that his staff would make the end of parties a top priority. Police reports from late 1950s London reveal that officers took pride in how many clubs they raided.[60] In 1957, an African and West Indian newssheet complained, "After robbing and persecuting [nonwhite colonial people] so much that cold and anti-social London seems a better proposition than life in the colonies—these very same exploiters confront West Indians in London and ask: Do you keep brothels? How many crimes have you committed?"[61] Such high-profile intervention by the state and police only reinforced stereotypes and exaggerated the numbers of migrants in the public perception. According to polls in the late 1950s, two-thirds of Britons wanted a halt to "coloured" immigration.[62]

News of the illusion quickly spread to immigrants' countries of origin. In early August 1958, Indian prime minister Jawaharlal Nehru lamented the "tendency in the United Kingdom for the colour bar to come into evidence in some places."[63] News spread to Malcolm X's home country, too. In 1955, a prominent African American journalist, Edward Scobie, wrote an exposé on British life for readers who were dealing with Jim Crow back home—just one of dozens of articles about British racism. "The ugly fact is that in spite of the lofty and sanctimonious acclamations of the English, when faced with the issue of color they are as guilty as the race haters or South Africa and the Dixie demagogues of America's South. Only John Bull prefers to hide behind a flimsy coverage of diplomatic hypocrisy."[64]

Such an avid reader as Malcolm X may well have come across such stories, or at least heard talk of them. He would certainly have heard of the anti-immigrant riots in Notting Hill, London, and Nottingham in late August and September 1958, which became headline news around the world. Black Harlem's newspaper, the *New York Amsterdam News*, reported on September 6 that "some 2,000 white teenagers rioted, smashing windows and throwing bottles at several houses [in Notting Hill] in which about 300 Negroes had taken refuge." (To orient readers who knew little of London, the paper explained that the riot occurred two miles north of Buckingham Palace.) In a summation that was likely all too familiar to Malcolm X, the *News* concluded that the violence was a result of competition for the lowest class of jobs, housing, and women.[65]

As the Trinidad-born, British-based broadcaster George Lamming saw things, the riots shattered any illusions colonial students in the "relative comfort" of Oxford or Cambridge might have had about Britain. Oxbridge students may have tried to dismiss "a cold stare, an enigmatic sneer, the built-in compliment which is used to praise, and at the same time remind them who and what they are." But the riots provided a reality check. "Oxford wakes up one morning to an appalling scandal. It is England's scandal. For the bells have tolled over Notting Hill Gate, and student or not, Oxford knows that the bell has tolled for all who suffer from a defect of colour."[66]

The following year, Antiguan immigrant Kelso Cochrane was murdered by a white gang in London—the first of the new wave of immigrants to be killed. A tall, physically strong young man whose teenage years had been somewhat similar to those of Malcolm X—in that he was thrown out of school and then drifted in a rage across the United States—Cochrane moved to Britain in the mid-1950s and worked as a carpenter. Late on Saturday evening, May 16, Cochrane walked to the local hospital because of a sore hand. He didn't make it home. In what the coroner described as a particularly "callous type of crime," half a dozen young men set upon him with a knife that pierced his heart. Cochrane was no saint, but the evidence showed that he was unarmed, sober, and entirely innocent. What made Cochrane's death particularly galling was that the police failed to make an arrest, even though witness statements made it abundantly clear who was to blame.[67] Again, the *Amsterdam News* carried the story on its front page.[68]

Black Britons had long organized for self-protection, to secure their rights, and to call for an end to empire. Dr. Harold Moody, a Jamaican doctor and committed Christian, founded the League of Coloured Peoples in 1931 to protect its members and promote better race relations in the United Kingdom and abroad.[69] During the later 1930s, a left-leaning anticolonial transatlantic network emerged, based in Britain, that included such luminaries as Trinidadian intellectuals C. L. R. James and George Padmore, Amy Ashwood Garvey (wife of Marcus Garvey), and future Ghanaian leader Kwame Nkrumah. The list of young leaders

resident in Britain who attended the fifth Pan-African Conference in Manchester in 1945, presided over by W.E.B. Du Bois,
reads like a *Who's Who* of future giants of national independence
movements. As the capital of the empire, London was the hub of
this international network.[70] Although the American arm of that
network collapsed during the early Cold War, London, home to
the Council of African Organizations, would remain an important site for black Atlantic intellectuals and anticolonial organizing. Malcolm X would give a keynote address at the Council
during his visit to England.

In the late 1950s, anti-immigrant riots, anger at the police, and
disillusionment with British life prompted unprecedented anti-
racist organizing in London and beyond. Hundreds of mourn-
ers—the numbers boosted by police informants—attended
Cochrane's funeral. (Poignantly, the opening hymn, "Thy Kingdom Come, O God," included the verse "Where is Thy reign of
peace / And purity, and love? / When shall all hatred cease / as
in the realms above?")[71] Claudia Jones, a Caribbean communist
who had spent her adult life in Harlem before being deported
to Britain in 1955, took a lead in transforming anger into political action. With Donald Hinds and others, Jones published the
influential West Indian Gazette, led demonstrations that connected freedom in the colonies to rights in Britain, supported
the cross-parliamentary party Movement for Colonial Freedom
(MCF), and founded the Notting Hill Carnival to celebrate
Caribbean and African culture.[72]

Such organizing was needed. While the riots earned sympathy from liberals, they also strengthened the call to halt immigration. A left-leaning tabloid newspaper, the *Daily Mirror,*
admitted that the rioting had "come like a kick in the pants to all
of us," and that it was embarrassing because "we have lectured

other countries," the newspaper called for "white hooligans [to be] properly punished" (which they were). Nonetheless, the *Mirror*'s final solution to "the stinking explosion in our backyard" was to limit immigration.[73] The MCF fought back. One flyer explained that Britain had more emigrants than immigrants during 1952–61, only one-fifth of immigrants were colored, nonwhite immigrants represented less than 1 percent of the total population, overcrowding was due to a lack of planning, and colored immigrants were the ones who suffered anyway.[74] But the very fact that immigrants were so few, and public opinion so strong, fundamentally weakened their lobbying power.

The Conservative government of the day introduced a Commonwealth Immigration Bill that came into law on July 1, 1962, to be reviewed annually. The act only allowed immigration by skilled workers with work vouchers (in practice, mostly from former white British dominions), but exempted Ireland from any restrictions. The leader of the Labour Party, Hugh Gaitskell, called it "cruel and brutal anti-colour legislation" (though his party did not repeal it when it took power in 1964). Nonwhite Britons agreed. A West Indian committee in London warned that "those people who were prejudiced against colored people might feel strengthened in their attitude by the Government decision to introduce this legislation."[75] They were proved right. Within a month of the act's passage, a mob two thousand strong responded to a fight between a white man and an Indian immigrant by storming through a West Indian section of London. There was only one arrest: a West Indian with an iron bar.[76]

Ironically, the prospect of an act restricting immigration had prompted a rush of migrants from Africa, the Caribbean, and South Asia trying to beat the deadline—more than 200,000 people during 1961 and the first half of 1962. Over half of the Indians and almost three-quarters of the Pakistanis who arrived in Britain in the fourteen years between the 1948 Nationality Act and the 1962 Commonwealth Immigration Act did so in the eighteen months before the latter became law.[77] For the first time, immigration rates did not correspond to British employment opportunities. Because this new wave of immigration came at a time when unemployment was rising, far from being extinguished, the immigration debate—and its attendant issues of housing and job competition—had become red hot by the eve of Malcolm X's visit. The fact that Britain's immigrant communities were growing and increasingly vociferous, not to mention closely networked to the Americas, Africa, and Asia, was part of the reason he chose to visit.

In Oxford, the ruckus over immigration coincided, in early 1961, with a government announcement that Britain's Central Ordnance Depot was to be relocated just north of the city as part of a wider military defense rationalization. News of the twin prospects of job opportunities and immigration restrictions spread through migrant grapevines. Although no records remain, staff at the depot remembered "a sudden influx of Pakistanis to Oxford over a period of about three months" at about the same time.[78] In 1961, Oxford's Pakistani residents formed a Welfare Association.[79] It was needed. By May 1962 the number of unemployed "colored immigrants" in the region had more than tripled, to 1,400, compared with the previous year. This had nothing to do with racism, explained the chair of the Regional Board for Industry; it was a result of Pakistanis' "physical shortcomings" for industrial work.[80]

Oxford was beginning to grapple with "the problem of the color line" for the very first time. And the course of this struggle would connect the city with the global struggle against racism.

THE HOUSING "COLOUR BAR"

> During Michaelmas [autumn] term of 1956, my
> landlady on Aston Street, just off the Iffley Road—
> the redoubtable Mrs Pike—explained to me that,
> while she had no prejudice against black students, she
> was prevented from taking any because of the extra
> costs caused by their skin colour rubbing off on the
> sheets.
>
> —Revan Tranter, Pembroke College student,
>   February 18, 2014

One month after the World Methodist Conference wrapped up, Jamaican student Stuart Hall arrived in Oxford on a Rhodes Scholarship to read English at Merton College. Like so many before him, Hall found his ideas of race and nation transformed by his time at the university, which he called the "summit of knowledge." In his own telling, Hall "came from this peculiar colored middle-class in Jamaica which was oriented toward Britain. . . . Most of my life had been spent thinking that the apogee of scholarly work and education was to get a scholarship and go to England to be finished off, and then come back, as it were, civilized."[81] However, "Three months at Oxford persuaded me that . . . I'm not English and I never will be."[82] Most of his friends were other "Third World students," and their "principal political concerns were with colonial questions."[83] Hall later chuckled at the irony of Rhodes's legacy: "The whole idea of the Rhodes scholarship was to gather together in Oxford and to give a superior education to the white sons of the empire. But of course gradually, you know, the colour of the Rhodes scholars got browner and browner."[84]

Like so many colonial students earlier in the century, Hall discovered leftist thinkers in Oxford, a group that had grown in size following the passage of the British Education Act of 1944, which provided free secondary education for 11- to 18-year-olds, and after the introduction of maintenance grants that covered the cost of university fees. Such students would form the bulk of support for anti-racist activism during Malcolm X's visit.[85] Hall was inspired by this increasingly assertive "intellectual minority culture," which stood against the "casual confidence of . . . the Hooray Henries."[86] Following the British invasion of Suez and the Russian invasion of Hungary, both in 1956, Hall helped forge a British "New Left" movement that was free from party loyalties, and founded a journal, the *Universities and Left Review,* which would later become the influential *New Left Review.*

Also like other colonial students before him, Hall came to his views on race and human rights through his observation of international affairs—in the case of his generation, a tumultuous era of nationalism and civil rights activism. India had gained independence in 1947. Ten years later, Ghana became the first African country to do so. In South Africa and the American south, demonstrators took to the streets and stayed off the buses—and hit the headlines in Britain. Such days of hope had a profound impact on Hall's racial consciousness. For him, it was because of "decolonisation and civil rights in the States that . . . no matter the colour of my skin, socially, historically, culturally and politically I made the identification with being black."[87]

What marked Hall's generation, though, was the way the concerns of "coloured" university students and Oxford-dwelling immigrants came together for the first time, with support from large numbers of white students. Politically active students from British colonies mingled with the city's rapidly growing communities of immigrant workers. "I actually played in a jazz band with a saxophonist and a drummer who were Oxford bus drivers and conductors who had migrated from the Caribbean with their families," Hall recalled. As he spent time with West Indian workers, he learned firsthand of the immigrants' disillusionment. "For most of the early period in England, I was struck by the very enormous difficulties these people were having to make any kind of life or win any recognition for themselves."[88]

In many ways, the life that overseas students led in Britain was very different from the immigrant experience. The students were temporary visitors and didn't have to face the workplace struggles that so bedeviled most immigrants.[89] At the elite universities in particular, students often came from privileged backgrounds, either on scholarships or with private means, and expected to return to leadership in their home countries. As one reporter put it, they were "the aristocrats of the coloured community."[90] Thus, with little direct stake in British race matters and little inherent solidarity with immigrants, colonial students were not immediately in the vanguard of the struggle for equal rights in the United Kingdom.

Where students did face the same problem as immigrants, though, was in finding a decent place to live—especially at Oxford in the late 1950s and early 1960s. The university's Delegacy of Lodgings reckoned that overseas students at Oxford were better off than most overseas students, since many had decent grants. But city-center housing was at a premium owing to the large swaths of land that lay on the River Thames's floodplain. The rapid expansion of foreign student numbers, following a 1958 meeting in Montreal that created a thousand new Commonwealth scholarships, only made matters worse.[91] By 1960, the university had more Commonwealth students than any university in the country outside London and, together with the various technology and extended education colleges in the city, offered well in excess of a thousand places to overseas students.

That same year, the mayor described foreign student housing as the city's "big problem."[92]

It was certainly too big a problem for the university to handle. Most Oxford colleges offered housing for first- and third-year students, but many second-years and virtually all graduates had to find private accommodation. The Delegacy of Lodgings kept a list of approved landladies whom students could approach and hoped it was long enough. But such a hit-or-miss system was problematic for foreign students, regardless of color. When prospective graduate student B. W. Greaves of Tanganyika wrote to the delegacy in May 1960, he received the stock reply: "I must warn you that the general situation in Oxford regarding accommodation is acutely difficult at the moment." The delegacy apologized that it was virtually impossible to find a place to stay in advance and advised Greaves to ask landladies in person on arrival.[93]

Asking in person, though, was precisely the problem (leaving aside the challenge of turning up in a strange country with nowhere to stay the first night). Time and again landladies refused to accept lodgers when they realized they were colored. As British settlers had done in China, some put "No Coloureds" signs in their windows or on their advertisements, sometimes adding "No Dogs." Most, though, turned away nonwhite foreign students with an apology rather than a scowl, claiming that they had no problem with race personally. Oxford landlady Rosalind Hayward wrote to the delegacy in 1962 insisting that "I am not in favour of any colour bar—in fact I have a Jamaican friend at the moment." But she was livid that the delegacy had sent a Nigerian student to ask her for a room when she had specifically asked for an "English or possibly American post graduate. . . . This is a tiny house, we are at very close quarters, [and through your] clumsiness you have hurt this woman's feelings."[94]

The feelings that landladies said they worried about most, though, were not their own. Time and again, they turned students away on account of what the neighbors would think. The excuse was so commonplace it became a standing joke among colored students. "Since I came 'ere I never met a single English person who 'ad any colour prejudice," said one of the characters in British playwright A. G. Bennett's 1959 play *Because They Know Not*. "When looking for a room everyone explained they would be happy to have me stay. It was the neighbour who was stupid.... Neighbours are the worst people to live beside in this country."

Although the "coloured student" housing problem intensified in Oxford during the 1950s, it was in fact widespread and dated back to the arrival of the first nonwhite students earlier in the century. The reach of the colored housing bar was strikingly consistent. Surveys either side of World War II in London found that 70 percent of landladies were unwilling to accept colored students—with the figure rising to 85 percent for dark-skinned African and West Indian students.[95] In 1960, in another large sample of London landladies, the figure for colored students generally was 80 percent.[96]

What was true in the capital was true in university towns across Britain. The early 1960s saw report after report of the lodging color bar. In 1963, a survey in Bristol found that only 3 percent of landladies would consent even to consider a colored student as a possible lodger.[97] In Sheffield, on receiving a silver bowl at a party to celebrate thirty-six years of service, a seventy-seven-year-old landlady insisted that her whites-only policy was not racial prejudice: "I like to mother my boys," she explained, "and I don't feel I could give a coloured student that kind of affection."[98]

Immigrants faced the same housing color bar. In a widely cited 1952 survey, 60 percent of landladies refused to take non-white lodgers—even though respondents included landladies in much poorer parts of London who could ill afford to be selective.[99] An unnamed "Nigerian in Yorkshire" complained to the Labour Party in 1955 that his landlady packed seven African men into a single room; but he had "no hope" of moving, since "if we go out looking for a room the whole street will be gazing at us. Some will even insult us."[100] News of British housing discrimination based on color spread to America.[101] In 1964, a leading African American newspaper, the *Chicago Daily Defender,* reported that "British attitudes" were similar to those of "northern and western Americans toward Negroes—little overt prejudices, no discriminatory laws," but many "landladies won't rent to a Negro or an Indian." As one landlady told an incredulous *Defender* reporter, "I've nothing against them dearie, but I can't stand the smell of curry."[102]

To make matters worse, the color bar was a cause as much as a consequence of racism. In the big cities, the refusal of middle-class landladies to take in dark-skinned lodgers forced nonwhite immigrants into areas associated with poverty, crime, and prostitution, thus reinforcing the stereotype that they were dangerous and dirty—and so unsuitable as lodgers in the better parts of town.[103]

Malcolm X may well have known of the housing problem from newspapers or meeting British students in Africa. When he came to England, he certainly recognized the phenomenon of stereotypes becoming self-fulfilling. In the United States, the formation of the ghetto was initially a response to the limited housing options for African American migrants, but the existence of ghettoes created stereotypes of black criminality and joblessness, prompting segregated school districting and suburban white flight—which in turn limited African American housing options further.[104]

The color bar also skewed prices in the rental market. Because rooms for nonwhite lodgers were in such short supply, some landladies took in nonwhite lodgers *only* because they could add what contemporary sociologists called "a foreigners levy," or what those who had to pay it called the "colour tax."[105] In a survey of 320 Oxford students in 1961, Oxford lecturer John Dawson found that African and Asian men paid on average 16 shillings more per week than white men, and African and Asian women 12 shillings more than white women.[106]

The housing color bar proved to be significant for many white Oxford students as well, because it was their first moment of real consciousness about race in Britain. Anthony Smith, who came to Oxford in 1958 as a member of the Labour Party and would go on to become head of the British Film Industry and president of Magdalen College, remembered being shocked by the "No Coloureds" signs in front windows. That led him to start a petition for open housing—though in a foretaste of battles to come, the university authorities rebuked him for "disturbing good relations between the University and the landladies."[107]

Responding to similar concerns on campuses across the country, and inspired by the mass student sit-ins in the American south, in May 1960 the London-based National Union of Students (NUS) discussed the possibility of a nationwide boycott of color-barred student housing.[108] Meanwhile, the British Council tried a more optimistic tack—an education campaign on the virtues of welcoming the foreigner. At a housing-crisis meeting of landladies in Oxford in 1960, Council representative Letitia Hartford help up the example of one landlady who had told her,

"I wondered how I as a housewife could make international relations better. Now I have taken in overseas students the world comes to me. My problem is solved."[109]

Such efforts were part of an emerging effort to promote better race relations at a time of increased immigration and a growing number of overseas students. Oxford had more than its fair share of goodwill advocates. Racial Unity—"a non-political, non-sectarian organisation formed to give general help on domestic, housing, and employment problems to immigrants"—held monthly coffee evenings "to bring together . . . overseas students who for one reason or another feel the need of further social contacts."[110] They tried to promote cross-cultural understanding, too. The highlight of 1953, for example, was a talk by Chief Nana Kobina Nketsia IV on "family life in the Gold Coast."[111] But such meetings informed the relatively few believers rather than challenging—let alone converting—the skeptics.

The color bar in housing, then, brought Caribbean, African, and Asian students and immigrants (and, to some extent, sympathetic white students) together. Claudia Jones made the potential national student "boycott on colour-bar digs" the headline story in the December issue of the *West Indian Gazette,* alongside a report on the eviction of three hundred West Indian tenants in London (following complaints about prostitution rackets).[112] And students identified with immigrants' complaints. In 1952, visiting African American journalist Roi Ottley concluded that the four thousand "Negro students" in postwar Britain had come to "see the whole British social system as a vast conspiracy against color" because of their difficulty in finding a place to live. For that reason, Ottley claimed, students became active in local politics. In London, they served as the "shock troops" of the "League of Colored Peoples."[113]

Ottley, though impressed by the troops' zeal, thought that "their efforts sometimes seem a bit pathetic." Apparently, they "have not learned the loud techniques of protest . . . nor are they formidable enough in numbers to form an effective pressure group. . . . The melancholy fact is: racial reformation in Britain is nowhere in sight, with no remedial machinery as in the U.S."[114] In 1952, Ottley was right. But by the time of Malcolm X's visit, loud cries of protest would be much more in evidence.

DISAPPOINTED GUESTS: BLACK STUDENTS
ON THE EVE OF MALCOLM X'S VISIT

> I am indeed grateful to the English. Grateful for
> rejecting me in order to discover myself.
> —Donald Hinds, *Journey to an Illusion*

In the summer of 1963, two Oxford lecturers advertised an essay competition, sponsored by the London-based Institute of Race Relations, for African, Asian, and West Indian students. A prize of £100 was on offer for the best essay concerning "attitudes towards the colour problem before [the writer] came to this country and the changes in these attitudes, if any, that may have occurred as a result of having spent time in Britain."[115]

Seventy-three students entered the competition. Of these, only seven had negative views of race relations in Britain before they arrived. Many of the rest reported that British Council orientation sessions in their home countries had given them a rose-tinted view of British race relations. But sixty-six wrote of facing discrimination in Britain: not just finding it hard to secure accommodations, but also numerous occasions when white people wouldn't sit next to them on a bus or at church, when milkmen kept their distance, when taxi drivers overcharged them, or when people called out "nigger" in the street.[116] Overall, there were more than five unfavorable comments to each favorable one. The lecturers concluded that the students' anger was "disturbing," especially since these students were likely to be leaders in the Commonwealth. They published the essays under the title *Disappointed Guests.*

The winning entry was submitted by Mervyn Morris, a Jamaican who came to Oxford's St. Edmund Hall in 1958, won a tennis blue (i.e., represented the university) in each of his three years at Oxford, earned a second-class degree, and wrote occasional essays for the BBC Caribbean service. Before coming to Oxford, Morris had made a conscious decision not to spend his time with other West Indians. Although he was the only West Indian in his year at St. Edmund Hall, he judged "that the centre of Oxford life is the college and that I must become integrated in the college community." Initially, he felt he was successful. During his somewhat lonely first weeks, he invited his peers to tea and went to their rooms for tea in return. By the end of the first year, he had made friends. "It does not embarrass me to like many facets of English culture," he wrote. He had heard from friends that "London can be very difficult," but, he thought, "life could seem fairly rosy if I concentrated only on Oxford."[117]

Eventually, however, Morris's experience turned sour. He suffered no violent hostility, but, arriving just after the 1958 Notting Hill riots, he did suffer occasional explicit incidents of racism that upset him. A teddy boy (member of a youth rebel subculture associated with gang violence) called him a "black bastard" on the train in London (though another white man countered, "He's the same colour as Louis Armstrong, man"). A white girl in a jazz club pulled away from him when she saw his color, and the only white girls who danced with him seemed to want to "test the mythical Negro virility." (Morris complained, "A West Indian can hardly be blamed for despising a woman who deep down regards him not as a man but as a foreign phallus.") The most painful incident was when the Lawn Tennis Association (LTA) decided that the combined Oxford-Cambridge team to play Harvard and Yale should, for the first time, be English only in the year that he and an Indian at Cambridge looked set to be in the team. (The captains eventually persuaded the LTA to reverse the decision.)[118]

What bothered Morris the most, though, were the more subtle, but frequent, incidents that left him feeling increasingly patronized, isolated, and finally excluded. Friendly students congratulated him on speaking English so well, or asked him how many wives he had, or assumed he was African, or made jokes about blackness.[119] Morris thought the problem was that Britons were in denial about their racism. He pointed to the government's claim that the Immigration Act was "for the benefit of immigrants" and quoted the justification made by residents who blocked an Indian family moving onto a housing estate in 1961: "This is not a matter of colour: we just don't want coloured families living on our estate."[120] He concluded: "The English are notorious for xenophobia. I believe the notoriety to be well earned."[121] How ironic, he observed, that the British aspired to be the moral leaders of the free world.

Living in Britain changed Morris. On a practical level, he grew longer hair, since no barber in Oxford knew how to cut it.[122] He found himself drawn to black culture for the first time. He enjoyed watching Senegalese dancers at Oxford's New Theatre, and he was proud of Lorraine Hansberry's play *A Raisin in the Sun,* about the travails of an African American family who moved into a white Chicago neighborhood, when it came to London's Adelphi Theatre in 1959. Morris felt he could identify, in a way the play's critics could not, with Hansberry's exploration of "the struggle going on within the personality of the Negro himself."[123] Above all, Morris had come to Britain with an idealized view of the mother country, but he went home a nationalist. "The important thing about the West Indies, or Jamaica, is that it is ours. We need now to persuade all our people that this is really so."[124]

Morris's experience was typical of those who submitted essays. Many of the lighter-skinned West Indians who entered the competition admitted that they identified as black and became Caribbean nationalists for the first time in England, and many African students took new pride in their African heritage. Patricia Madoo, a Trinidadian who went to Oxford's St. Anne's College, reflected, "The beginning of the disillusionment comes almost immediately." The incoming student sees white men doing menial jobs in the ports and on the railways—whereas at home, lighter skin meant higher class and thus better jobs.[125] Like Morris, Madoo began to identify with black immigrants and black culture in the face of rejection. "Gradually the efforts to be absorbed into English circles cease. Equally slowly a feeling of bitterness grows."[126] As in Morris's case, "the critical moment" was the Immigration Act, which gave "official sanction" to "national prejudice," followed by "an encounter with the officials [at the immigration desk] nasty enough to make her wonder what happens to the coloured people who are really trying to come in." Coming to Britain also gave Madoo a global vision. Reading of "some outrage in South Africa or the Southern USA," the visiting student, "by his unexpectedly intense fury and sorrow[, . . .] realizes that a transformation has occurred. He has become a black man, taking his side in the array of black versus white." Madoo, with lashings of irony, expressed gratitude for English racism. Having arrived with a presumption of light-skinned superiority, she departed feeling proud of her blackness and her homeland.[127]

Morris's and Madoo's stories recalled the nonwhite student experience since Victorian times. But what marked their generation in particular was the sheer number of students involved and the rise of student protest—in Britain and abroad. By the time of Malcolm X's visit there would be 40,000 overseas students in the United Kingdom, mostly from the Caribbean, Africa, and South Asia.[128] These young, disappointed guests joined with immigrant groups to campaign against the Immigration Act in Britain and in support of freedom movements worldwide. This protest against racial inequality in Britain and the empire was part of an interconnected global zeitgeist, which saw tens of thousands of students, from Greensboro, North Carolina, to Sharpeville, South Africa, risk their freedom, and sometimes their lives, in pursuit of racial justice. This was precisely the sort of global solidarity that Malcolm X was calling for.

On the face of it, the efforts of nonwhite students in Britain were less sacrificial than those of their counterparts abroad. There would be no U.S.-style mass sit-in movement, let alone a confrontation to match Sharpeville. Though growing in number, nonwhite visiting students were comparatively few, plus they were in a foreign country. But one striking aspect of their protest in the 1960s—and one that would have far-reaching consequences in Britain and abroad—was that Commonwealth students began to target the structures and ideological assumptions of the universities themselves.

British universities were ostensibly, and self-consciously, centers of enlightened thinking, with more than their fair share of left-leaning intellectuals. But some Commonwealth students critiqued them as bastions of imperialist, elitist, and even racialist thought. Prof. Hugh Trevor-Roper, Regius Professor of History at Oxford, invited such a critique. In a widely publicized series of lectures on European history published in 1963, Trevor-Roper railed against undergraduates who were "seduced" by "fashion" to learn about "black Africa. Perhaps, in the future, there will be some African history to teach. But at present there is none, or very little: there is only the history of the Europeans in Africa. The rest is largely darkness."[129] Across the Atlantic, Malcolm X heard of the slur and was outraged (though by the time the comments reached him, they had become wrongly attributed to the British historian Arnold Toynbee). In his autobiography, in 1965, Malcolm X condemned Toynbee's attempt "to bleach history" by saying that "Africa was the only continent that produced no history." Chortling over recent research into African civilizations, Malcolm X concluded: "He won't write that again."[130]

Well-meaning liberal academics came under fire every bit as much as the more conservative ones. Some students sought to revise established (Western) canons of literature by recovering, and privileging, narratives of Asian, African, and Caribbean history. None more so than a cohort of East African students in Leeds, the fourth-largest city in England, with the fifth-largest nonwhite student population. In 1964, Kenyan James Ngugi arrived on a scholarship from Makere University in Uganda, the leading colonial university in the region. Ngugi's family had been involved in the Mau Mau resistance (his mother was tortured), yet according to Ngugi it was his "experience of social and economic relations in Britain . . . that actually settled [his] socialist convictions."[131] Ngugi was appalled, not just by "air so filthy that you woke up to the sound of birds coughing," but also by the Immigration Act and police manhandling of student demonstrators. In a manner that Malcolm X would have appreciated, Ngugi rejected his name James for its imperial connection and took the name Ngugi wa Thiong'o. With his fellow East Africans, he set about "slaying the ogres of Cambridge and Oxford" who dictated the curriculum.[132]

There were aspiring ogre slayers in Oxford, too. Adil Jussawalla, an Indian reading English at University College, said it was nonwhite visiting students who first began to ask the "awkward questions [that] British intellectuals ... haven't asked themselves yet." Those intellectuals, he wrote, were quick to condemn the Holocaust, southern racists in the U.S., and apartheid, but the "empire remained beyond reproach."[133] Even so, Thiong'o judged Leeds a better place than Oxbridge from which to do so. "With nothing Oxbridgean to seduce the mind or eye, Leeds afforded a far better milieu ... to students seeking to shed the illusions of empire, for it was not hamstrung by ancient traditions."[134]

What Thiong'o couldn't have known was that the very ancient traditions that sought to restrain Oxford's Commonwealth students would actually provide a clear, high-profile target for student civil rights protest. In 1964, these protests would bring U.S. Black Power, anti-apartheid, British immigrant housing, and civil liberties movements into one struggle, and it would all happen on a single night—the night that Malcolm X came to town.

CHAPTER THREE

Antiracism Protests in Oxford, 1956-1964

A JAMAICAN AND THE OXFORD UNION

Racial discrimination in Oxford? "It exists," he says. "You just wonder when you are helping an old lady on to a bus whether she's embarrassed by your helping her." Next summer, he goes to the Bar and then home to politics, with a strong tipping as a future prime minister. Oxford old ladies boarding buses, please note.

—Report on incoming Oxford Union president Eric Anthony Abrahams, *Daily Mail*, October 8, 1964

Malcolm X may have been America's, and perhaps the world's, best-known black radical in late 1964. But within the University of Oxford there was an equally well known militant black leader, a charismatic Jamaican law student named Eric Anthony (Tony) Abrahams. In September 1964, Abrahams was elected president of the Oxford Union. It was Abrahams who formally invited Malcolm X to come to Oxford.

A gifted orator and an outspoken critic of racism who had recently returned from a speaking tour of the Middle East, Abrahams seemed to be something of a Malcolm X in the making. He certainly hoped so. Winning a Rhodes Scholarship to Oxford, becoming president of the Union, and then hosting Malcolm X were all steps toward fulfilling what he called in his application for the Rhodes Scholarship, "My most compulsive ambition . . . a career in public life."[1]

Unlike Malcolm X, Abrahams had enjoyed a life of privilege and good education. His father was a company director. Having attended a private preparatory school, then Jamaica College, Abrahams studied at the University College of the West Indies (UCWI) from 1958 to 1961, where he obtained the B.A. degree of the University of London.

The British colonial administration had founded the UCWI ten years prior to Abraham's arrival, with a view to training a reliable local leadership for imperial service. Yet despite its colonial mission, by the time Abrahams joined UCWI in 1958, the college was caught in the swirl of Caribbean nationalist politics. The faculty and administration were fast becoming black led. One student of the era, a self-confessed "country bumpkin," had gone to UCWI assuming "that only White People had the capacity to achieve. One could imagine my shock to discover that Black people could write poetry and that they could enjoy the music of Beethoven or Mozart."[2]

Black people were soon to enjoy independence, too. With Oxford alumnus Norman Manley as chief minister, Jamaica was part of the West Indies Federation of Caribbean islands, founded in 1958 to prepare for self-government. The federation collapsed in 1962, but Jamaica gained independence that year anyway, in August, as a separate state.

In this context of nationalist expectations, UCWI afforded Abrahams plenty of opportunities to hone the leadership skills that would impress the Rhodes Scholarship selection panel. He won prizes in debating competitions and was elected president of the debating society. As the college's premier debater, he traveled to competitions in the United States, including one in Wake Forest, North Carolina, in 1959—just a year before, and thirty miles away from, the first American student sit-ins against segregation in a downtown store in Greensboro. Abrahams would follow news of the student sit-in movement closely.

Abrahams also excelled at cricket, captaining his school and college teams. In 1960, cricket, especially cricket captaincy, was no mere recreation. That year, a campaign led by the celebrated Caribbean writer C.L.R. James had seen the Jamaican Frank Worrell become the first black player to be appointed captain of the West Indies cricket team for a test (international match) series. As the left-leaning, well-traveled Caribbean nationalist and pan-Africanist James explained in *Beyond a Boundary* (1963), acclaimed by many commentators as the greatest sports book ever written, black leadership of the West Indies cricket team was inextricably bound up with calls for self-respect, political independence, and nationhood.[3] It was during Worrell's tenure that the Caribbean islands gained independence. In August 1963, two days before Martin Luther King's "I have a dream" speech in Washington, the West Indies team beat England, in England.

One of Abraham's referees for his Oxford scholarship noted that Abraham's "leadership as captain of their Cricket XI received such attention" that he would have become president of the UCWI student union had he chosen to run.[4] Mumps and an eye infection prevented him from doing so. Even so, he was elected vice president of the college student union in his second year, and in that capacity he attended the 6th Congress of the

International Union of Students, held in Baghdad, Iraq, as the UCWI Guild of Undergraduates observer-delegate.[5]

In other words, the freshman student who arrived at Oxford in October 1962 was a young man with international and leadership experience, from a country that had gained independence only a month before. Unlike many Jamaican immigrants and visitors, he was also under no illusion about finding a racial utopia in Britain. Quite the opposite. A couple of years before he came to Oxford, his beloved younger sister, Hope, had started boarding school on the Isle of Wight off the south coast of England. Hope hated it. She reflected later that she "experienced a lot of racism there" and found the holidays even worse—the parents of a girl at her boarding school who took Hope in were clearly embarrassed to have a black visitor. Hope confided in her brother about the humiliation.[6]

So when Tony Abrahams came to Oxford, he found his personal goals already tied to a determination to challenge British domestic racism and imperial domination. Those personal goals were to make a name for himself in Oxford and then return to take a place in Jamaica's new government. "Even as a small boy I had an absorbing interest in all school activities which seemed to give scope for leadership talent," Abrahams explained in his Oxford application, "hence my youthful admiration for those who displayed this special quality."[7]

Abrahams may have excelled at leadership, but scholarly matters were another matter. He gained a 2.2 (a middling result) at UCWI. "His record up to the present has not been outstanding—in economics rather the contrary," admitted one referee. "It is on the personality side that he is strong."[8] His Oxford tutors tended to agree. Four colleges turned him down on academic grounds, and the fifth, St. Peter's, admitted him grudgingly. "He is obvi-

ously a man of character and a good person in himself," the master of the college wrote to the warden of Rhodes House, "but we
do feel very disquieted about his obvious academic weakness."⁹
The disparity between the school systems—even at the elite
level—in Jamaica and Britain didn't help. Latin was required
for law students at Oxford, but Abrahams hadn't studied it in
school. He tried to master some grammar the summer before
he arrived.¹⁰ Four weeks into his first term, the worried master
of St. Peter's wrote again to the warden of Rhodes House: Abrahams, though a "very nice man," had "no chance of completing
his degree in three years."¹¹

By that time, Abrahams probably didn't care. His sights were
set on the presidency of the Union, the launching pad for many
a political career. Studies and, following an injury, even cricket
slipped off his agenda. Christopher Hollis, a former Union president, described some of the qualities an aspiring candidate for
the position must have: "Human nature being what it is, it is
unlikely that [a would-be Union president] has not been at some
pains to curry favour with voters and to show himself both in
debate and in private life as perhaps a little bit more accommo-
dating and smiling to audiences and casual acquaintances than
sheer sincerity would demand."¹² With a combination of vaulting
personal ambition, savvy networking skills, and no little charm,
Abrahams fit Hollis's portrait perfectly. From the outset, though,
his personal ambition, much like that of Malcolm X, was tied in
with service to black advancement more broadly. When Hope
came to visit her brother at his first Union debate, he told her:
"Before I leave here I will be President of the Oxford Union. And
I'll fill the room with blacks."¹³

Abrahams's initial forays into Union debates showed promise.
Early in 1964, he was the third speaker in support of the motion

"This House would not fight for West Berlin." It was a "good enough effort," wrote one student journalist; "somehow, though, one is still waiting for him to make the really great speech of which he is so obviously capable."[14] Those speeches would soon come in debates about African independence and America's place in the world. By the spring term he had been elected the Union secretary. On June 12, 1964, Abrahams stood for election to be Union president in Michaelmas term (October to December). His rivals were the upcoming young British conservative Jonathan Aitken and a Pakistani radical, Tariq Ali. Both men were eloquent, charismatic, handsome, and ambitious rivals.

Ali was a more experienced political organizer than Abrahams. In Ali's own telling, he was born a left-wing agitator. His father was the editor of the largest-circulation newspaper in Pakistan until the government forced him to resign. Both parents were committed communists who often took him to "political happenings of one sort or another" and played Paul Robeson records at home.[15] The young Ali quickly developed a flair for street theater. At school he organized a demonstration at the local U.S. consulate to protest the death sentence given to an African American for "stealing a dollar in some backwood hellhole in the Southern United States."[16] At university he organized a demonstration in support of nationalist movements abroad. "Dozens of students were arrested; some were tortured."[17] Prevented by the government from further protest, Ali organized debates on seemingly trivial topics, such as whether Pakistanis should drink Coca-Cola (code for American imperialism). With politics in Pakistan heading for "an explosive climax," Ali "was not all that keen on coming to Oxford." He went, he said, because his girlfriend's father had moved to London—but when he did arrive in Oxford, he threw himself into the Union.[18] He was soon elected treasurer of the Union, and now aimed to be president.

Aitken was better connected than Abrahams. A speechwriter for the chancellor of the Exchequer during his holidays, the young president of Oxford's student Conservative Association had his career mapped out, beginning with the presidency of the Union and culminating with becoming prime minister— via stints in business, journalism, and the cabinet. The middle part of the career went according to plan. Aitken would write for London's *Evening Standard,* make millions in the Middle East, and win a position in Margaret Thatcher's shadow cabinet—and date a string of well-connected women, including Thatcher's daughter. Indeed, in 1967 Aitken felt so confident of his prospects that he published *The Young Meteors,* which listed those of his generation who would make it to the top with him, the actress Vanessa Redgrave and future chancellor Nigel Lawson among them.[19]

But the first step in Aitken's career plan proved too difficult. In the election for the Union presidency, Abrahams crushed Aitken by 420 votes to 229, with Ali in third place at 180 votes. Ali would win election to the presidency two terms later. As for Aitken, he would also fail in his final career goal—to become prime minister—when he became the first cabinet minister to go to prison, for perjury. Like Malcolm X, Aitken's time in prison led to a religious conversion—in his case, to Christianity—and he became an advocate of prison reform.

As the incoming president, Abrahams got to choose the motion and invite the speakers (three on each side) for the main debate—"the queen and country debate"—that would be held at the end of the autumn term. By tradition, the Oxford Union president invited the politician that he most admired. (Also by tradition, the Oxford Union president was the first speaker for the motion, and his Cambridge Union counterpart was the opening speaker for the opposition.) Abrahams's interest in the civil rights movement in America shaped his decision. The inspiring stories of sit-ins, freedom rides, and mass demonstrations and the horror pictures of white police attacks on children in Little Rock, Arkansas, and Birmingham, Alabama, were headline news in both Jamaica and the United Kingdom. But while the British mainstream media lauded Martin Luther King Jr.'s nonviolent approach, Abrahams, like many young Jamaicans, was more impressed by Malcolm X's call to win rights "by any means necessary." As Abrahams remembered later, "I saw him as very much the person who was making the most sense to me. I didn't believe in those days that nonviolence was going to be the answer. . . . So my hopes were on Malcolm X, not on Martin Luther King."[20]

Little wonder that when choosing his main guest speaker, Abrahams went with his hopes. Louis Nthenda's chance encounter with Malcolm X in Nairobi made an invitation possible. First, though, Nthenda had to convince Abrahams that it wasn't a hoax, and then Abrahams had to convince the BBC to televise the debate and pay for the costs. Nthenda provided Abrahams with Malcolm X's details in New York, and from that point on the Union took over the arrangements.[21]

Inviting Malcolm X to the Oxford Union was fraught with broader significance, given the state of Britain's empire and its immigration policies in 1964. As the Guyanan-born writer Jan Carew put it to Malcolm X the following February, "Tony didn't mind twisting the British lion's tail a bit when he invited you to take part in the Oxford Union debate a few months ago."[22] Abrahams's admiration for the American militant's uncompromising approach led him to select the motion "This house believes, 'Extremism in the defense of liberty is no vice. Moderation in the pursuit of justice is no virtue.'" And he did indeed "fill the room with blacks." One Union officer remembered later that he had never seen so many black faces in any setting as on the night that Malcolm X came to speak at the Oxford Union.

JACARI AND OXFORD

> People were raising money to bring a black student to Oxford, which shows an example of "Oxford consciousness." People were concerned enough to donate.
>
> —Hannan Rose, president in 1964 of the Joint Action Committee against Racial Intolerance, 2013

Abrahams also joined Oxford's new Joint Action Committee against Racial Intolerance (JACARI). In 1956, two students wrote to the proctors of the university asking permission to form a University of Oxford society that would raise money for a scholarship to be awarded to a black South African student.[23] (Oxford had a disciplinary system, dating back to the Middle Ages, whereby a senior proctor and a junior proctor—dons who were elected each year—oversaw the activities of students.) The proctors agreed, giving the idea their "general blessing," but told the students "to think of another name." The vice chancellor was worried it might otherwise "be regarded by the public as an official University creation."[24] This early hint of tension gave a foretaste of fallings-out between JACARI and the university authorities to come in the run-up to Malcolm X's visit. Still, permission was granted, and JACARI—a name without explicit mention of the university—was born. By 1959, the organization had 2,354 paid members and could justifiably boast of "being the largest university club."[25] Thus, unlike nonwhite students of previous generations, Abrahams entered a university that, seemingly quite suddenly, had a sizable number of students who were animated by, or at least sympathetic to, the cause of racial justice.

The rapid growth in JACARI's membership was due to the changing type of student at Oxford by the late 1950s. The expanded provision of Commonwealth scholarships led to increasing numbers of black and Asian students—some three hundred by the time of Malcolm X's visit (the second largest such cohort in the country, after London).[26] More significant, though, was the democratizing effect of the National Education Act and changes to Oxford's admissions policies, which, in the words of historian Joseph Soares, meant that during the 1950s the university's "world of Latin letters and privileged leisure was dismantled. Wealthy gentleman-commoners were virtually driven out and replaced by hard-working scholarly meritocrats."[27] Many of these meritocrats were active in the student Labour Party, the second largest university society after JACARI.[28] Although the two groups' memberships overlapped, JACARI had support from all student political parties and a wide range of student societies, including the student Christian movement, the humanist society, the Buddhist society, and the jazz society.

The main reason for the rise of JACARI, however, was that blatant racial discrimination was fast losing legitimacy in Britain. Hitler had given racism a bad name; the United Nations was championing human rights; and in the Cold War battle against the Soviet Union, so too was the British government. The imminence of the end of empire forced Britons to confront the prospect of forging a Commonwealth of willing African, Caribbean, and Asian members. This is not to say that Britain had become a racial utopia. Far from it. The riots in Notting Hill, the murder of Kelso Cochrane, and widespread opposition to immigration and to black immigrants living next door were testament to that—not to mention the British government's bloody suppression of nationalist movements in African and Asia. Yet at the same time, mainstream commentators and politicians were increasingly denouncing South African apartheid, American Jim Crow, and the British riots.

As in many Western countries, students were in the vanguard of this new sentiment. JACARI president Hannan Rose said that because of the university, "Oxford at that time was much more part of the world than any place in the U.K. People had a vague consciousness, even if they weren't sure of the details, of what was going on around the world."[29] Again, the situation should not be romanticized: even in Rose's telling, the Oxford consciousness was "vague." Tariq Ali complained that visiting students were often "incredibly reactionary" in their politics.[30] Not all Oxford students agreed with, let alone championed, a human rights agenda. And not all of those who joined JACARI were active members. One such student, David Griffiths, on looking back through his letters home, found little mention of "issues of race.... I guess I was more interested in meeting girls (largely unsuccessful)."[31] Many rights-conscious members were more concerned with issues of gender, sexuality, and especially class, which, to quote JACARI member Tym Marsh, "affected all of us who did not have it!"[32] Even so, in 1959 more than two thousand students paid to join a society that stood against racial intolerance.

JACARI's founding statement explained that the society "exists for two purposes: (1) To arouse among members of the University an interest in the problems of race relations in the Commonwealth today ... and (2) To find constructive ways of expressing a dislike of racial discrimination."[33] For most students in the late 1950s, "the problems of race relations in the Commonwealth today" meant South Africa, a British dominion (i.e., a country with close links to Britain but sufficient distance for British criticism not to mean self-criticism) that introduced racial apartheid in 1948. Many JACARI members had been involved in anti-apartheid campaigns since their adolescence, and each report of violence and injustice now pushed South Africa higher up the student agenda. After the Sharpeville massacre of March 1960, opposing apartheid became something of a signature issue for progressive students.

"Constructive ways of expressing dislike" initially meant raising funds for the William Brogden Memorial Scholarship (named after a JACARI committee member who died while at university). It was intended to be a "gesture of good will towards African people" who had just been excluded from South Africa's leading universities and to "show that members of the University feel very strongly about the problem of racial intolerance."[34] The fundraising was successful—JACARI's jazzmen hosted a concert in the town hall—as was selecting a student, Jeppe Mei, who had been admitted to read history at Wadham College, to receive the first scholarship.[35] However modest a gesture—and JACARI students made it clear that they wished to avoid "aggravating the tense situation in certain areas"—for some students, supporting the scholarship was their first moment of political engagement. As for Mei, after graduation he taught high school in Tanganyika.

When the white-only South African cricket team came to England in the summer of 1960, the apartheid issue touched closer to home. Demonstrations followed the touring team from match to match. (The other controversy on that tour arose when one of the South African team became the first visiting bowler to be no-balled for throwing.) As a university society, JACARI was not allowed to endorse the demonstrations. However, the JACARI president that term, P. S. Copping, wrote to the cricket authorities to "express displeasure about this and future tours until barriers are dropped," and JACARI members raised money to send cricket equipment to South African townships.[36]

JACARI members gradually escalated the ways in which they expressed displeasure. In February 1962, a delegation of six members, headed by the society's president, a young Christian socialist named Kenneth Leech, went to the Foreign Office to protest the British supply of arms to South Africa. One of the university proctors, scribbling on a newspaper report of the protest that Leech's visit was a "Break of Paragraph 10 of Rules for University Clubs," added the clipping to the fast-growing JACARI file.[37] In comparison to the student movement in the United States, this was hardly a radical action, and the proctor's file on JACARI was tiny in comparison with the FBI's file on Malcolm X. But for staid Oxford, it was clear that concern with apartheid and tensions with university authorities were growing.

Although initially JACARI's weekly speaker meetings were mostly about Africa, they were increasingly interspersed with talks about immigrant conditions and government policy in Britain. In December 1961, a JACARI delegation went to Parliament to try to persuade Oxford's Conservative MP, C. M. Woodhouse (later the fifth Baron Terrington), to vote against the upcoming Immigration Bill. Woodhouse insisted the bill was not a color bar. The students pointed out that immigration hadn't risen, just that the proportion of West Indians admitted into the country had increased; that problems of social inequalities (such as racketeering) were not being addressed; and that no attention was being paid to the root causes of immigration, such as unemployment in Jamaica.[38]

Back in Oxford, Kenneth Leech urged JACARI members to join the Movement for Colonial Freedom's upcoming march in

London's Trafalgar Square on February 4, 1962, in protest of the Immigration Bill. Chaired by Labour MP Fenner Brockway, who had introduced an anti–racial discrimination bill every year since 1955 to no avail, and with support from immigrant activists such as Claudia Jones and Ratta Singh, president of the Indian Workers Association, the Movement for Colonial Freedom had become the focal point of opposition to the bill. When the university proctors refused to let JACARI members join the march as a group, they went as individuals instead—together.[39] According to a JACARI flyer, the bill was really meant to "Keep Britain White" and actually "fostered race hatred." The flyer, in disgust, quoted Tory MP Sir Cyril Osborne, as reported in the *Daily Mail:* "This is a white man's country . . . and I want to keep it that way."[40]

Interest in British race relations led to interest in Oxford immigrants. In the spring of 1959, JACARI organized a talk on the "condition of coloured workers" in the city's car plants.[41] The following year, JACARI asked the proctors for permission to help the British Council canvass householders in order to find lodgings for non-European foreign students in Oxford. The proctors turned the request down, saying this was a non-university matter. JACARI president P. S. Copping wrote back to express frustration at students being denied the opportunity to help "alleviate in a small way a point of friction in race relations in Oxford itself."[42] Subsequent JACARI leaders would continue to make student housing a priority—and they would continue to have run-ins with the proctors.

By the time Malcolm X came to visit, JACARI's concerns also included the United States. In November 1963, the group welcomed the *Observer*'s special correspondent to present a talk titled "Civil Rights in America—Latest Developments."[43] There

Malcolm X and Oxford Union president Eric Abrahams outside the Oxford Union. The Zambian student on the left, Louis Nthenda, had invited Malcolm X to Oxford when they met in Kenya in October, 1964. The woman in the picture was a student journalist. December 3, 1964. (Getty Images)

Malcolm X, speakers at the debate, and members of the Oxford
Union Standing Committee, shortly before the debate. Minister
of Parliament Humphrey Berkeley is seated to Malcolm X's left.
December 3, 1964. (Gillman and Soame)

Eric Anthony Abrams, president of the Oxford Union, and Malcolm X, after the debate. December 3, 1964. *(Oxford Mail)*

A demonstration in London against the recent murder of Antiguan immigrant Kelso Cochrane and in response to the anti-immigrant violence in Notting Hill, London, the previous year. June 1, 1959. (Getty Images)

"How d'yer spell civilisation, Tosh?"

Commentators on both sides of the Atlantic suggested that those involved in anti-immigrant violence in Nottingham and Notting Hill, London, in 1958 had drawn inspiration from Arkansas governor Orval Faubus's defense of segregation at Little Rock Central High School the previous year. (Cartoon by Victor Weisz, *Daily Mirror*, September 5, 1958)

Malcolm X's travels abroad during 1964 and 1965 profoundly influenced his views of race, human rights, and Islam. Here he is with Sheikh Abdel Rahman Tag (right), future rector of Al-Azhar University, Cairo, the only Muslim university in the world. July 18, 1964. (Corbis Images)

Malcolm X invariably carried a camera with him on his travels. Here he is at JFK Airport, New York, after touring the Middle East. May 21, 1964. (Getty Images)

Matriculation photograph
of Eric Anthony Abrahams,
St. Peter's College, Oxford.
Michaelmas Term, 1962.
(St. Peter's College Archive)

Tariq Ali (center) and Eric Abrahams (on Ali's left) protesting outside the Oxford Union against the visit of the South African ambassador. This activity led to them being "gated," which made national news in the United Kingdom. June 18, 1964. *(Oxford Mail)*

Students in Oxford followed debates about immigration in Britain. Two weeks before Malcolm X's visit, Hannan Rose, president of JACARI, wrote a report for the Oxford student magazine *ISIS* on a controversial election in Smethwick, where anti-immigrant campaigners had warned, "If you want a nigger for your neighbour, vote Labour." (*Isis*, November 21, 1964)

White residents of Marshall Street, Smethwick, in the British Midlands, lobbied their local council and MP to prevent immigrants from buying homes there. During his visit, shortly after a bitter election over immigration, Malcolm X compared the treatment of "coloured people in Smethwick" to that of "the Jews under Hitler." February 12, 1965. (Corbis Images)

"When ours was planted it looked like a crocus too..."

Oxford students complained to the British Press Council that this cartoon, warning of the dangers of immigration by pointing to violence in the United States (including the recent death of Malcolm X), "distorts historical, political and social realities to express a view which is not merely the lowest taste, but is a direct and calculated insult to coloured peoples both in Britain and America." (Cummings, *Daily Express,* March 3, 1965, courtesy of the British Cartoon Archive, www.cartoons.ac.uk [University of Kent])

Activists demonstrated against Annette's hairdressing salon for operating a color bar. Thirty-six students, factory workers, a trade union official, and a university don were arrested following a sit-in protest. June 7, 1968. (*Oxford Mail*)

Three days after Malcolm X spoke at Oxford,
Martin Luther King Jr. preached in London. In
a statue unveiled in 1998 at Westminster Abbey,
London, his likeness took its place among the
ten "modern martyrs" said to have died in
"circumstances of oppression and persecution."
(Getty Images)

A plaque commemorating Malcolm X's visit to Marshall Street, Smethwick, was unveiled on February 21, 2012. The plaque was commissioned by the Nubian Jak Community Trust, which ran Britain's only black and ethnic minority national plaque scheme. (Corbis Images)

In the widely publicized "I, Too, Am Oxford" campaign, patterned on a protest at Harvard, students such as Brian Kwoba (shown here) published a series of photographs in which they stood outside iconic Oxford buildings, holding slogans to highlight what they called "othering" by the Oxford community. March 10, 2014.

were plenty of developments that year. In April, Martin Luther King and his allies had launched a city-wide action protesting segregation in Birmingham, Alabama, that provoked a violent response from the local police, prompted hundreds of demonstrations all across the country, and persuaded President Kennedy to introduce a civil rights bill to Congress. In August, King spoke to a quarter of a million people in Washington, D.C. The dramatic events were headline news in Britain, and thanks to the recently launched Telstar satellite, King's speech was relayed on British television. Pembroke College student John Wright, who came to Oxford "completely naive" on race matters, remembered being gripped by the drama of "the freedom marches, the brutality of Alabama police ... and the individual acts of black bravery on public buses and at school entrances."[44]

Thus, many of Oxford's students would be well prepared for a distinguished black American visitor the following year, though interviews with former students suggest a majority were somewhat wary of this particular visitor. Tariq Ali, an atheist, knew of Malcolm X only from his days with the Nation of Islam, which he called a "sinister outfit."[45] Wright agreed. "I remember ... being shocked by the violent attitudes and threatening behaviours" of black nationalists, and "I was also mystified by the Black Muslim movement.... It was all so far from my perceptions of English life."[46]

Support for JACARI sagged somewhat at the start of the 1960s, but in 1963, the year after Abrahams matriculated, the group's president, Pembroke student Michael Pinto-Duschinsky, welcomed a bumper crop of new members. News from America was part of the reason. So too was news from South Africa. The general secretary of the anti-apartheid movement and three former African National Congress political prisoners came to speak. Protest in Britain was also hitting the headlines. In Bristol, black social worker Paul Stephenson led a bus boycott—the first of its kind in the U.K.—to demand the end to the color bar in employment on the buses. He lined up high-profile supporters, including Labour MP Tony Benn and High Commissioner Learie Constantine of Trinidad, a former Test cricketer who had famously once sued a London hotel that denied him a room on account of his color. Bristol students marched in solidarity. The boycott forced the company to hire black workers; it announced the new policy on the day of King's "I have a dream" speech. Meanwhile in Oxford, JACARI started a survey of immigrant conditions. In late 1963, JACARI had to seek a bigger venue for its weekly meetings because Pembroke College's student common room, which held up to one hundred people at a squeeze, could no longer fit everyone.[47]

By the time Abrahams began his ascent of the Union political ladder, then, Oxford had a thriving new society that opposed racial intolerance. For many members, getting involved in JACARI changed their perceptions of, or even introduced them to, matters of racism and rights. "I learnt a great deal in those years from student colleagues," wrote Kenneth Leech, who went on to serve as a priest in inner city London and write influential books on Christianity and race. "Much of my early thinking about race and racism was clarified, expanded and challenged when I chaired JACARI."[48] Such interest and openness made Oxford fertile ground for Malcolm X. The university "was old and cold," he told a friend soon afterward, "but the students had open, inquiring minds."[49]

But the university society that ultimately did most to promote an "interest in the problems of race relations in the Commonwealth" turned out not to be JACARI. Rather, it was a society more associated with the British establishment and the host for Malcolm X's visit: the Oxford Union.

THE OXFORD UNION AND RACE

> The Oxford University Union, a debating society . . . has always played an important part in English political life.
>
> —W. E. B. Du Bois, "Race Student," 1943

Founded in 1823 and located in the heart of the university, the Oxford Union was charged with advancing education among the members of the university by organizing debates and addresses by distinguished visitors. It also provided a library, bar, and other recreational facilities. To join, university students had to pay a sizable fee (the equivalent of $300 in 2014 currency). Well-connected and ambitious students were eager to do so. In the early twentieth century, to quote the American literary critic John Corbin, "the Union held the elect of Oxford, intellectual, social, and sporting."[50]

From the outset, the Union engaged in politics. The motion for the opening debate of the first term each year was "This house has no confidence in Her Majesty's Government," and leading politicians would make their way from the Houses of Parliament to Oxford to make their case. For many Union members, though, the dream was to travel in the other direction. Winning a place on the Union's governing body, the Standing Committee, at the termly elections was seen as a good first step toward a political career. Being elected president was a step toward political stardom.

By the mid-twentieth century, the Oxford Union's reputation as a breeding ground for political leaders had a worldwide reach.

Writing in the United States in 1943, W. E. B. Du Bois noted in *Phylon,* the main black American scholarly journal of the day, that the Union "was considered to be the social ante-chamber of the English parliamentary system. Formerly, members of well-known English families occupied the post. Several presidents later became ministers of the Crown."[51]

Priding itself on being a forum for open discussion, the Union served as a platform for militant voices, including, on occasion, those of the most eloquent of nonwhite colonial students. During the First World War, South Asian students joined heated debates about the deployment of colonial troops. Some tried to win office in the Union as well. In 1923, the brilliant orator Solomon Bandaranaike, from the British colony of Ceylon (now Sri Lanka), won election to be secretary. The following year, he ran for the presidency but was defeated. He and others believed that many former-student life members had, breaking with custom, exercised their right to vote to deny him victory. Bandaranaike wrote later of the problems of being an Asian student at Oxford, saying that, ironically, "Oxford was the dearer to me because she . . . taught me to love my country better." He returned home an ardent socialist and nationalist, formed the Sri Lanka Freedom Party, became prime minister, and replaced English with Sinhalese as the country's official language.[52]

Ten years after Bandaranaike's defeat, Indian student Dosoo F. Karaka became the first nonwhite president of the Union. The hard-drinking, gambling, and womanizing student, who angered his parents by using up their savings to buy a part share in a race horse and by choosing to forgo the civil service to pursue journalism, fit comfortably into the Union social scene. Yet his hedonism was soon matched by a growing commitment to Indian nationalism. Like so many Indian students, he had arrived supportive of the imperial project. "I often wish that when we came to England for the first time we would not be so naive, so full of hope," he reflected later, only "to be battered about in our effort to acquire an English education." Though he appreciated that education, he resented the private school cliques, the condescension of some white students, and above all, that Indians were described as "wogs."[53]

Karaka's time at the Union could hardly have been more controversial. As secretary in 1933, he took the minutes for what became a notorious debate: "This house will in no circumstances fight for its King and Country." The motion was carried. Winston Churchill decried the debate as "abject, squalid, shameless." In the melee that followed the vote, someone ripped up Karaka's minutes book. For a time, he was put under police protection. Being elected president the next year, in a campaign that stirred racial passions, kept him in the spotlight. One journalist wrote after his victory, "Now that an Indian has been elected to the office of President of the Union, it no longer will be held in such high esteem."[54]

As president, Karaka created more controversy. In his opening speech he championed the "hundreds of thousands of men for whom the color bar has been a living hell." Over in the United States, the widely circulated *Baltimore Afro-American* newspaper approvingly quoted Karaka's call to arms: "The colored races are no longer asleep and are determined to win equality with the white race."[55] In his final speech, Karaka slammed his journalist opponent, winning cheers. He signed off by naming and shaming a whites-only university dining society, which barred members even from bringing Indians as guests.[56]

After Oxford, Karaka wrote a series of thoughtful articles in popular journals about the British color bar. It was somewhat

understandable, he conceded, that Britons read into their superior world status a superior innate culture. "Nothing is so stimu-
lating to self-assurance as success." But it was also "somewhat
unfair," he noted, anticipating the complaints of Asian and African students like James Ngugi in the 1960s, "to dump the ideas
of Western civilization on a country which was once steeped in
a glorious Eastern culture, and then to accuse the Indian of failing to conform to the standards of a civilization foreign to him."
Still, his victory at the Union encouraged him that the "new
generation of Englishmen, now students at the various Universities, have much less of these prejudices than the generation that
preceded them."[57]

The next Oxford Union generation fulfilled Karaka's hopes. It
became one of the more meritocratic institutions in the university, at least as far as race was concerned, where a silver tongue
was more prized than a white skin. Indeed, the reason Du Bois
wrote about the Union in 1943 was to hail the election of its first
"Negro" president, Cameron Tudor of Barbados. In Nazi Ger-
many, Goebbels reportedly denounced Tudor as "a slave boy
in Oxonian robes."[58] But in Oxford, the vice chancellor invited
Tudor to lunch to congratulate him.[59] A leading socialist in the
university scene, Tudor, reported the African American *Pittsburgh Courier* in a celebratory article, intended to "take an active
role in colonial politics."[60] And so he did, returning to found the
political party that would win election in 1961 and lead Barbados
to independence and eventually serving as deputy prime minister. Abrahams's eyes were set on the position one rank higher
in Jamaica.[61]

Indeed, by the mid-1950s the Union had taken a distinctly
leftward turn, with the student Labour Party group gaining something of a lock on the presidency. There was talk of

the "Tranter Machine," in recognition of the ability of Revan Tranter, a Yorkshire grammar school boy who was head of the Labour group, to turn out the necessary votes to control Union elections. The Union had a succession of South Asian and left-leaning white British presidents. Though the "atmosphere was predominantly white and male," according to one member from 1964, with plenty of "scornful and condescending heckling" by "Hooray Henrys," the debates, to quote another member from that year, were "often suffused with egalitarian idealism and the audience seemed to contain every colour of the social and political spectrum."[62] Or as Tariq Ali put it, "In those days it was the only forum for debate between Left and Right."[63] In spring 1963, Union members elected their first (white) South African president, Jeffrey Jowell, an outspoken critic of apartheid.

By the time Abrahams took office, the Union had just begun to admit women. The controversy over women's membership was, if anything, greater than that over nonwhite male students holding office. A campaign by women undergraduates at the turn of the decade had persuaded successive Union committees to put the issue to a vote. The first year, a majority of members— but not the required two-thirds—approved the motion. In 1962, though, the vote was decisive. Not that it put an end to opposition. Some members invoked a rule, not used since 1840, to blackball any women who put forward for membership.[64] The Union president, Indian student (and future playwright and screenwriter) Girish Karnad, proposed a motion—which passed—to remove the blackball rule, insisting that it was being misused against "the entire sex" rather than serving its original function of barring an unworthy individual.[65] When women were finally admitted, in February 1963, there were rumors of bomb threats.

The first women who joined the union then faced the chal-

lenge of gaining equal respect and winning elections to the
leadership committee. This was no easy task. The tabloid *Daily
Mail* described the first woman, Annabelle Levington, to join
the Union thus: "vital statistics: 36, 26, 38, blonde, reads English,
St. Anne's, boyfriend a cowboy in Australia." Levington was
more thoughtful in her comment: "I should not want to follow in
the steps of Gladstone, Asquith and Macmillan . . . but it's only
logical I should have the right."[66] One of the lead campaigners,
Judith Okley—who scratched out the word "him" from "all the
dues have been paid by him" on her union card—found Abrahams a willing ally as well as a close friend (and, briefly, boyfriend). Through his introduction, Okley was later able to spend
an afternoon with Malcolm X discussing women's rights. (In
1968, Geraldine Jones would become the first female president
of the Union.)

In addition to grappling with the issues of members' rights, the
Union tackled the broader issue of human rights in its debates. In
the two years before Malcolm X's visit, the Union had debated
such motions as "This house believes that Southern Rhodesia
should not be permitted independence until there is majority
rule" (with Kenyan nationalist Tom Mboya speaking); ". . . urges
sanctions against South Africa" (with Alfred Hutchinson of the
African National Congress speaking); ". . . deplores the Government's Immigration Bill" (with liberal politician Jeremy Thorpe
speaking); and ". . . supports Arab interference with Israeli trade"
(with Iraqi diplomat Edward Atiyah speaking—and collapsing
dead mid-speech), with strong majorities in favor each time.[67]
(Majorities of Union students also deplored the Americanization
of British culture, decided that God did not exist, and preferred
the Beatles to Beethoven.)

In other words, Abrahams was president of an institution

that had a recent, rich history of debating, internally and externally, the issues of human and race rights. And it was a tradition in which he was intimately involved. Abrahams was the lead student debater in the Southern Rhodesia and Americanization debates and was the chair when Edward Atiyah died mid-speech. "The speaker was very passionate," Abrahams remarked to reporters.[68] In his first week as president, Abrahams welcomed Solomon Bandaranaike's widow, Sirimavo, the prime minister of Sri Lanka (and modern world's first female head of state). Abrahams praised her late husband for being the Union's first non-white officer and for defeating a motion which held that "maintenance of colour barriers is civilisation." Abrahams also praised him for being the first Union officer to become head of state of a country other than Britain. "I need hardly say," he joked, "how much I hope he will not be the last."[69]

Malcolm X's invitation to the Union, then, was far less incongruous than it might have seemed to the outside world, especially with Abrahams in charge.

OXFORD AND MANDELA

> I have cherished the ideal of a democratic and free society in which all persons will live together in harmony with equal opportunities. It is an ideal which I hope to live for and to see realised. But, My Lord, if needs be, it is an ideal for which I am prepared to die.
>
> —Nelson Mandela, statement at Rivonia Trial, April 20, 1964

The students elected Abrahams to the presidency of the Oxford Union on Friday, June 12, 1964. That same day in South Africa, Judge Quartus de Wet sentenced Nelson Mandela, Govan

Mbeki, and six other African National Congress (ANC) leaders to spend the rest of their lives in prison. Mandela's appearance in Pretoria's Supreme Court may have been more than five thousand miles away, but the tremors from the trial would shake Oxford's dreaming spires.

The South African authorities hoped that the Rivonia Trial (so-called because the case was based on documents seized during a raid on an ANC hideout in the Johannesburg suburb of Rivonia) would silence the ANC leaders. Instead, following ninety days of interrogation in solitary confinement, it gave them a platform to speak to the world. They took full advantage. Mandela's powerful opening statement as an "African patriot" combined a searing critique of past atrocities, an optimistic vision for a future South African democracy, and a personal commitment to suffer for the price of freedom. As the proceedings unfolded, human rights activists around the world lobbied for justice.

In Britain, politicians, trade union leaders, clergymen, black activists, and members of the anti-apartheid movement condemned what many called a "savage" trial. Some 90,000 people signed a petition calling for justice. Hundreds of demonstrators descended on the South African embassy, including women wearing black sashes in solidarity with white women's anti-apartheid display in South Africa. Students on British campuses followed the case particularly closely. None more so than Thabo Mbeki, Govan's son, a student at the University of Sussex and many years later Mandela's successor as president of South Africa. For Mbeki, the surprising aspect of the final judgment was not the guilty verdict but the fact that the judge had not opted for the death sentence, which Mbeki had feared would be used to warn off outside interference.[70] Leaders of the global anti-apartheid campaign heralded the judge's decision as a victory.

Thanks to JACARI's organizational skills and the university's prestige, Oxford witnessed the most widely publicized student anti-apartheid demonstrations in the United Kingdom.[71] Oxford students' frustrations had been mounting before the trial—not just with the South African government, but with the university authorities as well.[72] By 1964, students were finding the proctorial system, which dated back to the Middle Ages, restrictive and insulting. Anger over Rivonia would, coincidentally, bring those frustrations to a head, transforming student concern about freedom in South Africa into a campaign for student liberties in Oxford. And because of Abrahams and Ali, and then Malcolm X, concern about racial justice abroad would also turn into a local battle about race.

Early in May 1964, JACARI leaders decided to organize a demonstration for whatever day the trial's verdict was announced, to be held in the cobbled city-center square surrounding the university's Radcliffe Camera, a circular eighteenth-century library. As was their duty, the students asked the proctors for permission. The proctors turned the request down on the grounds that, there being no date set for the verdict, the protest could not be adequately planned. Then JACARI heard that the university's Conservative Association had invited the South African ambassador, Cornel de Wet, to speak at Regent's Park College on June 12. With a definite date set for that event, JACARI secretary A. F. Shaw wrote to the proctors again, asking permission for a "line of demonstrators in Black Sashes" to picket Regent's Park College, while another group of demonstrators marched through the city center to end up at the college. The senior proctor turned Shaw down again.[73]

Shaw was incensed and wrote to tell the proctors so. But he spotted a way to circumvent their decision. The city's Ruskin College, an adult education college that had been founded "for working class men," was affiliated with but independent of Oxford University and thus beyond the proctors' jurisdiction. Ruskin students were planning their own protests, and Shaw urged all JACARI members to join them.[74] Meanwhile, JACARI sent circulars to eighty universities and colleges around the country to come to Oxford to join the protests against the ambassador. The national press picked up on the story.[75] The authorities, however, were distinctly unimpressed. The senior proctor warned Shaw that the university could take action against JACARI officers unless Shaw withdrew his call to students to join the Ruskin protest.[76]

JACARI leaders were in no mood to back down. Meanwhile, news from the United States kept passions high. In early 1964, the American Student Nonviolent Coordinating Committee launched an ambitious plan to send hundreds of volunteers to Mississippi, starting on June 13. The aim of the so-called Freedom Summer was to register thousands of historically disfranchised African Americans to vote, in preparation for the election that autumn. JACARI students decided to send a group to help during the upcoming vacation. For those who couldn't make it, the U.S. civil rights movement came to them. American student and JACARI vice president Frank Parker, a flamboyant figure with a red beard who would later serve as a voting rights lawyer, gave a speech at the final JACARI meeting of the year titled "The White Heat of Civil Rights."[77] White heat indeed. Barely a week after the Freedom Summer kicked off, three student activists—two of them white students from top universities in America, with whom JACARI members could readily identify—were shot dead. Meanwhile, Robert Serpell, JACARI's chairman, criticized the Civil Rights Bill that was being debated in the U.S. Congress as "only half a loaf."[78]

With world affairs engaging and enraging so many students—who, now that exams were over, had time on their hands—the proctors had reason to be worried. But they also had an ally. Oxford student societies were required to have a senior (faculty) member to advise them. JACARI's usual senior member, Kenneth Kirkwood—a South African–born professor of race relations who was an outspoken critic of apartheid—was on sabbatical at University College, Salisbury, Southern Rhodesia, as their first "Professor of Race Relations." His temporary replacement, Mary Proudfoot, a writer on economic development in the Caribbean and the dean of the all-women's Somerville College, was cut from a different cloth. She warned Shaw that going to Mississippi would "be enormously resented by all white Americans, whether sympathetic or not. And really I think rightly so."[79] She also insisted that protesting against apartheid would be counterproductive. "It is not a suitable technique for a serious university group. It will bring us up against not only the proctors but also the police. The end might be the dissolution of JACARI altogether."[80]

Unbeknownst to Shaw, Proudfoot sent regular updates about JACARI's plans and her best efforts to temper them.[81] Writing of Shaw with condescension, she told the senior proctor: "I think that he is just very young, very ernest [*sic*], and from a rather illiterate background."[82] At Proudfoot's insistence, nevertheless, Shaw retracted his advice to JACARI members to join the Ruskin march and shelved the plan to go to Mississippi. Thus when Shaw wrote to the senior proctor that he "reluctantly accepts this decision" not to disrupt the South African ambassador's visit, the proctors would not have been surprised.[83] As things turned out, Cornel de Wet canceled his visit, realizing that it was likely to coincide with the end of the trial and fearing trouble.[84] When the Rivonia Trial verdict was handed down on Friday the 12th, only a hundred or so students gathered at the martyrs memorial in the center of town, and only half a dozen of them were from JACARI—and they kept their distance from the Ruskin students.[85]

As for the national gathering of students, it turned into a weekend residential conference rather than a protest.[86] Students from Leeds, Hull, London, Belfast, Cambridge, Birmingham, Edinburgh, and Bristol made the trip to Oxford, where they attended seminars about race and protest in the United States, South Africa, and Britain. JACARI informed the proctors of the program, and the proctors approved, just asking for a tweak to the timetable to avoid a clash with lectures. In what would prove to be a significant move, the students formed a joint, nationwide group, called the Student Conference on Racial Equality. But on the weekend of the Rivonia Trial, they settled for talk rather than action. They sent a supportive telegram to Nelson Mandela: "Delighted to hear that you will live to fight again. We are with you."[87]

With him, maybe, but hardly fighting, let alone suffering. Not even marching or joining a picket, as things turned out, for fear of the proctors.

THE NIGHT THE SOUTH AFRICAN AMBASSADOR
SPOKE IN THE OXFORD UNION

BLOOD MONEY / no more arms for South Africa.
—Placard held by Tony Abrahams at protest of
South African ambassador's visit to Oxford,
June 17, 1964

Then the Oxford University Conservative Association (OUCA) overreached. They invited de Wet back to Oxford the following Wednesday, to speak in a room they had rented in the Union

building. "Now that the crucial day is over and the demonstration has taken place," explained the OUCA chairman, "I don't
think there will be any serious trouble." Proudfoot was not so
sure. "I hear, with gloom and misgiving," she wrote to the proctors, that the students are organizing a "bigger and better 'demo'"
outside the Lamb and Flag pub (where J. R. R Tolkien and C. S.
Lewis famously discussed their fantasy stories). Although she
went on record—as if she needed to—saying "how v. much I
dislike and distrust this 'demo' weapon, which the young now
find such fun," she worried that the tide had turned in favor of
student protest. The proctors, she noted, had to be wary, since
"a great many senior members of the University are supporters
of JACARI, so that, to take any formal action against this group
might well be to invite considerable trouble."[88] Proudfoot was
right about the likelihood of a demonstration and wider support for JACARI. And when the proctors ignored the warning
about formal action, her prediction of trouble also turned out to
be spot on.

When de Wet, with a police escort, came to Oxford, a crowd
of up to three hundred students gathered outside the Union in
the pouring rain, shouting "Go home de Wet" and "Free Mandela" and singing protest songs to the accompaniment of a gui-
tar.[89] There was no little excitement: three fire engines were
called out when students set fire to Conservative pamphlets.
There were some attempted high jinks too, including a failed
effort to let the air out of the ambassador's car tires. In the end,
though, the only serious incident was when a student threw a
penny at the meeting room window and broke a glass pane—a
gesture that the tabloid *Daily Express* reported as "Students burst
in through the windows and dived at the Ambassador."

In fact, the ambassador was able to speak without interruption, warning his audience that "multi-racialism" is "inevitably followed by a black dictatorship."[90] Direct contact between the ambassador and opponents of apartheid was limited to the delivery of two petitions calling for justice—one by city Labour councilors, the other by Serpell and Abrahams.[91] "The Proctors took no names" of troublemakers, wrote one student reporter, "because there were no obvious ones to take."[92] Still, the London *Times* transformed the story into one where "nearly 100 police fought with a crowd of anti-apartheid demonstrators."[93]

The ambassador headed home to London before a trip to Ascot racecourse. Two undergraduates shouted slogans at his car. The police arrested them. About sixty members of the crowd assembled outside the Union headed to the police station, where they lingered, waiting for their classmates to be released. There was no fuss, and the police seemed unconcerned.[94] What happens next is unclear. By best accounts, a couple of hours later a proctor turned up and questioned six students, including Abrahams and Ali. According to Abrahams, when the proctor went into the police station, a "bulldog" (university policeman) said they could stay outside. As the proctor saw things, though, he had told the students to go home. So when he came back out and saw them still standing there, he interpreted it as an act of defiance. Abrahams reckoned he was picked on for being the well-known Jamaican president of the Union.[95]

The next day, the proctors charged the six students with disorderly demonstrations and disobedience and for bringing the university's name into disrepute. They were banned from the university premises until the start of the next academic year in October, and for the first half of that term they were to be "gated," that is, required to be back in college by nine each evening.[96] They were also banned from joining any demonstrations for a year. Abrahams was fined £10 for good measure,[97] though the prospect of not being able to go out evenings and preside at the Union was much more galling. It says a great deal about the conservatism of student life in Oxford that this first confrontation with the proctors in the so-called swinging sixties was unintentional, and about the conservatism of university authorities that they came down so hard on the students for standing quietly outside a police station. But it says even more about racial tensions, frustration with the proctorial system, and the prestige of the Union that the Abrahams case became a cause célèbre in the city and in the press.

In an unusual alliance, the local Trades Council, representing some thirty thousand members, protested to the chancellor of the university about the severity of the punishment.[98] In what must surely have been a first, local Labour Party representatives even claimed to be concerned about the "disruption of the life and business of the Union," though their main targets were the proctors for supporting "the racial horror in South Africa, which was the cause of the protest."[99] Meanwhile, a group of national Labour MPs (who all happened to be former presidents of the Union) prepared legislation to amend the Oxford and Cambridge Act, which regulates those two schools' governance and workings, to prevent university authorities from taking such drastic action. It didn't pass.[100]

The students, though, proved more than capable of making the case for themselves. At the final debate of the term, the outgoing president, Lord James Douglas-Hamilton, faced a backlash over his decision to allow the Conservative Association to rent a Union room. Abrahams claimed that as a consequence, he and others had suffered at the hands of the police and the ambassador's party inside the Union premises. The Union president customarily chaired—physically sitting in the president's chair, calling on speakers and supervising questions—every debate in the chamber. To speak in a debate himself, though, the president had to vacate the chair in favor of an appropriate deputy. The young aristocrat duly did so in order to defend himself, insisting that he had given permission only for OUCA to rent the room and not for the police to enter the Union or for de Wet to speak. He agreed that "apartheid is the most detestable point of view that I can think of any Government taking," but defended free speech. "It will be a poor day when you can't let that man come along and express his repulsive views."[101]

Douglas-Hamilton's speech might have settled the matter, except the former Union president who replaced him in the chair, John McDonnell, happened to be a former president of the Conservative Association as well, and he got into a shouting match with another former president, and Labour supporter, Garth Pratt. Tariq Ali demanded that McDonnell apologize for OUCA's actions. McDonnell replied that he never apologized. Then the lights went out, and there was a mass exodus. When the lights came back on, members returned and voted in support of the president. Ali stormed out, with two hundred students behind him. Abrahams joined them. Later that evening, the dissenters returned. By this time, another ex-president of the Union, the South African critic of apartheid Jeffrey Jowell, had taken the chair. Abrahams proposed that the meeting adjourn in protest against the actions of the police and the behavior of de Wet's party. No doubt with relief at the prospect of a long and rancorous evening, the motion was carried.[102]

The following Thursday, the Union Standing Committee planned a response. They decided to compile a brief concerning misreporting of the event, which they would submit to the Press Council; write a letter of complaint to the *Times;* and send letters to former Union presidents in Parliament.[103] Some of the

MPs duly called on the proctors to relent—though their concern seemed to be that a gated president would be unable to oversee the Union's evening program, rather than a defense of Abrahams's rights or honor. Meanwhile Abrahams, using his legal training to good effect, pointed out to any reporter willing to write about him—and there were more than a few—the inconsistencies in the proctors' charges. The vice chancellor, following a meeting with Abrahams, thought his argument was "thin" and sided with the proctors.[104] But Abrahams's charm won over his college authorities. The vice master of St. Peter's, writing to Jamaica's Office of the High Commissioner, stated that "so far as the College is concerned his conduct has been excellent."[105] Ali, in contrast, didn't care for any authorities, and in an open letter denounced the proctors flat out as opponents of anti-apartheid sentiment.[106]

The students' campaign succeeded, in part. The proctors retracted the punishment of sending the students away until the autumn—not least because Ali and Abrahams, as foreign students, had no home in England to go to. In a nod to the power of the Union, they allowed Abrahams and Ali to stay out later than 9 P.M. on Thursdays, which was debate night. But otherwise the fines, gating, and restrictions from future protests remained in place.[107]

THROWING BRICKBATS AT AUNT SALLY

[We] are treated as the smallest children are treated in the kindergarten.

— Hannan Rose, Union committee member
and JACARI president, quoted in the *Daily Mail*, October 13, 1964

At the start of the next academic year, in October, the proctors tried to draw a line around the whole affair. The university set up a committee, chaired by E. T. Williams, warden of

Rhodes House, to review the power of the proctors, in particular "whether or not the present provisions governing their
exercise require modification."[108] The review "is very good
news," Abrahams told a national daily and, perhaps indulging
in ironic hyperbole, said: "There will be widespread joy among
undergraduates."[109] Some fellows, however, had concerns. One
defender of the proctorial system, writing to the university's in-
house magazine for faculty members, worried that if the university had treated the students as citizens who were answerable
to the police rather than to the proctors, "a considerably higher
proportion of the undergraduate body would now be in borstal
[youth detention center] than is the case under the present privileged position."[110]

At the same time, the proctors tried to counter the narrative
of harsh treatment of students. Reports abounded that the proctors' families had been subjected to harassing phone calls accus-
ing them of racism. All Souls College don Michael Dummett,
well known for his support of the anti-apartheid and civil rights
movements, wrote an article for the student press on behalf
of the proctors. He bemoaned the "profound and depressing"
contrast between the "idealism" of American students fighting
for civil rights and the "energies which ... are squandered" in
Oxford by "throwing brickbats at an Aunt Sally like the institution of the Proctors."[111]

But the proctors had only to look at the Union calendar for
Michaelmas 1964 to see that calm was not on the agenda. Malcolm X was due to visit for the final debate in the eighth (final)
week of term. Meanwhile, the first debate, about the affairs of
the previous summer, showed that the Union, too, had gotten
caught up in the brickbat throwing. Lord Douglas-Hamilton took
a break from his postgraduate law degree to fly down from Scot-

land and chair the first session. "I would ask the House to decide," he said to his successor, Tony Abrahams, "whether it is you or the Proctors who have brought disrepute." The House overwhelmingly decided, 600 votes to 1, that it was the proctors.[112]

Beyond the Union, the University of Oxford's student union—the representative student council—backed Abrahams, and criticized the proctors for being too hasty in their punishment, for selecting just a handful of students for censure, and for denying them their basic civil right to protest.[113] Beyond Oxford, the National Union of Students came out in support, too. Meanwhile Abrahams, from his platform as Union president, orchestrated a PR campaign with the consummate skill of the politician he aspired to be. He welcomed support from fellow undergraduates to pay the fines and from MPs and dons to persuade the proctors that "rustication would obviously have been inhuman."[114] He turned the charge of student harassment of the proctors to his own advantage by expressing sympathy—"I myself received many racialist letters condemning me"—and by denouncing the pranksters for "fail[ing] to appreciate the seriousness of the fact that the proctors have behaved oppressively against peaceful demonstrators." That oppressive behavior had continued, he complained, in that the proctors had forced him to decline invitations to speak at debating societies at other universities. "I console myself," he concluded in a sly dig, "with the rumour that the Proctors know that we were all innocent."[115]

As for Tariq Ali, he brought to Oxford some of the lessons he had learned in Lahore. On the eve of their gating, Saturday, October 10, and after an alcohol-fueled "freedom party," Ali and fellow Exeter College student R.I.P. Bulkeley burned an effigy of a proctor on the city center's Broad Street (the site of the 1555 burning of the Protestant reformers Nicholas Ridley, Hugh Latimer, and Thomas Cranmer). Ali and Bulkeley claimed to be following the tradition—after a mere five-century hiatus—of students burning a proctor, pointing out that burning only an effigy showed how moderate their own generation was in the big scheme of things.[116] For a student who had seen demonstrations stopped by bullets, tear gas, and prison, a disapproving proctor was hardly anything to worry about. Nonetheless, one university bulldog grumbled to a student reporter, "They've got a lot of guts."[117]

ANTI-IMMIGRATION ON THE EVE
OF MALCOLM X'S VISIT

> If you want a nigger for your neighbour, vote Labour.
> —Election slogan, Smethwick, 1964

While the students awaited the visit of the American firebrand Malcolm X at the end of term, national and local events raised concerns about rising racism in England. Indeed, it is striking the extent to which, by the autumn of 1964, local, national, and international affairs had become interlinked in student politics. At JACARI's speaker meetings, talks on American segregation, South African apartheid, African independence, and British race relations got equal billing.

Following a presentation by an American civil rights leader at the end of October, JACARI's November 9 and 16 sessions were speaker meetings about the "immigrant community in Britain."[118] The meetings were timely. During the general campaign for the November elections, the immigration issue moved to the front and center of British politics. In the industrial town of Smethwick in the West Midlands, keeping out immigrants became the ugly focus of a notorious electoral fight. By 1964,

4,500 recent immigrants, mostly from India and the Caribbean, had moved to Smethwick, representing 6.7 percent of the town's population. This caused tension because low-level manual jobs were increasingly hard to come by, and the waiting list for council housing had reached 4,000 people.

In the election campaign, the Conservative candidate, Peter Griffiths, a school headmaster, called for a ban on immigration for at least five years, the denial of council housing for anyone who had lived in Smethwick less than ten years, and separate school classes for immigrant children who spoke English as a second language. Griffiths argued, "Unrestricted immigration into this town has caused a deterioration of morals." The Birmingham Immigration Control Association threw its support behind him.[119] The national press tuned in. In a result that bucked the national trend toward Labour, Griffiths won, beating the shadow foreign secretary, Patrick Walker. One MP, Herbert Bowden, warned the House of Commons: "If the term 'Smethwick' becomes synonymous with ... Sharpeville or even [Little Rock,] Arkansas, it will be a bad thing for this country."[120] Malcolm X would have his own comments to make in a trip to Smethwick the following year, including a comparison with American racism. The new prime minister, Harold Wilson, was so incensed by the result that he condemned Griffiths as a parliamentary leper in his first speech in office.[121]

Leper perhaps, but he was not alone. Anti-immigration rhetoric began to infect British political discourse. The leading Labour campaigner against racial discrimination and immigration control, Fenner Brockway, lost his seat in Eton and Slough. Now, far from distancing themselves from anti-immigration sentiment, the Labour Party proceeded to embrace it. The party manifesto—reversing its opposition to the Immigration Act of

1962—promised to legislate against racial discrimination *and* to cut back on immigration. With a parliamentary majority of only five, and a Conservative Party calling for tough immigration controls, Labour quickly delivered on its promise, tightening immigration regulations for dependent relatives.[122]

For immigrants in London, this legislation was the last straw. Within weeks, they would organize a Campaign against Racial Discrimination (CARD) to challenge both political parties. Grant Kamenju, a Kenyan student who had studied at Leeds with Ngugi and would return to East Africa to overhaul the curriculum, steering it away from Western tradition, thought the only good thing to come out of the affair was that it exposed British racism. The world would see, he wrote, that a socialist government had "passed an 'Immigration Act' which amounts to an official endorsement of racialism, however disguised and dressed up in empty and hypocritical pious platitudes."[123]

Students in Oxford took note as well. Hannan Rose and friends from JACARI made the hour-or-so journey from Oxford to Smethwick to investigate. In a report for Oxford's student magazine *ISIS,* Rose accepted that "one of the worst things we could do is to say that there are no problems," not least for the immigrants themselves and their struggle for decent housing and employment. Over 400,000 nonwhite Commonwealth immigrants had come to Britain between 1959 and 1964 (more than in the period 1946–59). What frustrated Rose, though, was that at the general election, the "social problem of immigration . . . was transformed into a problem of race and politics." After Smethwick, he told fellow students, "we must now realise that it is not sufficient to deplore Apartheid and to be appalled by stories of Mississippi." Under the heading "Could It Happen Here?" Rose's article included a picture of American police shooting at African Americans in Harlem during riots in July of that year.[124]

If that sounded far-fetched to an Oxford audience, excerpts from speeches by anti-immigration campaigner Colin Jordan below the photograph suggested that the answer to Rose's question was "Yes, it could." Jordan, a schoolteacher, headed up the National Socialist Party and, at the time of Smethwick, was the most prominent white-supremacist spokesman in the country (a position he held until the mid-1970s, when he was caught stealing women's underwear from a shop in Leamington Spa). In an attempt to implicate every bogeyman he could think of, Jordan labeled the "Coloured Invasion" a Jewish conspiracy—abetted by the decadent upper classes, property and retail magnates, political party mandarins, the media, the press, rock 'n' roll, newly independent African nations, and the Communists—designed to squeeze hardworking British taxpayers and to create the "mongrel population" essential for the "long-term security of [those groups'] overlordship."[125]

For Jordan and his fellow travelers, British immigration policy had not gone far *enough*. The Tory Immigration Act was but a "piece of window-dressing . . . to disarm public feeling" but would make no dent in the rate of 120,000 immigrants a year. "Racial ruination" was sure to follow "in the wake [of] the African and Asiatic pour[ing] in." It wasn't even fair for "Coloured people": "What we hate is not you, as such," Jordan assured black Britons—with words that suggested the precise opposite—just "your presence in our land. . . . We believe in a square deal for you in lands of your own, where you can live your own way of life rather than exist as imitation White folk."[126]

Rose's article was not despondent, but rather frank and to the point. "Good race relations cannot be assumed," he wrote; "they must be created." The government needed to pass "a new Immigration Act that is not racial, to show that we intend to adopt a new course." Immigrants needed to be welcomed into the state rather than be used as a scapegoat. "The appointment of a coloured policeman . . . at the House of Commons . . . would be a good place to start." Above all, "we [need] to . . . create a multiracial society. . . . Integration must be our aim; there is a lot to be done before we get there." And young people were the ones to do it. The examples of the National Union of South African Students and the Student Nonviolent Coordinating Committee in the United States led him to hope that "students in Britain might take the lead in realising the urgency of the problems on our own doorsteps."[127]

First, though, the university's Conservative Association poured a little oil on increasingly troubled Oxford waters by asking the wrong person to speak at the wrong time—again. On this occasion, it was Evan Campbell, High Commissioner for Southern Rhodesia, who was invited to a meeting at Pembroke College. To avoid demonstrations, the proctors tried to persuade the association to cancel the visit. When that failed, they made sure Pembroke was "closely guarded by police and bulldogs." Ali and Abrahams turned up, but, wary of the consequences of violating the proctors' ban on protesting, there was no demonstration.[128] After all, a rather more important visitor was soon to come to Oxford.

RACE AND HOUSING ON THE EVE OF MALCOLM X'S VISIT

> 59.2% of the landladies interviewed would almost certainly refuse an application by a "coloured" student.
>
> —Survey on Oxford University lodgings, November 1964

Within a week after Rose's article appeared, and just days before Malcolm X's visit, JACARI took the lead in expressing "the urgency of the problems on [our own] doorstep." On November 25, JACARI released a sensational report about the color bar as it applied to Oxford student housing. The university had a clear policy of equal rights, regardless of race, and Oxford college rooms were open to all. Many second-year undergraduates and most graduates had to find lodgings in the town, and they did so by consulting the approved list of landladies compiled by the university's Delegacy of Lodgings. JACARI contacted the delegacy for the landladies' names and addresses. During the start of term, they visited 189 homes. Louis Nthenda, newly arrived from Malawi, was one of the volunteers who would ask to rent a room, be denied, and then be followed by a white student who would ask the same question. The headline results of the survey shattered the university's image: nearly two-thirds of the landladies on the approved list expressed racial prejudice, and more than half would not accept a nonwhite student as a lodger.[129]

To the JACARI students' surprise, the sentiment was pretty consistent, irrespective of the landladies' age or location. The landladies' xenophobia was also color specific. Although some landladies didn't want any foreigners at all, far more didn't want nonwhite students. In response to the question "Why will you not take nonwhite students?" the most common explanations were that such students were dirty, untidy, and would have too many visitors. Very few questioned the students' honesty or work ethic. But even more telling were the throwaway comments made during the interviews. The survey-takers reported that many landladies had an emotional reaction to the issue—and the overriding emotion was fear.

Following publication of the report, letters from landladies to the delegacy outlined precisely what they were afraid of. Some feared they might lose the basic right to decide whom they wanted to live in their private home. Using Cold War geopolitics to justify her stance, one landlady argued: "We are not living in Russia to be told who we should have in our houses." For others it was a religious issue. Writing from a smart terrace house in East Oxford, a Mrs. Lord explained that students who follow "Islam or Hindustan ... treat women differently[;] also they live differently [by] killing chickens and bleeding them at the back door." The biggest fear, though, was about sex. As one landlady reminded the delegacy, "People have daughters. I know of one case where a coloured man lived and when he left, the daughter of 14 was to have a child." This woman didn't want to leave a name, just "to convey to you what many people feel."[130]

For all the fear and intrigue wrapped up in the issue of race and housing, the JACARI report was, by design, a rather dull document—packed with methodological explanations, statistical tables, and control questions rather than juicy anecdotes and shocking backstories. (It would be published in condensed form in an academic journal the following year.) The undergraduate authors, JACARI leaders Clive Sneddon and Robert Serpell (both of whom went on to academic careers), thought that JACARI's demonstrations against the South African ambassador had gained a lot of publicity but achieved little—so they tried a different tack. "Could this university be shamed?" they asked. It turned out it could. Although housing was a perennial problem for immigrants and black students everywhere, the fact that this was a survey undertaken by students at Oxford meant the national press gave the story attention.[131]

Some landladies reacted in anger. The very day the report was publicized, one wrote to the delegacy, scathingly: "I know youth love to see their names in print." Another, a Miss M. Eagle, played the victim card. Since students were "paying a mere pittance—a mere quarter of what they would have to pay in an hotel," she complained, they had no right to "treat the house as a public institution. I wonder if the parents of the same students would be prepared to do the same [have no say in the choice of lodger] in their homes?" In a prescient warning to the delegacy, she predicted that the "recommendations of Mr Sneddon and Mr Serpell will result in yet a few more lodgings being closed."[132]

The students demanded that all landladies who wished to remain on the Oxford delegacy's list be required to sign a pledge to accept any student, regardless of color. Failing that, any landlady who refused to accept a nonwhite student should be stricken from the list. Meeting the day after the report was publicized, members of the delegacy—on the face of it—were more circumspect than some of the landladies. They "discussed at length possible ways and means of meeting" JACARI's favored "ideal" (thereby defining the call for a nondiscrimination pledge as something of a youthful impulse rather than a sensible solution). But the delegacy's bottom line was that there be enough rooms for students. In the final analysis, a pledge was not practical: "either landladies would reply, in which case (according to the results of the survey) the Delegacy's lists would dwindle to vanishing-point, or else (and this was more likely) they would decline to reply and the Delegacy would be faced with an impasse." So the delegacy decided to include a sentence about nondiscrimination in their information packet for landladies and to ask delegacies in other universities for advice . . . and to sit tight in hopes that the whole affair would blow over.[133]

There was little chance of that. One week later, Malcolm X came to town.

MALCOLM X ARRIVES IN OXFORD

The students all over the world are the ones who
bring about a change; old people don't bring about a
change.

—Malcolm X, Organization of Afro-American
Unity rally, Harlem, November 29, 1964

Malcolm X returned to New York from his eighteen-week African tour on the evening of November 24. The "controversial Muslim leader," wrote a reporter who intercepted him at the airport, declared that "extremism in defense of freedom is no vice."[134] The Oxford debate was clearly on his mind.

He headed to Harlem's Theresa Hotel (where he had met Castro) to recuperate with family and friends. Five days later, three hundred people attended a rally in his honor at the Audubon Ballroom in Harlem. "It's certainly good to be back," he told the crowd, "although I don't know how a black man can leave a black continent and come back to a white continent and say it's good to be back." He apologized that he couldn't speak for long and said he would hold a proper meeting two weeks later. "The reason that [my talk has] to be brief," he explained, "is that I have to leave the country again this week. I'll be back next Sunday, but I'm involved in a debate at Oxford University in England, outside of London, on Thursday."[135]

As it turned out, "brief" ended up being nearly an hour. Malcolm X spoke with pride about "his successful trip to Africa," with determination about petitioning the UN to get involved in American race affairs, and with anger about American involvement in the Congo and attempts by the United States Information Agency to discredit him. He spoke of lessons he had learned. An FBI agent passed on news from an informant at the rally to his superiors, no doubt with relief, that Malcolm X "no longer considered himself to be a racist," just "opposed to all people who are against the Negroes."[136] This was a changed man from the one who had set out on his world tour. The talk was somewhat scattershot, as befits an impromptu report. But the sentiments he expressed at the rally were the same ones he would develop, with clarity, cohesion, and force, at Oxford.

Malcolm X also spoke of practical lessons from Africa that could be useful for African Americans more generally. "I was able to steal a few ideas that they used, and tactics and strategy," he said. In particular, he was impressed by the passion and commitment of the best African nationalists. "A man who believes in freedom," he told his audience, "will do anything under the sun to acquire or achieve his freedom, and he will do anything under the sun to preserve his freedom."[137] Little wonder that he relished the chance to defend the motion "Extremism in the defense of liberty is no vice."

The only part of the FBI agent's report that reached the bureau's director, J. Edgar Hoover, was the fact that Malcolm X "stated he will go to London and would debate at Oxford University." In an urgent teletype message, the New York agent suggested that Hoover request the FBI's London team to cover the debate. The director did so, immediately.[138]

Hoover needn't have worried. The BBC would be there broadcasting. But worry he did even so. "It is desired," he told his London agents, "that you attempt to determine the nature and purpose of subject's trip."[139]

In fact, the purpose of the trip to Britain wasn't a secret. Malcolm X told his Harlem audience many of the reasons: "You and I have to link up with our people who are in Paris—when I say our people, you know, us; we have to link up with our people who are in London, England." It was part of his broader concern "to link up with our people who are in the Caribbean, in Trinidad, in Jamaica, in all the islands, and we've got to link up with our people who are in Central America and South America." Malcolm X was hopeful. He had jotted down the names of numerous black students in Britain during his African journeys, with whom he hoped to connect. "Once we get together, brothers, we can get some action, because we'll find we are not the underdog."[140]

What he didn't explain to the audience was why he was going to start his trip to Britain in Oxford. Part of the reason was practical. He had been invited, and thus the cost of his travel to England would be covered—no small matter for a man with no financial backing and, as students were surprised to discover, holes in his shoes. (There would be no fee, though. Abrahams wrote to say how much he appreciated "the gesture" of his attendance.)[141] But practicalities were only part of the reason for accepting the invitation to the Union. Malcolm X had been invited to speak at the London School of Economics (LSE) as well, and he chose Oxford instead.

He would still go to London during his first stay in England (and the following February, he would speak at the LSE), but where better to start the English leg of his travels than at Oxford, that most famous of universities at the intellectual heart of the empire, where a self-confident showman who loved debating could shine? The Oxford Union also appealed for the prestige and legitimacy it would confer on him and his cause. Although his reputation was growing, Malcolm X, to his enduring frustration, still lacked the institutional base of other African American leaders and continued to be dismissed by much of the mainstream U.S. press as a violent extremist. The motion he was to debate suited him perfectly, and he trumpeted the invitation to American audiences and the media both before and after his return. If such an august, historic institution as the Oxford Union would hear him, so too should the powers that be in America.

In his letter to Abrahams accepting the invitation, Malcolm X said he did so "without hesitation" because Oxford students were "on fire" against racial discrimination.[142] No records remain to explain how he knew about this fire—as he admitted later, "I honestly didn't know what to expect when Tony Abrahams phoned to invite me to Oxford."[143] What mattered is that by the time he accepted the invitation, Malcolm X was looking forward to meeting a coming generation of outstanding African, Caribbean, and South Asian students who were pushing their own rights agenda. When Lebert Bethune asked Malcolm X about going to "one of the most sacred of European institutions, . . . he pointed out to me that the office of presidency of the Oxford Union was held then by a black Jamaican, who was proposing the motion for debate[, and] that the incoming president for the following term was a Pakistani."[144]

Malcolm X flew out of John F. Kennedy airport at 10 P.M. on November 30. FBI agents watched him leave. He arrived in London at 9:35 the following morning, spent the night, and then took the train to Oxford.[145] Abrahams immediately put his guest at his ease. Malcolm X was impressed. Whereas "Negroes at Harvard and Yale always looked to me as if they were being apologetic," he later said, Abrahams "walked around Oxford like he owned it."[146] With the star-struck white Union secretary, Henry Brownrigg, in tow, Abrahams escorted Malcolm X to the Randolph Hotel.

Later that day, Abrahams gathered a group of leftist students in the President's Room of the Union to meet Malcolm X. When he was asked how he took his coffee, Malcolm X said, "Integrated"—that is, with milk. It was an old joke of his, but new on the students. One of the group was Judith Okley, one of the first women members of the Union. Although she hardly knew of Malcolm X, she was struck by the fact that "people were in awe of this guy," so much so that "some of them could barely talk" in his presence. "The ironic thing," she thought, "was that he wasn't very black, and his hair was almost reddish."[147] Malcolm X and the students engaged in small talk. He spent the rest of the day getting acquainted with the city, some of its students, and especially Abrahams. Louis Nthenda acted as his host, meeting him after breakfast each day and escorting him around the town.

On the morning of the debate, Malcolm X read the tabloid *Daily Express*. The front page reported that the pope was in India, it was so cold in Britain that one school had sent children home, and the female star of the hit TV show *The Avengers*, Diana Rigg, had quit. It was the main story on page two, though, that caught his eye. Complete with a map of troop movements in Stanleyville, the Congolese capital city of "hell and horror," the *Express* had an inside account of the crisis titled "Savage Simbas Hit Back." The topic was close to Malcolm's heart. At his recent rally in Harlem, he explained that the so-called rebels "call themselves Simbas, which means lions, you know. . . . They're freedom fighters, and your and my heart should be with theirs." The *Express* reporter saw a government-hired "mercenary . . . gun down four Congolese . . . who may have been good men. . . . They may or may not have been Simbas."[148] Angered at the atrocities, and angry that the British press had labeled the Simbas savages, Malcolm X took the paper with him. He would quote from it at the Union and then again back in America.[149]

Characteristically eager to learn more about his new environment, Malcolm X asked Abrahams to invite Okley to his hotel room. He did not want to seem improper, so he insisted she come with at least one other person and that the women hide in the bathroom when the waiter came with tea (though the waiter might have found it odd that one person needed three teacups). Having encountered plenty of sexism during her time in Oxford, Okley was grateful that "he did not treat us like little white floozies. He treated us like equals, like intelligent beings."[150] In his autobiography, Malcolm X wrote of a white American female student who had come up to him after a talk, asking how she could help to end American racism. True to his Nation of Islam ideology, he had dismissed her. If he were to meet her again, he wrote, he would have talked with her.[151] He clearly viewed this Oxford meeting as an opportunity to find out about white women's concerns. "He was interviewing us," Okley recalled later.[152] He also used his trusted camera to take pictures of them reflected in the mirror.

That evening, dressed in suit and tie, he joined the other speakers and Union committee members for a candlelit silver-service dinner in the Union's paneled dining room. Then he headed to the debating chamber, where a packed crowd and television cameras were waiting.

CHAPTER FOUR

The Debate, December 3, 1964

PROLOGUE

Mr. Chairman, tonight is the first night that I've have
ever had opportunity to be as near to conservatives
as I am.

—Malcolm X, Oxford Union debate,
   introductory remarks

Malcolm X had to wait over an hour before he was called to
speak. Usually when he gave a speech, he was the featured
speaker, and the way the Oxford speech has been remembered
in the history books since, it would be easy to assume that that
was the case here. But no: at the Union, he had to take his turn in
line, the third speaker in support of a motion proposed by Tony
Abrahams, and the fifth speaker (of six) overall.

To be sure, Malcolm X was the main attraction of the evening. But part of the attraction was to see how he coped in a
debate, Union style. That style included bravado and innuendo,
point scoring and repartee, a confrontational context in front
of a crowd of curious and confident students that turned talk

into theater. Malcolm X rose to the occasion with gusto and panache. Indeed, it would be accusations from his opponents and interruptions from the audience that prompted Malcolm X to deliver some of the more memorable lines in his speaking career.

Tony Abrahams began proceedings, calling up various Union officers to give their reports.[1] Malcolm X heard an advertisement for a Christmas Pantomime, the list of recent purchases for the Union library, and the news—delivered in a desperate salesman-style tone—that the upcoming Union ball had nearly sold out . . . but there were *just a few* tickets left. That joke got almost the biggest laugh of the evening. Abrahams then introduced and roasted the main speakers: for the motion, the Scottish nationalist, communist, and writer Hugh McDairmaid, who was "more successful as a poet than a politician," having got barely a hundred votes in the previous parliamentary election; against the motion, the liberal Conservative MP Humphrey Berkeley (who would later campaign for gay rights), a "radical Tory that we have produced tonight just to show that such things do exist"; for the motion, Malcolm X, who "like Tariq A. is a Muslim—the difference is that one is a red Muslim and the other a black Muslim"; and finally, against the motion, Labour peer Lord Stoneham, who had stood in at two hours' notice for someone who was standing in for someone else. The audience roared with approval at Abrahams's jibes. This was hardly the respectful introduction that Malcolm had received at the University of Ghana, or even Harvard for that matter.

As the outgoing president, Abrahams opened the debate (and because Abrahams was speaking, the committee chairman, Tariq Ali, took the chair). In an earnest speech, he explained that his team was supporting the words of the motion rather than the views of the person who uttered it and asserted that the roll call of famous moderates in history, "from Pontius Pilate to Neville Chamberlain," lent weight to their argument. In a droll response, Abrahams's Cambridge counterpart, Christian Davis, mocked Abrahams's "passionate speech, which ran through the whole gamut of human emotions from A to B," told a few jokes about Oxford, and then argued that although extremism might sometimes be the lesser of two evils, "it was always a vice." In a lengthy speech, Davis maintained that because different people had different views of liberty, the idea that people should defend it with extreme measures was "silly, irrelevant, and dangerous." (Later, Lord Stoneham observed that it was the two student speakers who were silly, because they had spent most of their time making irrelevant jokes.)

Hugh McDairmaid followed with a brief, intense speech that described "moderation in all things" as the "most abominable doctrine in the history of mankind" and praised those Scottish heroes who had never submitted to the English. Berkeley, rising to speak in opposition, lampooned both McDairmaid and Malcolm X for changing their names (Hugh McDairmaid, a Gaelic name, was a replacement for Christopher Grieve) and declared, to much laughter, that "any motion that can unite an apostle of racial absolutism with an apostle of economic absolutism"—referring to Malcolm X and McDairmaid, respectively—"must in my view clearly be wrong," particularly when the two extremists supported a thesis "propounded by a man [Barry Goldwater] who voted against civil rights and anything remotely suggestive of socialism." Liberty for Mr. McDairmaid, claimed Berkeley, "means the enlightened policies of Mr. Brezhnev," the premier of the Soviet Union. "Liberty for Mr.

X means racial segregation. . . . He is North America's leading exponent of apartheid."

Then Malcolm X stood to speak. He took his time to gather his thoughts. As Lebert Bethune later learned from Malcolm X himself, "he had been angered by the flippant drawing room comedy manner of Humphrey Berkeley." He may have been frustrated, too, at being lumped with a Scottish communist on an evening of banal student joking. Malcolm X confided in Bethune later: "It took an effort of will to keep me from trembling."[2] There was hushed silence, a marked contrast to the laughter that had just reverberated around the hall. He started with a joke that went down well, about being in such close proximity to conservatives. Stumbling a bit, he began to respond to Berkeley, then abruptly, in mid-sentence, remembered to thank his hosts (though he mistakenly thanked the chairman, Ali, rather than the president, Abrahams, for inviting him) before continuing his response.

Then Malcolm X found his footing. He mocked Berkeley without getting personal, referring to him more effectively as "that type." This was actually an old rhetorical trick of Malcolm X's but with a new color. In previous talks about the docile, accepting "house Negro" (as opposed to the militant "field Negro"), Malcolm X had often riffed with disdain on "that type." Now, "that type" referred to a type of white person—reminiscent of his repeated use of "the white man" or even "the man" in earlier speeches. True to his new belief in human brotherhood post-Mecca, "that type" no longer meant every white man; but he still expressed disdain for "that type" who endorsed any "person as being right just because his skin is white." In a clever play on the Union's parliamentary style of calling other speakers "my honourable friend," Malcolm X would repeatedly start to refer to Berkeley by saying "my friend," then quickly catch himself and substitute "that type." It brought a laugh every time. Tony Abrahams admitted later, "I have never been as sorry for a man as I was for Humphrey Berkeley that night, because Malcolm took his speech and, I mean, he just tore him up."[3]

And then Malcolm X started on his prepared speech. He had been able to rest and prepare for a couple of days, and it showed. His speech was brilliantly crafted, interweaving humor and gravitas, personal stories and high politics, and observations about Oxford, America, and the world. Malcolm X focused squarely on the motion of the debate, arguing that he was unfairly stereotyped as an extremist and that it was the American powers that be who were the real extremists. Thus he had a responsibility, on behalf of humanity, to oppose oppressive forces, even if it was by extreme means.

Some of Malcolm X's speech was new material, especially about the Congo, which was a fast-developing crisis, and about the way the media misrepresented people's motives, since his own thinking on that issue was still developing. Most of his speech, though, he had given before, including such themes as his contempt for American foreign policy, his criticism of American civil rights legislation and nonviolent civil rights protest, his commitment to resist oppression by any means necessary, his support for human rights, his belief in the brotherhood of man, and his devotion to Islam. What made the speech so effective was the way in which he adapted his material to the occasion. What made the speech so significant was its singularly clear statement of his thoughts at the end of a year of travel and that it was broadcast and widely reported—barely two months before he died.

THE IMAGE OF THE EXTREMIST

[Malcolm X] spoke to the Union last term and made
a very good impression. . . . He was much more
reasonable that he was alleged to be.

— Union president Neil MacCormick, quoted
in the *Oxford Mail*, February 22, 1965

The quote that informed the Oxford motion may have been
Barry Goldwater's and chosen by Tony Abrahams, but a debate
on extremism was the ideal topic for Malcolm X nevertheless. He had risen to fame, or rather infamy, as the ultimate
extremist—a Black Muslim and nationalist, a prophet of hate
and an advocate of violence. Despite his public commitment to
human rights, Sunni Islam, and the United Nations during his
travels in 1964, the image continued to stick. Coming to Oxford
reminded him of that. Time and again, Malcolm X met Oxford
students who expected him to be angry or dangerous. Indeed,
that is why his appearance at the Union attracted such interest, both locally and nationally. In his speech, Malcolm X mentioned a conversation with a female student over coffee or dinner the previous day. ("For those minds of yours that run astray,"
he added, "there were several of us" at the meeting—a serious
point of honor that was delivered as a joke to the student audience, which enjoyed it as such.) The student had told him, "I'm
surprised that you're not what I expected." Malcolm X asked
what she meant. She confessed, "Well, I was looking for your
horns." "I have them," Malcolm X replied, "but I keep them hidden, unless someone draws them out."

At the debate, that someone was Humphrey Berkeley. The
Conservative MP's caricature of his opponent as a racist Black
Muslim played right into Malcolm X's hands, allowing him to
defend his reputation without seeming oversensitive, and then

to challenge his accuser and "that type." "Evidently he has been misinformed," Malcolm X suggested, with a generosity that he clearly didn't mean and would quickly contradict. No, he did not support apartheid, segregation, or racialism. The issue was not Malcolm X's position, but the prejudice of Berkeley's type. "When you find people like this—I mean that type; when a man who they have been taught is below them has the nerve or firmness to question some of their philosophy or some of their conclusions, usually they put that label [of extremist] on us, a label that is only designed to project an image which the public will find distasteful."

In rebutting Berkeley, Malcolm X was able to make a wider point about who set the terms of the debate about race and extremism. "I just take time to make these few things clear" about Berkeley's views, Malcolm X explained, because one of the tricks of "that type" is to "create images of a person who doesn't go along with their views and then they make certain that this image is distasteful, and then anything that that person has to say from thereon, from thereon in, is rejected." For Malcolm X, "that type" included policy makers and opinion shapers in both America and Europe. "During recent centuries the West has been in power, and they have created the images, and they've used these images quite skillfully and quite successfully."

Such images held power, and they reinforced the color line. "And this is actually true," Malcolm X said; "usually when a person is looked upon as an extremist, anything that person does in your eyesight is extreme." When applied to the question of violence across the color line, "as long as a white man does it, it's all right. A black man is supposed to have no feelings [and] love his enemy no matter what kind of attack, verbal or otherwise—he's supposed to take it. But if [a black man] stands up in any way and tries to defend himself, then he's an extremist." For Malcolm X, the irony of the image of the angry black man was that it hid the reality of the dangerous white supremacist. "Usually they end up trying to put all those characteristics on us," he had told the Harlem rally on his departure, "to hide their own guilt."[4]

Noting the power of images, Malcolm X had recently become concerned about the media's use of imagery. In the weeks surrounding his Oxford visit, he jotted down more thoughts in his personal notebook about the media than any other subject. This was not something he had devoted much time to in previous speeches. But in the Oxford debate, he mentioned newspapers and the press twenty-five times. "When the people who are in power want to, again, create an image to justify something that's bad, they use the press.... The powers that be," he continued, "use the press to give the devil an angelic image and give the image of the devil to the one who's really angelic." Or "they'll take a person who is a victim of the crime and make it appear he's the criminal, and they'll take the criminal and make it appear that he's the victim of the crime."

Malcolm X was encouraged that the powers that be seemed to be losing their grip. "Now, there was a time," he told the Oxford audience, "when the dark world, people with dark skin, would believe anything that they saw in the papers that originated in Europe. But today, no matter what is put in the paper, they stop and look at it two or three times and try and figure out what is the motive of the writer." And as the dark world grew increasingly skeptical of media-created images, it was beginning to challenge them. "In the past," Malcolm X explained, "the oppressor had one [yard]stick and the oppressed used that same stick" to judge who was an extremist. But "today the oppressed are sort of shaking the shackles and getting yardsticks of their own, so when they say 'extremism,' they don't mean what you do, and when you say 'extremism,' you don't mean what they do."

Still, there was much work to be done. Malcolm X had told the rally of OAAU supporters in Harlem before leaving for Oxford, "it should be emphasized over and over and over by you and me that we aren't racists. One of the worst categories to let them put you in is the category of racist."[5] Malcolm X came to Oxford to emphasize that point through both his argument and his demeanor. Indeed, simply by coming to Oxford, Malcolm X challenged the category of extremist to which he had been assigned. He was clearly aware of the symbolic value of his appearance at the Union. If his words were taken seriously in this most august of English institutions, they should also be listened to in America. An extremist to be dismissed from the public square he was not.

By addressing the motion directly, Malcolm X sought to turn the tables on the definitions of extremist versus moderate. Playing on the word *extremism* as meaning forceful or confrontational, he told his audience that the West's creation of negative racial stereotypes explained "why today we need a little extremism, in order to straighten a very nasty situation out." In the remainder of his speech he would spell out, "extremely," that while he was not racist, "that type" in America most certainly was.

ISLAM

I must wear two hats: Muslim & Nationalist.
—Malcolm X, undated speech notes,
late 1964

After responding to his opponent's accusation that he was an extremist, Malcolm X introduced himself as a Muslim. "My religion is Islam. I believe in Allah, I believe in Mohammed as the apostle of Allah." He would repeat his creed when concluding his speech, adding: "I believe in fasting, prayer, charity, and that which is incumbent on a Muslim to fulfill in order to be a Muslim. In April, I was fortunate to make the Hajj to Mecca." In between these two declarations of faith, however, Malcolm X didn't mention Islam at all.

By December 1964, Malcolm's spiritual journey from child of a Baptist preacher to angry atheist to Nation of Islam spokesman to Sunni Muslim seemed complete, though he remained eager to learn more. After leaving the Nation of Islam, he had seized every opportunity to understand what he called "Old World Islam." He found the latest chapter in the story of his faith deeply satisfying. In the Middle East and at Islamic meetings, he spoke at length of his devotion. "I am proud and thankful to Allah for blessing me to be a Muslim," he told one audience in Egypt.[6] "I am now striving to live the life of a true Sunni Muslim," he stated in a letter to the *Egyptian Gazette.*[7] His personal notebooks suggest that he was excited by the growth (albeit minor) of Islam among African Americans and thought that it heralded major change, since Islam had originally spread among the downtrodden in the East a millennium or so previously.[8]

In private conversations with non-Muslims, too, Malcolm X spoke openly and passionately of his religion. "Islam not only makes all the scattered pieces of my life fit," he explained to Jan Carew two months after the debate, "it glues them together. So even though sparks still fly inside my head, I can control them before they start fires"[9]—as his performance at Oxford demonstrated. Carew was impressed by his faith and his works. "There was something mesmeric about Malcolm's asceticism, his passionate devotion to Islam. He was possessed with all the fervor of a new believer." As Malcolm X himself explained, "it was as if he'd rinsed his brain, his spirit, his whole being with fresh spring water."[10] On wistful reflection, Carew wished "that I could embrace a religion with the same passion and certainty."[11]

Yet in public secular contexts in 1964, Malcolm X said little about religion or Islam. This marked quite a turnaround from his first public speeches, where, typically at some length, he defended Elijah Muhammad and the Nation of Islam and spoke of Allah's call to black America and impending judgment of white America. Leaving the Nation, however, allowed Malcolm X to focus on other matters. Indeed, he had begun to leave religion out of political speeches shortly before he left the Nation—one of the reasons his position within the Nation had become so fraught, in fact.[12] Once free of the Nation, he clarified his decision to separate religion and politics. In his most famous speech, "The Ballot or the Bullet," delivered in a church on April 3, 1964, he said: "Islam is my religion, but I believe my religion is my personal business. It governs my personal life, my personal morals. And my religious philosophy is personal between me and the God in whom I believe."[13]

In that speech, Malcolm X also explained why he kept religion out of politics. "If we bring up religion we'll have differences, we'll have arguments; and we'll never be able to get together." In turn, this explanation allowed him to highlight the reach of American racism. In the lived experience of an African American, he noted, religion mattered little because "you catch hell whether you're a Baptist, or a Methodist, or a Muslim, or a nationalist." Much better, he suggested, "if we keep our religion at home, keep our religion in the closet, keep our religion between ourselves and our God."[14]

Founding both the Muslim Mosque Inc. (MMI) and the Organization of African American Unity (OAAU) in 1964 allowed Malcolm X to institutionalize his separation of religion and politics. As head of the Muslim Mosque—or as he had put it in Nasser's guestbook, as the "leader of Islam in U.S.A."—he could appeal to the Arab world for support in building, and expanding, the African American Muslim community. His outreach in 1964 seemed to promise success. He wrote home with delight when Arab supporters pledged funds for twenty scholarships for members of MMI to study in the Middle East—his joy heightened by the fact that Elijah Muhammad received funds for only one scholar (and that was his son).[15] The OAAU, by contrast, did not mention religion once in its founding document. Its five priorities were unity among people of African descent (which by definition meant downplaying religion), self-defense, education, politics and economics, and the morality and integrity of the African American community.[16]

By separating religion and politics, too, Malcolm X could put on his OAAU hat without undermining his religious credentials, and vice versa. "When I come to a meeting sponsored by the OAAU," he told the predeparture Harlem rally, "I put my religion in this pocket right here, and keep it here." But because he led the Muslim Mosque, his religious commitment could not be in doubt. Indeed, he reassured Muslims in the Harlem audience who might be "nervous" about the political emphasis of his speech that "when I talk like this, it doesn't mean I'm less religious; it means I'm more religious."[17] It was a successful strategy—asserting his Islamic faith but not letting it interfere with his political project. As one of the leading Christian ministers in the Black Power movement, Rev. Albert Cleage, reflected after Malcolm X's death: "He was a Muslim, I am a Christian, and yet I can think of no basic matter upon which we disagreed."[18]

While Malcolm X took care to separate his faith and politics in public, in private he saw them as intertwined. By late 1964, Malcolm X was convinced that Islam best encouraged human rights. In public, he sometimes referred to his faith as a way to reinforce his fierce commitment to black rights. "That's why I am a Muslim," he told the Harlem rally, "because it's a religion that teaches . . . if someone steps on your toe, chop off their foot."[19] In Oxford, explaining why he "put religion in his pocket" served to highlight the urgency of the race problem. "At the same time that I believe in that religion," he said, "I have to point out that I am an American Negro. And I live in a society whose social system is based upon the castration of the black man, whose political system is based upon the castration of the black man, and whose economy is based upon the castration of the black man."

Thus, in the context of his public speeches in late 1964, the unusual aspect of Malcolm X's Oxford speech was not that he said so little about Islam, but that he mentioned that he was a Muslim at all—twice. That he did so was to rebut his image as an angry black Muslim extremist—an image that he had long resented. At Columbia University in late 1963, when he was still in the Nation, he complained that the "press has referred to us as Black Muslims, which we aren't. We are black people who are Muslims because we believe in the religion of Islam."[20] Now that he had embraced Sunni Islam, the reputation still held. Even Abrahams introduced him as a Black Muslim. Hence, Malcolm X's brief testimonies during his speech in Oxford focused on going to Mecca, following Islamic rituals, and living as a true Sunni Muslim. "If there is something wrong with that," he said pointedly, "then I stand condemned."

Viewers of the televised debate would have needed to pay close attention to understand the distinction he drew between

Black (Nation of Islam) Muslims and black (Sunni) Muslims, though, especially since the BBC pundits in the studio continued to refer to him as a black (i.e., Black) Muslim even after the debate, while condemning his "wildly exaggerated" picture of the U.S.A.[21] Given his contempt for Western media, Malcolm X was likely not surprised at that treatment.

Having defended his reputation and suggesting that calling him an extremist meant calling every Muslim an extremist, Malcolm X went on the attack. Standing at the lectern, he condemned the ways in which America psychologically castrated the black man, starting with a withering critique of American intervention in the Congo—a topic that brought together his long-standing anger at American racism, his recent experiences in Africa, and his new concern about the role of the media.

CONGO

> Never believe what you read in the newspapers—
> they're not going to tell you the truth. The truth isn't
> in them. Not when it comes to the Congo. They can't
> tell the truth.
> —Malcolm X, speech to supporters in Harlem,
>   November 29, 1964

Events in Congo appalled Malcolm X. In 1961, forces loyal to pro-Western Moise Tshombe had murdered the pan-Africanist Patrice Lumumba, Congo's first prime minister after winning independence from Belgium. In the summer of 1964, Tshombe seized power and recruited white South African and European mercenaries to destroy his opponents. Malcolm X loathed the man. In all his speeches, Malcolm X reserved his greatest contempt for Tshombe. He was "the worst African ever born," he said at the Harlem rally before his departure for Europe, and the "man who in cold blood, cold blood, committed an international crime—murdered Patrice Lumumba."[22]

By the time Malcolm X returned to New York from Africa in late November 1964, the conflict in the Congo had degenerated into a full-blown humanitarian crisis. Tshombe's mercenaries had gained the upper hand over the opposition "Simbas." Fearing capture and execution, the Simbas had rounded up many hundreds of white European and American expatriates as hostages. The Belgian and American governments launched what they called a rescue mission. Some two hundred hostages were killed, including missionaries. While those battles were raging, Tshombe's mercenary army swept back into the major cities, killing thousands of Simbas. More than one hundred thousand Congolese would die during the years of civil war.

Malcolm X's concern for Congo was tied up with his commitment, at the end of 1964, to an international black struggle against white supremacy. By this time his fierce global vision, which had once set him apart from other American civil rights activists, was increasingly the mainstream position among African American leaders. James Farmer, head of the Congress of Racial Equality and one-time critic of Malcolm X, called on the United States to stop supporting Tshombe. The *Chicago Defender* backed the call: "There is, after all, an interrelation between the African longing for unfettered sovereignty and the American Negro's dream of unconditional citizenships and unqualified acceptance."[23] The very day Malcolm X flew to London, the *Defender*'s editor urged his readers to condemn brutalities in the Congo as much as in Mississippi: "The sad fact stares us in the face that much of the disaster that befell the Americans and Europeans in the Congo is attributable to white arrogance and a mistaken sense of invincibility in a black man's land."[24]

Most African leaders thought the same. Kenyan foreign minister Joseph Murumbi charged the United States and Belgium with issuing "hypocritical statements" to "cover premeditated aggression."[25]

Malcolm X took the critique of American foreign policy one step further. It was not just aggressive racist arrogance that the United States was displaying in the Congo; it was colonialism, plain and simple. Just as a basketball player, when cornered, passes the ball to a teammate, he explained, the waning European powers had passed their control of Africa to the United States. As for Tshombe and Lyndon Johnson, "they're sleeping together. When I say sleeping together, I don't mean that literally. But beyond that they're in the same bed. Johnson is paying the salaries, paying the government, propping up Tshombe's government, this murderer."[26] At the airport, as he left for England, he blamed the deaths of white people in the Congo directly on President Johnson for his "support of Moise Tshombe's hired killers." The "Congolese have been massacred by white people for years and years," he declared. And, using the phrase he had applied to Kennedy's assassination, and which had gotten him into so much trouble, he concluded: "Chickens come home to roost."[27]

Little wonder, then, that Malcolm X brought up the Congo situation in Oxford, especially since the story was headline news in the British press, too. The reason he devoted more than a third of his speech to the Congo, though, was that it reinforced his argument about the media's creation of extremist images. "The Congo situation is a nasty example," he said, "of how a country, because it is in power, can take its press and make the world accept something that's absolutely criminal." What particularly angered him was the way the press framed the story as being about good against evil—but the wrong way around. He told the

Oxford students that because the pilots who dropped bombs on defenseless village women and children were called "American-trained" and "anti-Castro," they were seen as good, while the rebels were presented as evil "savages" who were "raping white women, molesting nuns." "Hired killers" were dignified by the term "mercenaries." As for Tshombe, that "paid-killer cold-blooded murderer" was dignified by the title Prime Minister.

Malcolm X may well have read the *New York Times* before he flew to England. On November 27, the paper reported a white nun's horror as she was forced to walk down a street naked before being beaten and threatened with being eaten. She had wanted to die. Only the arrival of Belgian troops saved her.[28] The day before his Oxford Union speech, the same paper wrote of "a confused farrago of primitive and sadistic Congolese rebels."[29] And if Malcolm X had picked up the *Times* on his return, he would have read that the Simbas "believe in magic and deck themselves with leaves and animal skins."[30]

In Oxford, when Malcolm X mentioned that he had read a clear account of the situation in Congo in the *Daily Express* that morning, some students laughed, presuming he was joking about the ability of the tabloid to be clear about anything. He was not. Malcolm X thought the *Express* told something of the truth of the mercenaries' indiscriminate slaughter of Congolese. He would quote from that article at greater length on his return to Harlem. In his mind, the British press was slightly better than its American counterpart, even though, he told his Union audience, the "American press . . . has tricked your press into repeating what they have invented."

Malcolm X's main point was that the murderous extremism of the Congolese government was "never referred to as extremism because it is endorsed by the West, it is financed by America, it's made respectable by America, and that kind of extremism is never labeled as extremism." That kind of extremism, though, was indefensible, "since it's not extremism in defense of liberty." And "if it is extremism in defense of liberty—as this type just pointed out," he went on, with another jab at Berkeley—"it is extremism in defense of liberty for the wrong type of people." Those in the West, even those in Oxford, even "my friend" Berkeley, would not condone America's and Tshombe's action if they recognized it for the murderous extremism it was. "It's condoned primarily because it has been glorified by the press and has been made to look beautiful, and therefore the world automatically sanctions it."

At this point in his argument a member of the audience challenged Malcolm X's portrayal of the Simbas as justifiably extremist by asking, "[What] sort of extremism would you consider the killing of [white] missionaries?" Malcolm X addressed the question head on: "It was an act of war." And, in a nod to his context: "I'd call it the same kind of extremism that happened when England dropped bombs on German cities and Germans dropped bombs on English cities." Once people recognized there was a war, "then anybody that dies, they die a death that is justified." Reminding the students that America and Belgium had escalated the war in the first place, Malcolm X mentioned the discussions in the international press about whether sending in paratroopers had been the right tactic. "Some of the refugees that were questioned on television . . . a couple of days ago pointed out that had the paratroopers not come in, they doubted that they would have been molested."

Far from wrongfooting him, then, the question allowed Malcolm X to reiterate a point he had made before coming to Oxford and would often make again—that by describing hostages as "white hostages," newspapers "give the impression that they attach more importance to a white hostage and a white death, than they do the death of a human being, despite the color of his skin." It was contemptible "to make a distinction between the type of dying according to the color of the skin." To be sure, Malcolm X acknowledged, news of such deaths as those of the white missionaries do not "go by me without creating some kind of emotion." But pivoting to his new commitment to the potential brotherhood of man, regardless of race, Malcolm X argued that it was time to "begin thinking in terms of death being death, no matter what type of human being it is." When people did that, the issue of extremism versus moderation would become moot.

In the meantime, while injustice raged, he emphasized a favored theme: the right of a black man to defend himself, even though the American press labeled such a man "an extremist . . . or as a rabble-rouser." Now this theme also spoke to his new advocacy of human rights. "We are not human beings unless we ourselves band together and do whatever, however, whenever, is necessary to see that our lives and our property is protected." He would expand on this idea of fighting back, justifiably and by any means necessary, for the remainder of the debate.

AMERICA

> I don't believe in any form of unjustified extremism.
> But I believe that when a man is exercising extremism,
> [when] a human being is exercising extremism, in
> defense of liberty for human beings, it's no vice.
>   —Malcolm X, Oxford Union debate

The final section of his speech was also prompted by a student's intervention. In this case, the student criticized the fact that Malcolm X had "projected, rather successfully, a quite upsetting image of that 'type.'" Members of the audience started to heckle the questioner. Malcolm X, eager to respond, asked the audience to quiet down so he could address the comment. And so, for the final third of this speech, he went into detail about exactly what he thought of "that type." For all that he had developed a human rights agenda and no longer considered white people inherently racist, Malcolm X had not moderated his view of the American government's culpability for racism one bit. Here, in a foreign country and in front of a strategic audience in the chamber and a national audience on television, was an ideal opportunity to indict his homeland.

For Malcolm X, the issue was not just that the American social, political, and economic system was "based upon castration of the black man." Reverting to his points about image, Malcolm X denounced America's "subtle, deceptive, deceitful methods to make the rest of the world think that it's cleaning up its house." During his tour of Africa, Malcolm X had learned of the propaganda value of the American Civil Rights Bill that had been passed in 1964, and it angered him deeply. At the Harlem rally in late November, he told the crowd that in every African country the U.S. Information Service window displays pictures showing the passage of the bill to make "it appear that the civil rights bill created a paradise in the United States for the 22 million Negroes." In his view, "the United States Information Service ... will make that propaganda machine that Goebbels had, under Hitler, look like child's play."[31]

In Oxford, Malcolm X argued that the Civil Rights Bill of 1964 counted for nothing when three civil rights workers were killed in Mississippi soon after its passage. Then, turning Humphrey Berkeley's charge about his support of apartheid on its head, he charged: "American democracy was as racist as South

Africa or as racist as Portugal or as racist as any other racialist society on this earth. . . . The only difference between it and South Africa," he continued, was that "South Africa preaches separation and practices separation, [whereas] America preaches integration and practices segregation." To convey his contempt for his home country, he told the students: "I have more respect for a man who lets me know where he stands, even if he's wrong, than the one comes up like an angel and is nothing but a devil."

As he had done in many of his major speeches while in the Nation of Islam and afterward, he then explained why civil rights bills and legal decisions made so little difference in the lived experience of black Americans. It came down to the procedural rules, especially regarding seniority, that steered the composition of Congress's committees. "Of the thirty-six committees that govern the foreign and domestic direction of that government, twenty-three are in the hands of southern racialists," he pointed out. These committees could make sure civil rights bills were so "chopped up and fixed up that by the time it becomes law, it is a law that can't be enforced," not even in northern cities like Boston or New York City. And "if a society doesn't enforce its own laws, because the color of a man's skin happens to be wrong, then I say those people are justified to resort to any means necessary to bring about justice."

Although Malcolm X's talk of committees and government structures may have appealed to the Union students' minds, he closed his critique of American racism with an appeal to the heart. A moderate or nonviolent or "wishy-washy love thy neighbor" approach would surely fail, he said, because "the racialist never understands a peaceful language." African Americans knew "*his* type of language" all too well. "We have been the victim of his brutality, we are the ones who face his dogs who tear the flesh from our limbs. . . . We are the ones who have our skulls crushed, not by the Ku Klux Klan, but by policemen. We are the ones upon whom water hoses are turned, practically so hard that it rips the clothes from our back, not [just] men, but the clothes from the backs of women and children, you've seen it yourself." The students had indeed seen it, on British television news. Oxford students, even those who had challenged the proctors, could hardly argue with a man who represented that sort of suffering.

HAMLET

> Tony Abrahams told me afterwards that it really shocked them when I laid that quotation on them.
> —Malcolm X to Jan Carew,
>   in *Ghosts in Our Blood*

Malcolm X concluded his speech by calling on historical greats to support his argument. First he mentioned the American founding father Patrick Henry and his famous cry, "Give me liberty or give me death." He had made much of Henry and the American revolution in previous speeches back home. But whether out of sensitivity to his British audience or an awareness that Henry would be little known, Malcolm X swiftly changed tack and summoned the greatest of all English writers, William Shakespeare.

This was Malcolm X's first reference to Shakespeare in any of his major speeches, perhaps in any speech thus far. But in Oxford, his time in prison learning Shakespeare by heart now came in handy. Not that he admitted to the depth of his familiarity with the bard (or the place where he'd gained it). "I only read about him passingly," he insisted, and feigned unfamiliarity with

"Hamlet, I think it was who said, 'To be or not to be'?" To much laughter, he added, with the timing of a comedian: "He was in doubt about something."

And then Malcolm X quoted the next line of Hamlet's speech, simply adding one word—*moderation*—to bear on the motion at hand: "Whether it was nobler, in the mind of man, to suffer the slings and arrows of outrageous fortune—moderation—or to take up arms against the sea of troubles and, by opposing, end them." Malcolm X rested his case: "And I go for that," he said. "If you take up arms, you'll end it, but if you sit around and wait for the one who is in power to make up his mind that he should end it, you'll be waiting a long time."[32]

Reinforcing the message that he was an extremist only in his concern for justice, not in his consideration of color, he concluded: "And I, for one, will join in with anyone—don't care what color you are—as long as you want to change this miserable condition that exists on this earth. Thank you." The students responded with enthusiastic applause. Although Malcolm X ultimately lost the vote, 228 to 137, he had won plenty of admirers.[33]

Tellingly, Malcolm X did not quote the next line of Hamlet's speech, of the fate of the extremist. "To die, to sleep—No more." Within three months, that would be his own fate.

CHAPTER FIVE

After the Debate, 1964-1968

MALCOLM X'S TRAVELS IN ENGLAND

I hope that the Afroamerican Community in Paris,
as well as in the whole of Europe, will realize the
importance of us sticking together in unity and
brotherhood and doing something to solve our own
problems.

—Malcolm X to supporters in Paris, by
telephone, February 9, 1965

The rest of Malcolm X's trip to England that December was
organized by the Federation of Islamic Students Societies, an
independent group founded in 1961. When he heard that Malcolm X was coming to Oxford, Ebrahimsa Mohamed, the federation's secretary and a student at Manchester, contacted the head
of the Islamic Center in Geneva, who knew Malcolm X from his
earlier visit there. Ebrahimsa arranged talks to student Muslim
groups in Manchester and Sheffield on Friday, the day after the
debate, and to an Islamic society in London on Saturday.[1] On
his trip, Malcolm X stayed at the homes of British Muslims and
joined prayers at local mosques.

Much as he wanted to wear his Muslim hat, Malcolm X found himself wearing his black activist hat instead. In Manchester, his talk became a matter of controversy because extremists were forbidden to speak on campus. The visit to Oxford came in handy, just as Malcolm X had hoped it would: Muslim students pointed out that if the Oxford Union had welcomed him, then so should Manchester's student union. The union finally accepted the point, but too late in the day for any publicity to be organized. The sponsoring students simply put up posters saying "Malcolm X Speaks" outside the main debating hall. The hall was packed an hour before the speaker arrived.[2] Both before and after the lecture, Malcolm X was interviewed on television about his views on race.

In Sheffield as in Oxford, Malcolm X arrived in the middle of a conflict over race. In late November, a university magazine had published an article that supported the voters in Smethwick and said "black immigrants were inferior and should 'get home.'" On December 3, outraged students held what the local newspaper called a "massive protest meeting" to challenge the magazine's "racialist tendencies."[3] The following day, Malcolm X arrived on campus. The secretary of the Sheffield Islamic Circle, G. U. Siddiqui, was frustrated by the "unfortunate coincidence that he is coming when the racialist question is in the Union. . . . His visit has nothing to do with it."[4] The circle felt compelled to ask the (white) student union vice president to introduce Malcolm X, to counter suspicions that he had been invited for racialist motives.

As in Oxford, too, Malcolm X's presence meant the national press picked up the local story. The *Sun,* a national tabloid, warned that the "bearded Mr. Eoin Hodgson, student union president"—using the adjective to stereotype him in a way that reinforced Malcolm X's point about press bias—expected "a lot of stirrers there."[5] According to the local newspaper report, some seven hundred attended and hissed during a speech that didn't pull any punches when it came to the Congo.[6] The student union responded with a petition, signed by more than two hundred students, stating that the newspaper account "grossly misrepresented what took place" and pointing out that "Malcolm X is the only person in the history of the Union who has received a standing ovation from 700 students." The union secretary said they would use "any means necessary" to secure a return trip. One student sent a clipping about the contretemps to Malcolm X in Harlem. No doubt he was delighted to see such a strong challenge to a media misstatement—and pleasantly surprised that the editor of the newspaper admitted it had been in error.[7]

If the first tour of Britain was about networking with Muslim students, his next trip was designed to build solidarity with African and Caribbean students. The Council of African Organisations (CAO) in London, a network of African student groups, invited Malcolm X to give the keynote address at its first congress, at Africa House in February 1965—focusing on the topic "In Solidarity with Southern African and Afro-American Struggle for Freedom"—and offered to pay his costs.[8] Like the invitation to Oxford, it was too good an opportunity to turn down.

Malcolm X returned to England on February 5, staying for a week, during which time, among other things, he gave the keynote address at the congress; spoke at the London School of Economics; attended a launch party for a new militant black British magazine, *Magnet*; and gave a lengthy interview to the African cultural magazine *Flamingo*. He tried to visit Paris again, to speak at a rally on African and African American solidarity sponsored by the French Federation of African Students, but he was turned back at the airport. He addressed the Paris audience by telephone instead. At every turn, Malcolm X called on African and Caribbean students to join with African Americans in a global struggle.[9]

Finding himself with unexpected spare time in Britain, Malcolm X visited the immigration hotspot of Smethwick, near Birmingham, with the BBC.[10] Anti-immigrant activists were incensed. Smethwick's mayor, Clarence Williams, declared: "It makes my blood boil that Malcolm X should be allowed into this country."[11] True to form, Malcolm X stoked the controversy. His comment on Smethwick's new anti-immigration MP, Peter Griffiths—"I wouldn't wait for them to set up gas ovens"—hit the headlines on both sides of the Atlantic.[12] So too did Griffiths's call in the House of Commons for the "undesirable alien [to be] refused entry to this country."[13]

In the final analysis, Malcolm X's two tours of England were a triumph. He spent time in four of the country's largest cities; met dozens of aspiring African, Caribbean, Asian, and Middle Eastern leaders; and received widespread, approving attention from the black British press. The *West Indian Gazette,* for one, devoted a full page to his keynote address at the Solidarity Congress.[14] Even the British mainstream press acknowledged that the stereotype of an angry black Muslim did not fit the man. "Since breaking with his old leader Elijah Muhammad a year ago," reported the *Guardian,* "Mr X has talked more and more like an African Nationalist and has moved more formally towards Islam."[15] This was precisely the point that Malcolm X had hoped to make. In America, the African American press reported on his performance in Oxford and reception in England with pride, and the mainstream press, too, described his trips to Britain as successful.[16]

Malcolm X returned to America on February 13. He planned
to return to Britain again that summer.

MALCOLM X AFTER OXFORD

> My reason for being here is to discuss the Black
> revolution that is going on, that's taking place on this
> earth, the manner in which it's taking place on the
> African continent, and the impact that it's having in
> Black communities, not only here in America but in
> England and in France and in other of the former
> colonial powers today.
> —Malcolm X, rally in Rochester, New York,
>   February 16, 1965

Just as in Africa and the Middle East, Malcolm X's trip to
Oxford, and his travels in France and then England more generally, challenged his thinking. That was his intention. Although
he was invited to Britain to give public lectures and was never
short of comments for the media, in private meetings he preferred to ask questions, and he loved to observe local people, his
camera ever at the ready. In Paris, he sought out Africans in the
cafes.[17] In Birmingham, he visited a pub on a street where immigrants now lived. Legend has it that the strict Muslim ordered
a pint.[18] In Oxford, he met with students over cups of tea and in
discussion groups—and to their surprise, he plied them with
questions. Indeed, he particularly enjoyed his time on British
campuses. "I love to hear from students, especially their ideas
and opinions and conclusions," he wrote to one admirer from
Sheffield (who had addressed her letter "Malcolm X, OAAU,
Harlem, New York" and asked the mailman to forward "by any
means necessary"). Hearing from students "adds to my own
understanding."[19]

Time in England and France added to Malcolm X's take

on both racial discrimination and black resistance. Prior to his European travels, Malcolm X's vision of an international black movement stretched to most continents except Europe. He spoke of only two categories of black people: those fighting imperial rule in the former colonies and African Americans fighting racism in the United States. Black Europeans were not on his radar. Insomuch as he spoke of Britain and France at all, they were colonial powers that had caused untold problems in the past; but they were not countries that held much interest for him in the present. At Yale in 1962, Malcolm X had scoffed: "Today, when the sun rises, we can hardly find the British Empire."[20] The new evil empire was the United States. "Only Americanism is more hypocritical than colonialism," he told a rally in Harlem in 1963. "America's democracy is nothing but hypocrisy." And as a result, "America is the last stronghold of white supremacy" because "the black revolution has swept white supremacy out of Africa, out of Asia, and is getting ready to sweep it out of Latin America." Europe didn't even merit a mention.[21]

During his tours of England, however, Malcolm X quickly recognized that, as he told reporters in Smethwick, "Britain has a colour problem"[22]—and it was strikingly similar to the American color problem. In his notebook, between his time in Oxford and the return to London, Malcolm X jotted down his thoughts about the black image in the white media "Press calls us racists ... crime statistics fed to *white* public ... false image skillfully created ... Justify Police State ... Riots." This was the American story, but it was also, he noted with an asterisk, "Same in England," with the same consequences for the "Colored Community."[23]

At a rally in New York on December 20, 1964, following his first tour of England, Malcolm X condemned England as a satellite state of America. At that stage, he commended France for refusing to fall into that orbit, saying rather that "France wants America to be her satellite."[24] But after being turned back at Paris airport in February, he changed his mind. "France has become a satellite of Washington, D.C.," he told his French supporters on the phone. Still smarting from the rejection, he raged: "The French Government is probably the worst racist government there is." The fact that "every other lowdown person has been permitted to come to France," including that "despot of the worst sort" Tshombe, made the insult even worse. Malcolm X handed the French security forces an English penny "and told them to give this to de Gaulle because, from my point of view, his government and country were worth less than a penny."[25]

Learning about Britain and France and then connecting them to America changed Malcolm X's analysis of the causes of white supremacy. He now thought of the three democratic capitalist regimes as an inextricably linked white power structure. "The interests in this country are in cahoots with the interests in France and the interests in Britain," he told supporters in New York on the evening of February 14, the same day his house was firebombed by opponents in the Nation of Islam. "It's one huge complex or combine . . . an international power structure" of politicians, business, and the media that worked "to suppress the masses of dark-skinned people all over the world and exploit them of their natural resources."[26] This was an important development in Malcolm X's thinking. His critique of white power shifted from a simple anti-American and anticolonial position to a more nuanced, international, somewhat socialist perspective—a shift that reflected his concerns about the media and dovetailed with his commitment to human rights and advocacy of intervention by the United Nations.

Yet even as he grew more concerned about the global reach of institutional white privilege, Malcolm X was encouraged to meet so many black Europeans. In his journal, he noted that "there are 4 types of Blacks [and] 4 spheres of white influence: Spanish America, British & French . . . and U.S." All told there were "over 100 million *Afros* in [the] West, *inside* the Western Power Structure." Perhaps because it was new information for him, Malcolm X took every chance to educate his fellow African Americans, in speeches, about the "increasing number of dark-skinned people in England and also in France."[27] Or as he put it to supporters in Harlem, "We've got a whole lot of our people over there, brothers. I saw them."[28]

In his mind, the "whole lot of our people" augured well for black resistance "over there." In speeches to supporters in America following his final trip to Britain, Malcolm X explained: "The only reason that England's problems haven't been highly publicized" was simply "because America's problems have been so highly publicized." Yet in some ways Britain and France actually faced a more "precarious position" than the United States, because they had "a sort of commonwealth structure that makes it easy for all of the people in the commonwealth territories to come into their country with no restrictions." What it meant was that "the three major allies, the United States, Britain and France, have a problem today that is a common problem."[29]

Part of the common problem facing Britain, France, and the United States was "the outside or external phase of the revolution, which is manifest in the attitude and action of the Africans today." That was "troublesome enough" for the three major allies. But what excited Malcolm X most was that the "common problem is the new mood . . . of the Black people within continental France, within the same sphere of England, and also here in the United States." The inspiration for the new mood was African resistance to the European empires. But the effect of the new mood was being seen within the Western democracies. "Now the powers that be are beginning to see that this struggle on the outside by the Black man is affecting, infecting the Black man who is on the inside of that structure," he explained. "I hope you understand what I'm trying to say," he emphasized. "Just as the external forces pose a grave threat, they can now see that the internal forces pose an even greater threat.... The newly awakened people all over the world pose a problem for what's known as Western interests, which is imperialism, colonialism, racism, and all these other negative -isms or vulturistic -isms."[30]

For Malcolm X, this internal resistance within the Western power structure had immense, and tantalizing, potential. But there were also challenges. "The internal forces pose an even greater threat only when they have properly analyzed the situation and know what the stakes really are." He warned of the danger of "divisions between these internal forces"—specifically, between black communities in different Western countries. Malcolm X thought his role was to forge a united front, by establishing the OAAU in America and Europe. In his view, his expulsion from France and the controversy he had caused in England meant his work was already paying dividends. As he explained to supporters, "Just by advocating a coalition of Africans, Afro-Americans, Arabs, and Asians who live within the structure, it automatically has upset France, which is supposed to be one of the most liberal—heh!—countries on earth, and it made them expose their hand. England the same way. And I don't have to tell you about this country that we are living in now."[31]

The British example of alliances among immigrant groups from different nations gave him further encouragement.

"Recently," he told supporters in New York two days after the firebombing, "the West Indians in England, along with the African community in England, along with the Asians in England began to organize and work in coordination with each other, in conjunction with each other. And this has posed England a very serious problem."[32] Jan Carew felt it was English racism rather than African independence that led to the unity in Britain. Black in a British context, he noted, had a very broad definition. "The English did us a favor, Malcolm. They've lumped us all together as 'niggers'—Asians, Africans, West Indians, the lot. They compel us to unite whether we like it or not."[33]

In many cases, in fact, they did not like it. One Indian immigrant to Britain who had spent time in America complained to an interviewer in 1967, "When I was in U.S.A. I was not considered as a coloured man."[34] Claudia Jones was frustrated by the continued island mentality of immigrants from different parts of the Caribbean. Nonetheless, race protest in Britain was characterized by solidarity across national lines, whether it be Jamaican, Pakistani, and Zambian students hosting Malcolm X in Oxford, or Indian, Pakistani, African, and Caribbean workers associations joining together in housing and job protests. Malcolm X thought the unity among immigrant groups in Britain was likely to get stronger in the short term. "I can forecast that since all of you have, more or less, just arrived," he said to Jan Carew, and because you "are able to talk the same language and play the same games," it "will help for a while" in terms of working together.[35]

"During 1965," Malcolm X forecast in his travel journal, "we shall see the longest, hottest and bloodiest summer yet witnessed by . . . the Black Revolution." And, he mused, that means "trouble for old John Bull."[36] Malcolm X looked forward to seeing that trouble in person on return visits. He did not get the chance. On

February 21, just eight days after his return to the United States, as he was about to start a speech in Harlem, he was shot dead by members of the Nation of Islam.

THE AMERICAN CIVIL RIGHTS
MOVEMENT AND BRITAIN

> More and more I have come to realize that racism is a world problem.
> —Martin Luther King Jr., at a meeting with British activists in London, December 1964

If Malcolm X, who already had a global vision of black politics, was influenced by his time in England, it is little surprise that his fellow African American travelers to Britain were similarly stimulated by their experiences there. None more so than Rev. Martin Luther King Jr., whose speech at St. Paul's Cathedral in London followed Malcolm X's debate in Oxford by just three days. In his early years of leadership, King did not share Malcolm X's pan-African outlook or his contempt for American ideals. When King famously declared, "I have a dream," it was "a dream deeply rooted in the American dream." Although in accepting the Nobel Peace Prize in 1964 he spoke of world peace and placed the American civil rights movement in a global context—one of his first mentions of international affairs[37]—even then he only referred to the "black brothers of Africa and brown and yellow brothers in Asia, South America, and the Caribbean." Black Europeans did not get a mention. According to King's speechwriter Clarence Jones, the subject never came up.[38]

King didn't come to Britain to learn, but to teach, or rather, to preach. Much like Malcolm X speaking at the Oxford Union, speaking at St. Paul's Cathedral enhanced King's status at home—in his case, as an international religious statesman at a time when southern opponents were denouncing him as a communist. Preaching "under Sir Christopher Wren's mighty dome" and attracting thousands "to its huge doors" was front-page news in the American press.[39] Also, as in the case of Malcolm X, speaking abroad provided King with a platform to espouse his philosophy to a wider audience. Clarence Jones recalled that King and his team "accepted the invitations to England to get their message out."[40] Benefiting from a Church of England public relations officer, King was able to partake in seven media interviews during his two-day London visit.[41]

One point King sought to make, given Malcolm X's presence in Britain at the same time, was that "the doctrine of black superiority is just as dangerous as the doctrine of white superiority." The *New York Times* got the message, reporting that King was trying to counter the "activities of Malcolm X . . . who [was] also in London."[42] There was also the question of money. "In the dark hours," King wrote to one British donor, "we will always remember the many people in England who encouraged our work . . . by their very tangible expressions by which our movement is continued."[43]

Whatever his intentions, though, King did learn from his time in Britain. Like Malcolm X, he was struck by similarities between Britain and America. Before King left the United States, Clarence Jones had typed up a speech for an address at a London public meeting. But once he got to London, King jotted notes on London Hilton Hotel paper denouncing the "segregation and discrimination that is emerging" in Britain and "that you have quite rightly deplored in others."[44] He told reporters that the "festering boils" of black neighborhoods in Britain were deteriorating into U.S.-style ghettoes.[45]

When King returned to Britain in 1967 to receive an honorary degree from the University of Newcastle, he noted that "Britain is now in the position that the northern cities of America have passed through.... There is a latent prejudice leading to discrimination in housing and jobs. It is from [that] a black ghetto is developing in Britain."[46] By this time, part of the reason King accepted such invitations abroad was that he was increasingly critical of the American dream. Yet in turn, one of the consequences of his travels to Europe was the development of his critique of Western capitalism, militarism, and foreign policy. In other words, his international travels led him to similar views of the Western power structure as those held by his old nemesis, Malcolm X.

Of course, most African Americans didn't come to Britain. And for them, African independence was a far greater inspiration than the travails of black Britons. Good news of anticolonial movements abroad, especially Ghanaian independence in 1957, helped galvanize the mass nonviolent protest against segregation that erupted across the southern United States in 1960. As James Baldwin, the novelist most associated with the American civil rights movement, famously put it: "At the rate things are going here, all of Africa will be free before we can get a lousy cup of coffee."[47] Even so, bad news of anti-immigrant riots in 1958 in Britain, a country with full civil rights, served as a bleak counterpoint and strengthened the arguments of those, such as Malcolm X, who advocated self-defense and rejected integration. The American press, white and black, covered the British race riots of 1958 in depth. News from Europe, in short, strengthened what would later be called a Black Power perspective, right at the outset of the civil rights movement.[48]

Malcolm X's expulsion from France, a country with a reputation for transcending the color line, rammed the warning home two years before the Black Power slogan first came to prominence in Mississippi. Or rather, Malcolm X himself rammed it home, with a characteristically punchy one-liner: "I have never been prevented from entering Mississippi," he told reporters. "General de Gaulle has too much gall."[49] After his death, many of Malcolm X's African American critics felt at liberty to agree with him. James Baldwin, who lived for many years in Paris, happened to be speaking at a joint meeting of JACARI and the Oxford Union soon after Malcolm X's death. "Malcolm and I did not agree on a great many things," he said, but "we and our families were menaced by the same indifferent forces. . . . This war, this plague, this disaster is clearly not any longer local."[50] .

In life and in death, then, Malcolm X championed the global struggle for civil rights. Part of his legacy was that future American Black Power leaders would instinctively look abroad, even to old John Bull, for inspiration. Stokely Carmichael, the Trinidad-born activist who oversaw the American student movement's adoption of Black Power in 1966, accepted an invitation to speak at a conference in London in 1967 precisely because "Black Power formations had begun to emerge in the African/Caribbean immigrant communities in Britain. This seemed a perfect opportunity to establish contact and exchange ideas with these emerging forces."[51] This exchange duly confirmed Carmichael's interpretation of the race problem not in terms of Jim Crow specifics, or even colonial oppression, but as a product of an international system of racialist Western democracies. "We're talking now about the U.S.," Carmichael told reporters, but "you can apply a little of it to London."[52]

African American activists also used news from across the Atlantic to bolster their fight against discrimination at home.

Malcolm X publicly denounced American racism as "a cancer spreading all over the world" that was manifesting itself in Britain.[53] Although entries in his journal suggest that this was indeed his viewpoint, for others such rhetoric was entirely tactical, used to pressure southern segregationists. During the 1950s, virtually all African American press coverage of the black experience in Britain had been negative, reflecting anti-imperial sentiment. The rise of the American civil rights movement, and particularly the massive resistance to it, marked an about-turn in reportage. "Race relations in England, in the past, have been on a higher plane of conviviality," reported the influential *Chicago Defender* after the anti-immigrant riots of 1958—thereby ignoring virtually all of its own reports from the previous decade. "Nevertheless, America's brazen, vulgar display of racial hatred has assumed the virulence of a communicative disease which is infecting the mind and soul of the stolid Englishman."[54]

But black activists were not the only ones to use British news for their own domestic purposes. The mainstream American media picked up on bad news from Britain to defend America's reputation. Or at the very least, they echoed Malcolm X's observation that Britain and America had a "common color problem," to make American racial tensions seem less exceptional. As the African American *Pittsburgh Courier* put it, the white press's amazing alacrity in picking up on all the gory, gruesome tidbits that could be extracted from the recent series of "race riots" in England represented an attempt by "some white Americans to expiate their own sins."[55] "Radio station announcers," a West Indian visitor to New York noted ruefully, would "interrupt a programme to splash—not without satisfaction—the news of Britain's race riots." Meanwhile, U.S. liberals, observed one British reporter, had "a mixture of slight *schadenfreude* and genuine sorrow." Said one race relations man: "It's like the headmaster getting into trouble." As for Governor Orval Faubus of Arkansas, orchestrator of the Little Rock crisis in which white mobs sought to bar the first black children from going to the city's previously all-white high school, he enjoyed telling British reporters to shove it. "What about that shindy in Nottingham?" he asked the *Daily Express.* "We have sympathy for you."[56]

THE AMERICAN CIVIL RIGHTS
MOVEMENT . . . IN BRITAIN

Your Fight Is Our Fight!
—A banner outside the American embassy
in London, in solidarity with the March
on Washington, 1963

British activists certainly drew connections between themselves and their American counterparts. A lead editorial in March 1963 in the black London weekly the *West Indies Observer* described racial discrimination in Britain as "Mr James Crow, Esq."[57] In February 1965, Trinidad-born, London-based Michael de Freitas went to hear Malcolm X at the London School of Economics and was captivated. Sharing Malcolm X's rage at white dominance, de Freitas told Jan Carew later that he "decided there and then to set up a Black nationalist movement in Britain."[58] He accompanied Malcolm X to Smethwick, changed his name to Michael X, and created the short-lived Racial Adjustment Action Society (its acronym, RAAS, a Jamaican obscenity).[59]

Those comparing the situations of black Britons and African Americans had a compelling narrative to tell.[60] Both countries, which had large white majorities, professed a commitment to individual rights regardless of race, but in practice there was plenty of discrimination. British sociologists wrote of a "British dilemma" (support for Commonwealth citizens abroad but immigration restrictions at home) to match the famous "American dilemma" (a creed of freedom yet support of segregation).[61]

Some of the landmark moments of racial strife in the two countries were indeed uncannily similar. The antiblack riots in Nottingham and London in 1958 followed hot on the heels of mobs defending white-only schools in Little Rock, Arkansas, and neighborhoods in Levittown, Pennsylvania. The outrage that followed the 1959 murder of Antiguan immigrant Kelso Cochrane in London paralleled that surrounding Emmett Till's murder in Mississippi in 1955. Southern U.S. politicians who played the "nigra" card had their counterparts in British anti-immigrant politicians. The British Race Relations Act of 1965 followed the American Civil Rights Act of 1964. Striking, too, were the similar justifications for racial discrimination on both sides of the Atlantic. In angry letters to the Oxford proctors, local landladies defended the housing color bar by unwittingly invoking the American shibboleths of homeowners' rights, anti-communism, and the dangers of black men's sexual promiscuity.

The flow of people between the two countries made the connections stronger. The new ease of air travel enabled African American leaders to make quick trips to Britain, and in reverse, white students, including members of JACARI, and politicians flocked to the United States to observe civil rights protests first-hand. For Britons who could not afford to make the journey, television allowed them to follow events from the comfort of their own homes. (The classic years of civil rights protest coincided with the first generation of mass British TV ownership.)[62] With U.S. civil rights demonstrations staged for dramatic effect, the British media followed the action like a soap opera. So, too, did the fast-expanding black British print press—not least because the editors of the most influential newspaper, the *West Indian Gazette,* and the most popular glossy magazine, *Flamingo,* had both come to London from the United States. In other words, by the time Malcolm X came to Oxford, news and ideas and people traveling between Britain and the United States were barely delayed by the Atlantic crossing.

Since the situations were so similar, and the American story so well known, British activists were inevitably influenced by their American counterparts.[63] British Black Power groups hailed Malcolm X as their inspiration. The Campaign against Racial Discrimination (CARD), the most high-profile British civil rights organization of the era, was formed following discussions between British activists and Martin Luther King in December 1964. In 1967, formation of the United Coloured People's Association, a London-based Black Power group, coincided with a visit by Stokely Carmichael. "The Black masses," explained the association, suffered "middle-class-so-called Black leadership and sophisticated la-di-da organisations being forced" on them. "America tried it too, and found out that the Grass Roots have a way of picking their own leadership, with Newark, Detroit, Watts and Cleveland to prove it."[64]

Tactics associated with American protest regularly turned up in Britain. The Bristol bus boycott was styled on the famous Montgomery original of 1955, which had propelled Martin Luther King to international fame. Paul Stephenson, the leader of the Bristol protest, who hailed King as an inspiration, had visited the United States shortly before launching the boycott, at the invitation of civil rights leaders there.[65] The student sit-ins in American restaurants had their counterparts in the popular "freedom drink-ins" in British pubs. Operation Guinness in Lewisham was a particular hit.[66] There was a London Black Panther group.[67] And even the Ku Klux Klan jumped in, hoping to establish British hate groups. As one Klan spokesman boasted to British reporters, "We have told them how to organise."[68]

British politicians also framed discussions of civil rights in the light of news from across the Atlantic. Godfrey Hodgson, the London *Times* correspondent on racial conditions in the 1950s, later chuckled when he recalled the "rush to bring inappropriate remedies across from America." He had good reason to recall the rush: when a cross-party group of MPs sought to find a solution to the immigration problem, the first thing they did was go on a fact-finding tour of the United States. He had reason to chuckle as well. When the prime minister appointed the archbishop of Canterbury to head a committee on racial conditions, the prelate declared that he was "anxious to learn of similar problems in America first hand." So when the Temptations came to London in 1970 to promote their new album, he invited them to his Lambeth Palace residence—and blessed them ahead of their upcoming tour.[69]

On the face of it, then, protest in Britain appeared to be something of an offshoot of the American story—the racial equivalent of the postwar Special Relationship between the two governments, in which Britain was very much the junior partner. After all, Tony Abrahams invited Malcolm X to speak in his country, not vice versa. The Atlanta-based civil rights journalist Calvin Trillin, who traveled through Britain in 1965, certainly drew this conclusion. Writing in the *New Yorker,* Trillin explained that he felt he was "watching an old familiar play performed by an inexperienced road company." Even a death threat sent by a "deputy wizard" of the British Klan, Trillin noted, ended in impeccably polite British terms: "Faithfully yours."[70]

Yet although Britons often looked to America, there was no uniform transatlantic movement, even if British activists claimed there was. Michael X was a case in point. He shared the same hustling background, took the same surname, and tried to claim the mantle from his hero, declaring (after Malcolm X's death, conveniently) that Malcolm X had chosen him to be his leading apostle in Britain. But lacking Malcolm X's integrity, intellect, or international vision, Michael X was mostly posturing, and RAAS was an organization in name only. He gained some belated respect in 1967 when he became the first person to be convicted under the hate speech section of the Race Relations Act for describing whites as "vicious, nasty people." Ironically, the hate speech section had been designed to silence white supremacists.[71] (Michael X was later hanged for murder in Trinidad.)

Moreover, for all the apparent similarities between the two countries, the differences were marked. Britain's immigrant community was more recent, much smaller, and from a wide range of countries. Britain also did not have formal Jim Crow segregation. Thus, the classic tactics of the American civil rights movement, such as mass confrontations with white-supremacist sheriffs, were not readily transferable. In any case, British immigrants had plenty of other examples of protest from around the world to draw from, not to mention a tradition of protest of their own. Black Power, with its explicit international vision, was a better fit for those angered by immigration restrictions and frustrated by the moderate response of major black equality organizations. Its Islamic connections appealed to Britain's Bengali community in particular—hence Malcolm X's popularity in Britain. Even so, American Black Power's calls for black community control, cultural nationalism, and armed self-defense were somewhat lost in translation because nonwhite Britons represented less than 3 percent of the population, half were from Asia with their own long-established cultural traditions, and virtually none owned guns.[72]

American white-supremacist ideas and organizations did not find an easy passage to Britain either. At the first public meeting of the Klan in Britain, in the upstairs room of a Birmingham pub, the audience of just thirteen men and two women was outnumbered by reporters and TV crews (although granted, the presence of a large press contingent is testament to the hold the American Klan had on the British imagination). The meeting broke up after just ten minutes when the landlord asked them to leave.[73] In any case, white British hate groups, already well entrenched, resented the implication that they needed American help. Colin Jordan, head of the National Socialist Party, told reporters, "We ain't nothing to do with this childish organisation [i.e., the Klan]."[74]

Rather than import the American civil rights movement wholesale, then, activists in Britain borrowed the American model for their own purposes and used it at their own timing. Paul Stephenson's bus boycott in Bristol, for example, followed its Montgomery predecessor by seven years and was about the right to a better job in the company rather than a seat at the front of the bus. The first British sit-ins began three years after their American counterparts and were few and far between. Members of the Operation Guinness group, moreover, met no opposition—at least not in the first ten or so pubs they visited. It is unclear whether they were barred from subsequent pubs because of their color or because they had already drunk almost a dozen pints of beer. The British Black Panther Party, for its part, formed before the American Panthers had begun to establish international affiliates, and most likely did so without their knowledge.[75]

In short, American styling was a strategic choice by British activists to strengthen their campaigns and to legitimize their own complaints. Sympathy for the U.S. civil rights movement was widespread across Britain. When white supremacists bombed an African American Baptist church in Birmingham, Alabama, in 1963, killing four young girls, residents of Llansteffan, Wales, raised funds to replace the church's stained-glass window. Yet mainstream British commentators routinely contrasted American horrors with British decency. The Welsh stained-glass artist who went to Alabama, for one, was "entirely dismayed by what I discovered" over there.[76]

Naming discrimination in Britain as Mr. Jim Crow, Esq., and equating British protest with the American version, therefore, was potent rhetoric. Michael X certainly made capital out of Malcolm X's reputation, and his organization, RAAS, gained attention, briefly, from a mainstream press expecting the rise of Black Power in Britain. Similarly, Tony Abrahams had much to gain, in terms of boosting his own profile, from associating with his hero. During the Bristol bus boycott, Paul Stephenson made the comparison with the U.S. civil rights movement explicit, telling reporters, "People are saying that it is worse [here] than it is in the deep south of America" because of restrictions on immigration and the British denial of discrimination. Such complaints found their way into the mainstream liberal British press.[77]

Initially, British Black Power advocates struggled to gain followers, stressing connections with the United States to gain legitimacy with black Britons. In their first year, the British Panthers numbered less than a dozen members. But by importing the Black Power aesthetic, they allied themselves with a powerful brand.[78] Many of the Black Power groups that emerged in Britain used Malcolm X's image and words on their mastheads, despite the fact that his slogans did not easily translate to British contexts.[79] In particular, they trumpeted the threat "By any means necessary," even though they had no intention of pursuing an armed struggle. Fittingly, such tributes earned the small, unarmed cadre of British Black Power activists unwarranted attention from white authorities looking for unrest.

To increase the likelihood of getting legislation passed, liberal British politicians and so-called race relations experts trumpeted the fact that they had modeled their proposals on American examples. The Race Relations Act of 1965 was virtually xeroxed from U.S. federal and state legislation (although that legislation was against de jure discrimination, which had little impact on de facto employment and housing discrimination in Britain). Lobbyists used the news of American riots in the late 1960s to strengthen the bill.[80] By the same token, news of American violence spurred passage of a more restrictive Commonwealth Immigrants Act in March 1968, restricting entry to those born in Britain or with a parent or grandparent born in Britain. Conservative MP Enoch Powell was not satisfied, however. The following month, after his first visit to the United States, Powell delivered his infamous "Rivers of Blood" speech, warning that "the tragic and intractable phenomenon which we watch with horror on the other side the Atlantic . . . is coming upon us here by our own volition and our own neglect."[81] Meanwhile, American Ku Klux Klan leaders, equally proud of their British connections, invited Powell on a lecture tour.[82] Britain passed a yet more restrictive act in 1971, allowing entry only to those with a work permit relating to a specific job.

OXFORD AFTER MALCOLM X

Fear! Elderly Europe, weary-liberal, as well as
reactionary, feared Malcolm.
  —Lebert Bethune, "Malcolm X"

Just as Malcolm X and other African American leaders learned
from and were influenced by their time in Britain, so did British
activists learn from their American visitors. Precisely what the
influence was on British protest varied from place to place. Each
community had its own story to tell. In Oxford, the influence
Malcolm X had was mixed, and where his influence was most
significant, it was also, for hosts and guest alike, unintended.

The Union quickly moved on from Malcolm X's visit. Two
nights after the debate, in the same building, members celebrated
the end-of-year ball to a backdrop of rhythm and blues. Tariq Ali
drank champagne from a slipper and led a chorus of left-wing
members in a rendition of "The Red Flag." The students' main
concern seemed to be whether any of the female guests would
wear a topless dress, which, according to the designer who introduced the attire in Paris that summer, was a statement of gender equality and women's liberation. None did. "I am very disappointed," Abrahams told reporters. "I was assured by reliable
sources that they would come."[83] An event less in keeping with
Malcolm X's piety and priorities is hard to imagine.

Militant politics returned to the Union two terms later when
Ali was elected president. But this had everything to do with Ali's
background and disposition rather than Malcolm X's visit. Ali
was a controversialist at heart. He even invited George Wallace, the outspoken segregationist governor of Alabama, to come
and speak. (Wallace's secretary replied that the governor "would
seriously consider" the invitation; he turned it down.)[84] Ignor-

ing the proctor's restrictions, Ali made high-profile appearances in demonstrations against the Vietnam War, including giving a Nazi salute outside the American Embassy when police tried to move him on.[85] After Oxford, he moved to London and became a prolific author, filmmaker, left-wing commentator, and editor of the *New Left Review.*

For Abrahams, the Malcolm X visit helped to cement relations with the BBC. After graduating in the summer of 1965, he was offered a job as a reporter—thus becoming the first black reporter at the corporation. Abrahams was delighted and had no fears about being a "black first." "I've no doubt there'll be a certain amount of resentment," he told reporters. "When I was President of the Union, I got a lot of abusive letters about my colour. But I've been around long enough to take it in good humour."[86] His color certainly suited the BBC. A 1965 documentary about Jamaica, *A Little Bit of Madness,* had led to criticism that the corporation reinforced negative stereotypes of West Indian immigrants. Its popular long-running light entertainment program *The Black and White Minstrel Show* hardly helped. The appointment of Abrahams provided cover, and the BBC's director general appeared proud to announce the breakthrough.[87] On his return to Jamaica, Abrahams would serve as the youngest ever director of tourism and then in the cabinet before hosting a popular breakfast radio show that covered political and social issues.

Malcolm X made a greater impact on JACARI than on the Union. However, his contribution to the students' antiracist campaign was anything but straightforward. Indeed, the authors of the JACARI report on the student housing color bar had feared that his visit—which was at the invitation of the Union, not the JACARI leadership—would be counterproductive. Their intention had been to use a scientifically rigorous study in order "to make a splash," as JACARI leader Clive Sneddon later recalled. The arrival of Malcolm X, though, inadvertently bound the survey up with revolutionary politics and, to the authors' frustration, led some journalists to dismiss them as "trendy lefties" rather than to engage with the problem of housing discrimination.[88]

Ultimately, though, the media attention that accompanied Malcolm X's visit enhanced the shame factor more than it undermined the survey's credentials. The very week of the debate, Oxford's Delegacy of Lodgings met in something of a panic. Although they opposed discrimination, they also feared losing landladies when student rooms in the city were at a premium. The secretary of the delegacy wrote to other universities seeking urgent advice. Mrs. E. M. Talbert at the University of London, not picking up the purpose of the request, replied: "I have always 'got away with it'" by explaining that "almost everyone is barred one way or another—60% of my landladies won't take women . . . three won't allow lodgers with beards. . . . I sometimes wonder whether it is a bit hypocritical," she confessed, "but it has worked up to now."[89] In the end, the delegacy rejected JACARI's proposal to remove any landlady who was unwilling to promise to accept "colored students," but agreed to issue nondiscrimination guidelines.[90]

The housing affair rumbled on. Ironically, some of the student delegates to Oxford's mock United Nations General Assembly the following Easter were denied rooms. The national press picked up on the story. In response, the delegacy agreed to insert a nondiscrimination clause into landladies' contracts.[91] This was "an improvement on the old position where the problem was swept under the carpet," but JACARI thought more still needed to be done.[92] In March 1966, a Jamaican student claimed that he had been prevented from visiting white students in their rooms at the all-women's Somerville College. It was annoying for him, but "particularly serious" for "coloured students at the college who have to live under the shadow of this prejudice. For them it must be like being operated on by a surgeon who hates your guts."[93] In May, Oxford's student newspaper reported that the Delegacy of Lodgings was reluctant to enforce its nondiscrimination guidelines because some landladies had dropped off the list in protest.[94] A month later, JACARI students complained that the university's first major reform commission in a generation had ignored the housing issue completely.[95] They launched a "friendship plan" to meet new students and help them to find accommodation—and provide moral support when they were turned away.[96] In 1970, after continued complaints, the university resolved its dilemma by relinquishing control of undergraduate residences in the city altogether.

A year after Malcolm X's visit, JACARI formed a national body, the Student Conference on Racial Equality (SCORE), to encourage "similar action in other Universities ... to force authorities to take a position AGAINST discrimination, rather than tacitly accepting it." More generally, SCORE's aim was to bring together all "those most concerned with race relations in Britain" by hosting an annual conference.[97] News from around the country was initially encouraging. Leeds and Sussex banned segregation from their student housing. The National Union of Students lobbied the government to enact antidiscrimination legislation. SCORE insisted that ending housing discrimination was only the first step, that the ultimate goal was to ensure visiting students had no "fear of being rebuffed." Radical nonstudent groups were impressed by SCORE's efforts.[98] Ultimately, however, SCORE did not become the militant equal of America's

Student Nonviolent Coordinating Committee (SNCC). It did try to support SNCC from a distance, though. In 1966, it hosted a fundraising photo exhibition about SNCC, "the most active civil rights group in the Southern States," and held workshops about the international student movement in order to "put Britain's current problems in a world context."[99]

JACARI also turned its attention to other forms of discrimination in Oxford. In February 1967, fifty students joined pickets to protest the city council's attempts to remove a group of gypsies from a parking lot.[100] The following year, students were among the three dozen people arrested for staging a sit-in at Annette's hair dressing salon in West Oxford when Annette refused to give appointments to African and Asian customers. The charge was obstructing the highway. Following intermittent protests for more than a year, students had picketed the salon for two weeks straight in the run-up to the sit-in. In a prearranged challenge, an African student entered the shop and asked for an appointment. When he came out frowning, pickets rushed into the salon. Many passersby didn't support them, though some didn't really care either way. One older woman warned the protesters, "If you don't let me in I will box your ears." (She pulled a man's hair instead.) The husband of the proprietress insisted it was just that the staff did not have the skill to cut African hair.[101]

Organization around race equality issues continued outside the university as well. The Oxford Committee on Racial Integration (OCRI) was formed in early 1965 to "combat racial intolerance in Oxford City." OCRI was one of many councils around the country that won grants from the government for a full-time community relations officer. Although Bristol's Paul Stephenson condemned the councils as nothing more than a white liberal attempt to prevent racial tensions, rather than a genuine effort to end discrimination, OCRI was far more antiracist than most, serving as a local branch of CARD and earning a reputation for political militancy.[102] OCRI's leadership was independent of the church and trade unions and was intellectually interested in the problems of race.[103] The university played a vital unofficial role. JACARI members were involved from the outset and the group's founder, Michael Dummett, was a fellow of All Souls College. Dummett, who had spent time in Alabama during the Rosa Parks–inspired bus boycott, shared Stephenson's critique of other local liaison committees, calling them a confidence trick whose "fundamental aim is to keep the black minority under control."[104] He was determined to make OCRI something different.

Dummett's wife, Ann, was Oxford's first community relations officer—and she had plenty to do. Oxford was one of four areas in England where the number of immigrant children more than doubled during 1965–67.[105] Housing was a major problem. Ann Dummett told reporters, "I must admit coloured people with children are in a desperate situation."

As for employment, progress was very much a case of one step forward and two steps back. One big step forward came in October 1967, when Hans Raj Gupta became the first Indian to hold the post of inspector in a bus company in Oxford, and most likely in the country. He had been a conductor since 1961.[106] Two steps back came the following January, when Gupta was attacked outside his house following threats by telephone. In Parliament, the home secretary, James Callaghan, confirmed that the Gupta family had been placed under twenty-four-hour protection.[107] OCRI's newsletter, meanwhile, carried testimonies of immigrants' unhappy experiences at work. In 1972, one West Indian man reported that, even after twelve years working at an Oxford plant, daily unpleasantness continued: "I've got to the stage where I just work on and pray to God to give me courage until the day is over."[108]

In the end, OCRI's record was mixed. Oxford's Pakistani Welfare Association, one of the first in country and based around the city's first mosque, which opened in 1965, refused to associate with it.[109] The Indian equivalent, however, worked with OCRI closely—somewhat unusually, since in most towns militant Indian associations saw community relations councils as part of the problem. One of OCRI's major contributions was to serve as the leading critic of the national Community Relations Committee (CRC) that oversaw and funded local community relations groups. After the CRC issued a thirteen-page guidance document in 1969, Ann Dummett complained that the proposals "do not include the words race, racialism, prejudice, immigrant, black, white, equality, justice or colour." Instead they spoke of "harmonious community relations." As she put it, "These are not the terms in which we can ever being to solve our problems." She resigned from her position soon afterward.[110]

The Dummetts joined various efforts to lobby the government for immigrant reform, and both published widely. Drawing on her Oxford experience, Ann Dummett's *A Portrait of English Racism* (1973) argued that white Englishmen and women almost always defined a racist as someone "who held a position to the right of whoever is giving the definition."[111] Malcolm X would have approved of a study that explored the framing of racism. That, after all, was the central issue in his Oxford speech. Ann Dummett acknowledged Malcolm's influence on her methodology. When choosing his name, she noted, Malcolm X declared: "You shall not say what I am. *I* shall tell you what I am."[112] Hence she sought to present the actual voices of immigrants rather than rely on stereotypes and hearsay.

The most far-reaching legacy of Malcolm X's visit and the race protests of 1964 in Oxford, however, was not related to the issue of black equality at all. Rather, it was the undermining of the system of university discipline. Students had found themselves at loggerheads with the proctors over the right to protest apartheid. When the proctors singled out Ali and Abrahams for the worst punishment, the students demanded a change to the proctorial system. As a student newspaper put it, "'Down with the Proctors' or 'Burn the bastards in effigy': these are some of the standard cries of Oxford's reforming students against the deadly, antiquated and absurd system of discipline that the Proctors represent."[113] Abrahams quickly became the lightning rod for nationwide student demands for civil liberties. And then JACARI released its survey, and Malcolm X swung into town.

The university set up a committee to review the power of the proctors. The outcome was a compromise in which the proctors retained the power to ban undergraduate newspapers and magazines after "proper discussions and warnings," the assumption being that "citizens of Oxford have to be protected from abuse." Still, this was progress, suggested JACARI president Hannan Rose. Some other, "quite radical changes to the system" also gave undergraduates the right to defense, right of appeal, and right to know on what matter they were being summoned—in English rather than in Latin, as had traditionally been the case.[114]

The fact that there were any concessions at all emboldened the students, though the token nature of those concessions exasperated them. A series of demonstrations followed, fueled by anti–Vietnam War militancy and news of student protest elsewhere in Europe and America.[115] When the proctors temporarily banned the main student newspaper in October 1968, some 150 students dressed in subfusc (formal academic attire) marched from the Union Society to the proctors' office to present a petition against "proctorial tyranny" signed by more than a thousand students.[116] The Labour society proposed mass sit-ins. The proctors backed down. Student newspapers hailed the inspiration of recent sit-ins at the London School of Economics rather than those in the American south less than a decade before—an example, if one were needed, of how quickly transatlantic tactics were appropriated and repackaged for domestic purposes. Nor did they remember the earlier Oxford protests against proctorial control: the reaction to the arrest of a militant Jamaican president of the Union following demonstrations against apartheid, a student who drew further renown from the visit of America's most famous black radical.

Epilogue

We read stuff like the *Autobiography of Malcolm X.* We had Malcolm X albums. I remember in the Youth League there was a record that went around from member to member called *Message to the Grass Roots, speeches by Malcolm X.*

> —Linton Kwesi Johnson interview, London,
>   August 2, 2011

I think as a student of colour you can feel comfortable. Yet as a black student you do have to accept that in a lot of situations it is likely that you will be the only non-white person in a room and that can sometimes get exhausting. I accept that this is not an Oxford specific problem . . . Still, I don't think the university can absolve itself from all blame.

> —Oxford undergraduate historian interview,
>   April 4, 2014

Born in Jamaica in 1952, Linton Kwesi Johnson moved to England in 1963 and studied at Goldsmiths College in London. In 1969, he joined the Black Panther Youth League, which had a thousand or so members, and later the Brixton-based Race Today Collective. A master of words and rhythm, Johnson organized poetry workshops and became known as the father of "dub poetry"—a term he coined to describe the way reggae DJs combined music and verse. His third and most famous book of poetry, *Inglan Is a Bitch,* was released in 1980, on the eve of a confrontation between some five thousand residents of Brixton and the police. Reflecting on his years in the Youth League, Kwesi Johnson remembered the influence of American Black Power figures—not just the American Black Panthers who hit the headlines in the late 1960s, but also Malcolm X, who had been killed some years before. "It was the most formative period of my life and has helped to shape me and make me into the person I am today."[1]

Kwesi Johnson's story could be retold through the lives of any number of black British activists. Malcolm X's influence continued long after his death, in Britain as well as the United States. Obi Egbuna, the Nigerian-born Black Power activist and founder of the British Black Panthers, was a member of the Council of African Organizations in London when Malcolm X came to visit in 1965. Egbuna, who dated the formation of British Black Power to the visit to London of American Black Power leader Stokeley Carmichael, was clearly profoundly influenced by Carmichael's hero, Malcolm X. Egbuna spoke, as Malcolm X did at Oxford, of the international dimensions of the Western power structure, a structure that needed resisting, to use Malcolm X's oft-used phrase, "by any means necessary."[2] Tony Soares, who headed the Black Liberation Front, a small black separatist group in London that broke away from the British Black Panthers in 1970 and attracted the attention of British police, collected recordings of Malcolm X's speeches.[3]

Darcus Howe, who also joined the British Black Panther Party, met Malcolm X in Notting Hill and shook his hand. "I have never seen such a remarkable personality in my life. I've met prime ministers, I've met presidents, I've spoken to Nelson Mandela," he commented. Howe felt that Malcolm X "legitimized that part of me which 'respectable' Trinidadian and English society feared and despised." Meeting Malcolm X, as well as Martin Luther King during his visit in December 1964, made Howe feel part of a global movement, and he sought to give "a local habitation and a name to the black power movement spawned in the United States."[4] In 1970, Howe and eight others were arrested in the so-called Mangrove Nine case, after they protested against repeated police raids on the Mangrove Cafe, a Caribbean restaurant and meeting place for black activists. Howe would continue to speak out against discrimination through his work as a journalist and filmmaker. With Tariq Ali, who had met Malcolm X in Oxford, Howe produced the influential 1980s multicultural current affairs television program *The Bandung File*, named after the 1955 meeting in Bandung, Indonesia, of the leaders of newly independent states.[5]

.   .   .

Half a century after Malcolm X's visit to Britain, the color bar in housing and employment had been removed, and the American-styled Black Power organizations of the late 1960s and early 1970s had long since dissipated. In Smethwick, the previously, defiantly, all-white Marshall Street—the scene of the anti-immigration campaign where Malcolm X spoke of "gas ovens"—had become a multicultural community. In February 2012, the Nubian Jak Community Trust (NJCT), which ran Britain's only black and ethnic minority national plaque scheme, placed a blue plaque commemorating the visit of the "international civil rights campaigner" on number 30 Marshall Street—the first home to be bought by a nonwhite person, in 1971. "I'm not saying that racism has been totally wiped out here," commented Harbhajan Dardi, assistant general secretary of the Indian Workers Association, which had invited Malcolm X to Smethwick in 1965. "But the relationship between races is 100 times better." "Malcolm X," Dardi continued, "shone a spotlight on a blatant discriminatory policy that the British people were not prepared to stand for."[6]

In Oxford by this time, 21 percent of students were from black, minority, or ethnic (BME) backgrounds.[7] Indeed, the days of the color line in Oxford student housing were so far distant that most people I've spoken to in Oxford about this project found it hard to believe that such problems could have existed at all. Many students and academics had no idea that Malcolm X had been to visit the university, either—and without exception, those who did know were aware of the speech but not of the campaign for racial equality that was the backdrop to his visit.

More generally, in British popular memory, the history of civil rights is an American story, not a British one. Half a century after the visits of Martin Luther King Jr. and Malcolm X, the American civil rights movement is among the top five most popular history subjects in British high schools. In 1998, Martin Luther King's statue was unveiled above the west entrance to Westminster Abbey. But no modern black British campaigner was celebrated in the Abbey, and black British history is rarely a part of high school curriculum. Focus on American civil rights icons can help Britons think about the history of the struggle for racial justice, but it can be used to forget about it, as well.

And yet, half a century after Malcolm X's visits to England, campaigners insist that race equality is far from being realized. In August 2011, civil unrest rocked the country. Darcus Howe told a BBC reporter that the violence was a response to police harassment of young black men. "I don't call it rioting. I call it an insurrection of the masses of the people. It is happening in Syria, it is happening in Clapham, it's happening in Liverpool, it's happening in Port of Spain, Trinidad, and that is the nature of the historical moment." When the reporter suggested that Howe was no stranger to riots himself, he replied, in exasperation, "I have never taken part in a single riot. I've been on demonstrations that ended up in a conflict. . . . Have some respect for an old West Indian Negro."[8] The "have some respect" interview went viral, not just in Britain but in the United States as well. For many "African-American and Latino/a youths unfamiliar with the U.K.'s racial politics," observed historian Robin Kelley, the interview "internationalized what often felt like a uniquely American phenomenon of police constantly harassing . . . black and brown people."[9] It was a reminder, if one were needed, that learning about race traveled in both directions across the Atlantic. The call for respect also echoed Malcolm X's exasperation, when speaking at the Oxford Union, at the way the American media ignored his call for human rights.

Howe was far from alone in his critique of contemporary British politics and society. In Smethwick, the Nubian Jak Community Trust's rationale for erecting a plaque in 2012 lay in part in a resurgence of anti-immigrant sentiment at the ballot box. The British National Party (BNP), formed in 1982 with membership restricted to "indigenous British" people, rose to prominence with calls to halt immigration and offers of grants for repatriation. In 2010, the party received over half a million votes in the general election. At the local level, the BNP won more than fifty council seats—two of them in Smethwick. The NJCT explained that, following the unrest of the previous year, "hopefully the plaque will serve as a timely reminder of Malcolm X's influence here." Harbhajan Dardi agreed: "We would not want to see a return to racial intolerance or bigotry and hopefully this plaque will remind people to stand united against that." Underpinning this hope for the future was a somewhat rose-tinted view of Malcolm X's role in the past. "Malcolm made an impact on understanding and awareness in the community. People came to know the reality that we're all human beings regardless of the colour of our skin."[10]

In Oxford in 2012, the student-led Campaign for Racial Awareness and Equality (CRAE) published a report, "One Hundred Voices," detailing some of the grievances of BME students. Many spoke of the isolation they felt; some complained of the cost of assimilation. "I think I've successfully made myself fit in [to Oxford] and, in that process, I've actually lost myself," one said. In a nod to the historic roots of the issue in the university, one student expressed shock that the African Studies Library was based in Cecil Rhodes House, named after the colonial advocate of Anglo-Saxon influence. Another condemned the prominence of Hugh Trevor-Roper's portrait in the history faculty, given the Regius Professor's notorious dismissal of African history fifty years previously, which had earned a mention in Malcolm X's autobiography as well.[11]

Two years later, CRAE stepped up the challenge to the university, updating the 100 Voices Report and—as JACARI had done in 1964—releasing a survey to quantify their complaints. The survey made for stark reading. Some 60 percent of BME students thought that "racism is a problem in Oxford" (in contrast to 60 percent of white students who thought it was not), and almost two-thirds thought there were insufficient "safe spaces in which to discuss race and ethnicity." On March 10, 2014, CRAE leaders organized a race summit with senior faculty within the university, including the vice chancellor, to explain that individual experiences of racism "stem from structural and institutional issues at the collegiate University." In response, the university made seven commitments to change, including greater candor on the issue of race, a curricular review, and greater respect for diversity in the university community. Most CRAE leaders were delighted by the response. Others noted the lack of a timetable for action.[12]

There were striking links between the CRAE campaign and its predecessors. As in previous generations, some students recognized that their time in Oxford transformed their thinking on racial identity—including their own. Pembroke student Michael Joseph reflected that, "having never experienced anything other than being a minority [at school in England], getting involved in a group whose sole focus was racial equality and meeting people with different backgrounds and experience of activism" meant "I have become much more aware of my own racial ideology since I got here." Joseph would go on to become a leader of CRAE.[13]

To coincide with the race summit, an "I, Too, Am Oxford" campaign posted pictures on Tumblr of more than sixty BME students standing in front of iconic Oxford buildings. Echoing the complaints of previous generations, they held up whiteboard signs conveying attitudes they had encountered at the university ("Why do you speak such good English?" or "Oh, you're from Ghana . . . My cousin's nanny is from Kenya"). National and international media picked up on story. As in the 1960s, British student activists borrowed strategies from the United States. The campaign took its cue from the recent, much publicized "I, Too, Am Harvard" initiative—which in turn took its name from the poem "I, Too, Sing America," written by the Harlem-based African American poet Langston Hughes nearly a century before.

In a final reminder of Malcolm X's visit, the most prominent discussion of race at Oxford during the 2013–14 academic year came at the Union, at an end-of-Michaelmas-term speech by a renowned African American leader. Jesse Jackson, a former colleague of Martin Luther King Jr. and prominent civil rights activist thereafter, criticized Oxford for admitting only six "black Caribbean" students out of a new intake of 2,635. Acknowledging that the issue was also about educational opportunities before the application stage, Jackson called for "positive access" to ensure the "greatness" of Oxford education and to save students from "being cheated of a multi-cultural and multi-racial experience in a world that is multi-cultural and multi-racial."[14] One black British undergraduate at the Union that evening, who wished to remain anonymous, found it "refreshing to actually see someone look out into the audience of mostly white students and say, 'Why there aren't more black students here? This is a problem: it's not because they're not good enough. What has stopped them getting here?' It was interesting to me," she explained, "that someone outside the UK, not associated with the university, made what seemed like such an obvious point but one that I had been waiting to be vocalized."[15]

NOTES

PROLOGUE

1. Union Society termcards [academic calendars], Oxford University Societies, Box U3, John Johnson Collection of Printed Ephemera, Bodleian Library, University of Oxford (hereafter cited as John Johnson Collection).

2. "This Is Malcolm X," *Sun*, December 3, 1964, 7.

3. See http://vault.fbi.gov/malcolm-little-malcolm-x/, pts. 1–14.

4. Jan Carew, *Ghosts in Our Blood: With Malcolm X in Africa, England, and the Caribbean* (London, 1984), 68.

5. Email from Henry Brownrigg to author, September 10, 2010.

6. The full quotation was, "I would remind you that extremism in the defense of liberty is no vice. And let me remind you also that moderation in the pursuit of vice is no virtue" (Barry Goldwater, acceptance speech, 28th Republican National Convention, San Francisco, July 16, 1964).

7. Lebert Bethune, "Malcolm X in Europe," in *Malcolm X: The Man and His Times,* ed. John Henrik Clarke (New York, 1969), 232.

8. The full audio and a partial video recording of the speech are widely available online, e.g., http://blackfreedomstruggle.modhisox

.ac.uk/chapter9.html (under People, Malcolm X, ... debating at the Oxford Union).

9. "Malcolm X a Speaker in Oxford Debate," *Guardian,* December 3, 1964, 8; "Malcolm X on the Sin of Moderation," *Guardian,* December 4, 1964, 24.

10. Bethune, "Malcolm X in Europe," 232. See also Tariq Ali, *Street Fighting Years: An Autobiography of the Sixties* (London, 2005), 104.

11. Although Malcolm X's speech at Oxford has since been widely acclaimed as one of his finest, the visit itself has generally occupied at most a curious footnote in historical writing about the civil rights movement. Historians interested in his growing international vision have understandably been drawn to his travels through the Middle East and Africa instead. Most studies of Malcolm X mention the speech only briefly (if at all) in terms of Malcolm X's oratorical skills. Even Manning Marable's widely praised recent biography, *Malcolm X: A Life of Reinvention* (New York, 2011), gives the Oxford visit but a passing mention. For works that cite the debate as an example of Malcolm X's oratorical skills, see Dennis D. Wainstock, *Malcolm X, African American Revolutionary* (Jefferson, N.C., 2009), 135; Eugene Victor Wolfenstein, *The Victims of Democracy: Malcolm X and the Black Revolution* (London, 1989), 135; and Louis A. DeCaro Jr., *On the Side of My People: A Religious Life of Malcolm X* (New York, 1996), 252. Kevin K. Gaines, *American Africans in Ghana: Black Expatriates and the Civil Rights Era* (Chapel Hill, N.C., 2006), 202, briefly discusses the debate in the context of Malcolm X's views on extremism. Works by contemporaries that discuss the debate include Bethune, "Malcolm X in Europe"; Ali, *Street Fighting Years;* and Carew, *Ghosts in Our Blood.* In the run-up to the fiftieth anniversary of the debate, there has, thankfully, been renewed interest in Malcolm X's speech. Graeme Abernethy, "'Not Just an American Problem': Malcolm X in Britain," *Atlantic Studies* 7, no. 3 (2010): 285–307, explores the symbolism of speaking at one of the intellectual centers of the British Empire. Saladin M. Ambar, in "Malcolm X at the Oxford Union," *Race & Class* 53, no. 4 (April–June 2012): 24–38, and his forthcoming book *Malcolm X at Oxford Union: Racial Politics in a Global Era* (Oxford University Press), discuss Malcolm X's evolving thought on

nationalism and racialism in the context of racial controversies during British and American elections. Sohail Daulatzai's research focuses on the links between Malcolm X's talk and present-day challenges; see "Malcolm X at Oxford (Almost) 50 Years Later: On Malcolm, Empire, and the Muslim International," paper presented at Oxford University, June 4, 2013. For an introduction to Malcolm X's travels in Britain and elsewhere, see Marika Sherwood, *Malcolm X Visits Abroad: April 1964–February 1965* (Savannah Press, 2010).

12. On putting off replies to other invitations, see Correspondence, Speaking Engagements, 1964–65, box 3, folder 19, Malcolm X Collection: Papers, 1948–65, Manuscripts, Archives and Rare Books Division, Schomburg Center for Research in Black Culture, New York Public Library, New York (hereafter cited as MXC). On his willingness to accept such invitations at less pressured times, see, for example, Malcolm X to Morton Bobowick, July 30, 1964, ibid.; on the Oxford invitation, see Eric Abrahams to Malcolm X, November 27, 1964, International Correspondence, England 1964, box 3, folder 15, MXC; and on his willingness to accept unusual invitations for money, see Elsa Franklin to Malcolm X, January 12, 1965, and Don Brown to Miss Marilyn Lennon, n.d. 1965, Radio and Television, 1961–65, box 3, folder 20, MXC.

13. On Malcolm X's schedule, see James Shabazz, Muslim Mosque Inc. press release, April 13, 1964, Muslim Mosque Incorporated, Press Releases and Schedule of Activities, 1964, box 13, folder 6, MXC. On missing his family, see Malcolm X to Betty Shabazz, August 4, 1964, Correspondence, Shabazz, Betty, 1960–64, box 3, folder 2, MXC. See also Malcolm X to Betty Shabazz, July 26, 1964, ibid., where he asks her to "kiss the babies for me."

14. The baby, Gamilah Shabazz, was born on December 4, 1964, while Malcolm X was overseas.

15. The Nation of Islam claimed it had purchased the house for him in connection with his ministerial responsibilities.

16. On the organization in a shambles, see Malcolm X to Muhammad Taufik Oweida, November 30, 1964, and Malcolm X to Muhammad Sourour El-Sabban, November 30, 1964, Other Correspondents, 1962–65, box 3, folder 4, MXC.

17. Malcolm X to Betty Shabazz, August 4 and July 26, 1964. Malcolm X planned to be based in the U.S. for most of 1965 to rebuild his organization; author interview with A. Peter Bailey, June 9, 2011.

CHAPTER 1

1. For all quotations on his trip to Cairo, see notes in Travel Diary, 1964, Diaries, box 9, folder 6, MXC.

2. See speech notes, 1964, MXC.

3. FBI report, May 22, 1964, in folder titled Malcolm X Little, no. 100-399321, sec. 11, serials 109–126, available at http://vault.fbi.gov/malcolm-little-malcolm-x/malcolm-little-malcolm-x-hq-file-12-of-27/view.

4. On the post–World War One zeitgeist, see Adriane Danette Lentz-Smith, *Freedom Struggles: African Americans and World War I* (Cambridge, Mass., 2009); and Stephen Tuck, *We Ain't What We Ought to Be: The Black Freedom Struggle from Emancipation to Obama* (Cambridge, Mass., 2010), 136–69.

5. Opening of the UNIA Convention, Liberty Hall, New York, August 1, 1920, printed in *Negro World Conference Bulletin,* August 2, 1920, in Marcus Garvey, *The Marcus Garvey and Universal Negro Improvement Association Papers,* ed. Robert Abraham Hill, vol. 2 (Berkeley, 1983), 479.

6. Theodore Kornweibel, *Seeing Red: Federal Campaigns against Black Militancy, 1919–1925* (Bloomington, Ind., 1998), 106.

7. Report by Special Agent P-138, New York, August 21, 1920, in Hill (ed.), *Marcus Garvey Papers,* 2:612.

8. Quoted in Kimberley L. Phillips, *Alabamanorth: African-American Migrants, Community, and Working-Class Activism in Cleveland, 1915–45* (Urbana, Ill., 1999), 187.

9. Robert Trent Vinson, "'Sea Kaffirs': 'American Negroes' and the Gospel of Garveyism in Early Twentieth-Century Cape Town," *Journal of African History* 47 (July 2006): 281.

10. For an overview of Malcolm X's early life, including his parents' decision to organize for Garvey, see Manning Marable, *Malcolm X: A Life of Reinvention* (New York, 2011), chaps. 1–3.

11. Unless stated otherwise, quotations from Malcolm X about his life are from Alex Haley and Malcolm X, *The Autobiography of Malcolm X* (London, 1965).

12. Marable, *Malcolm X.*

13. See, for example, Alex Haley's interview of Malcolm X, *Playboy,* May 1963, in *Malcolm X: Collected Speeches, Debates, and Interviews (1960–1965),* ed. Sandeep S. Atwal, PDF document.

14. Prepared script for radio show, n.d., in Speeches, MXC.

15. Christopher Hollis, *The Oxford Union* (London, 1965), 217.

16. Author interview with Judith Okley, August 21, 2013.

17. "Arabs Send Warm Greetings to 'Our Brothers' of Color in U.S.A.," *Pittsburgh Courier,* August 15, 1961, C1.

18. "Africa Eyes Us," *Amsterdam News* (New York), August 22, 1959, 10.

19. Foster Bailey, "Nkrumah Tells Rally in Harlem Negroes Form U.S.-Africa Bond," *New York Times,* October 6, 1960, 18.

20. Peniel E. Joseph, *Waiting 'Til the Midnight Hour: A Narrative History of Black Power in America* (New York, 2006), 42.

21. The quotes in this and the next paragraph are from the Harvard Law School Forum speech of March 24, 1961, in Atwal (ed.), *Malcolm X: Collected Speeches.*

22. Prepared script for radio show, n.d., in Speeches, MXC.

23. Malcolm X and George Breitman, *Malcolm X Speaks: Selected Speeches and Statements* (New York, 1966), 14–16.

24. Quoted in David Zirin, review of *42,* www.thenation.com /blog/173905/review-42-jackie-robinsons-bitter-pill.

25. Robert Penn Warren interview with James Famer, June 11, 1964, http://whospeaks.library.vanderbilt.edu/interview/james-farmer-jr.

26. "The Last Interview," Malcolm X and the *Al-Muslimoon* Staff, from *Al-Muslimoon* magazine, February 1965, available in part at www .malcolm-x.org/docs/int_almus.htm.

27. Fulton Lewis, "Washington Report," March 26, 1964, in FBI files, folder titled Malcolm X Little, file no. HQ 100-399321-A, sec. 1, December 15, 1956–March 21, 1964, available at http://vault.fbi.gov/mal colm-little-malcolm-x/malcolm-little-malcolm-x-hq-file-23-of-27/ view.

28. Dick Schaap, "The Paradox That Is Malcolm X: All Charm and All Contradictions," *Herald Tribune,* March 22, 1964, available at http://vault.fbi.gov/malcolm-little-malcolm-x/malcolm-little-malcolm-x-hq-file-23-of-27/view.

29. Letter to Mr. Ahmed Mohamed Nour, Sudan, from Malik El-Shabazz, March 21, 1964, International Correspondence, MXC.

30. "Interview with Malcolm X," conducted on March 19, 1964, by poet and jazz critic A.B. Spellman, appeared simultaneously in *Monthly Review* and *Revolution.* It can be accessed at http://monthlyreview.org/2005/02/01/interview-with-malcolm-x.

31. Travel Diary, Thursday April 16, 1964, MXC.

32. Travel Diary, Friday April 17, 1964, MXC.

33. Travel Diary, Saturday April 18, 1964, MXC.

34. Travel Diary, Wednesday April 22, 1964, MXC.

35. Travel Diary, Tuesday April 21, 1964, MXC.

36. Travel Diary, Saturday April 25, 1964, MXC.

37. Travel Diary, Sunday April 26, 1964, MXC.

38. Malcolm X, "Black and White," *Guardian,* February 27, 1965, 8.

39. Travel Diary, Saturday April 25, 1964, MXC. He continued: "People: white, black, brown, red and yellow all act alike, as one, as Brothers. People with blue eyes and blonde hair, bowing in complete submission to Allah, beside those with black skin and kinky hair, as they give the same honor to the same God, they in turn give some (equal) honor to each other."

40. Travel Diary, Friday April 24, 1964, MXC.

41. FBI files, NY 105-8999, "Foreign Travel of Malcolm X," 102, http://vault.fbi.gov/Malcolm%20X/Malcolm%20X%20Part%2021%20of%2038 (PDF).

42. "A Warning to White America," letter to the *Egyptian Gazette,* August 25, 1964.

43. Malcolm X, "Black and White," 8.

44. Travel Diary, Thursday April 30, 1964, MXC.

45. "At Ibadan, Nigeria," FBI files, NY 105-8999, "Foreign Travel of Malcolm X," 91, available at www.negroartist.com/writings/FBI%20files/malcolmx14b.pdf. See, too, U.S. Information Agency, "Reports on

Public Opinion in Africa: Attitudes and Aspirations of African Students in France,"1963, 139.

46. Notes on speech in Ghana, May 1964, in Travel Diary, MXC.

47. "At Ibadan, Nigeria," 93.

48. Press release noted in Travel Diary, following entry of May 17, 1964, MXC.

49. Travel Diary, May 17, 1964, MXC.

50. Transcript, New York radio show, June 8, 1964, FBI files.

51. Travel Diary, May 17, 1964, MXC.

52. Bruce Perry, *Malcolm X: The Last Speeches* (New York, 1989), 132–33.

53. FBI files, NY 105-8999, "Foreign Travel of Malcolm X," 115–16. For more on his relationship with Ossie Davis, see "Malcolm X and Ossie Davis," *Michigan Citizen,* June 17, 2012, available at http://michigancitizen.com/malcolm-x-and-ossie-davis-2.

54. "Malcolm X Seeks UN Negro Debate," *New York Times,* August 13, 1964.

55. J. Edgar Hoover, telegram to FBI New York office, June 5, 1964, http://vault.fbi.gov/Malcolm%20X.

56. FBI headquarters file on Malcolm X, https://archive.org/stream/MalcolmX-FBI-HQ-File/100-HQ-399321-14_djvu.txt, 39.

57. Malcolm X to Betty Shabazz, July 26, 1964, International Correspondence, box 3, folder 2, MXC.

58. "Malcolm X Gives Africa Twisted Look" *New York Journal American,* July 25, 1964.

59. Malcolm X and John Lewis, *Malcolm X Speaks to Young People* (New York, 1969), 26.

60. Malcolm X to Betty Shabazz, July 26, 1964, MXC.

61. Marable, *Malcolm X,* 373.

62. "There's a Worldwide Revolution Going On," February 15, 1965, in Atwal (ed.), *Malcolm X: Collected Speeches . . . (1960–1965).*

63. Malcolm X to Betty Shabazz, August 4, 1964, International Correspondence, box 3, folder 2, MXC.

64. Email from Louis Nthenda to author, February 18, 2014.

65. Lebert Bethune, "Malcolm X in Europe," in *Malcolm X: The Man and His Times,* ed. John Henrik Clarke (New York, 1969), 229.

66. Ruth Porter, "Paris Meeting Hears Malcolm X," *The Militant,* December 7, 1964, 5.

67. Bethune, "Malcolm X in Europe," 229.

68. Porter, "Paris Meeting," 5.

69. Malcolm X, "The Black Struggle in the United States," *Présence Africaine,* no. 54, 1965.

70. Bethune, "Malcolm X in Europe," 231.

71. Porter, "Paris Meeting," 5; Malcolm X, "Black Struggle."

CHAPTER 2

1. Antoinette Burton, *At the Heart of Empire: Indians and the Colonial Encounter in Late-Victorian Britain* (Berkeley, 1998), 129.

2. John Ruskin, *Lectures on Art, Delivered before the University of Oxford in Hilary Term,* 1870 (Gutenberg ebook, 2006), 21; available at www.gutenberg.org/files/19164/19164-h/19164-h.htm.

3. Burton, *At the Heart of Empire,* 127–28.

4. John Jones, *Balliol College: A History* (Oxford, 1988), 219.

5. Burton, *At the Heart of Empire,* 127.

6. Vijay Prashad, *The Darker Nations: A Biography* (New Delhi, 1987), 39.

7. R. Hooker, "The Pan-African Conference 1900," *Transition,* no. 46 (1974): 20–24.

8. *Sunday Chronicle* article from July 15, 1919, cited in "Negro Hatred in England," *Argos* (Cardiff), July 18, 1919, folder 01/04/04/01/14/01, Institute of Race Relations Archive, London (hereafter cited as IRR). The article said the average Englishman "knows nothing of the negro's inborn and ineradicable savagery, and still less of his unspeakable bestiality where women are concerned."

9. Cecil Rhodes, "Confession of Faith" (speech), June 1877, available at http://pages.uoregon.edu/kimball/Rhodes-Confession.htm.

10. Catherine Hall, *Macaulay and Son: Architects of Imperial Britain* (New Haven, 2012), 229.

11. James Corsan, *For Poulton and England: The Life and Times of an Edwardian Rugby Hero* (Leicester, U.K., 2009), 127.

12. Jones, *Balliol College*, 219; Burton, *At the Heart of Empire*, 129; Richard Evans, "The Victorians: Empire and Race," lecture delivered April 11, 2011, Museum of London, available at www.gresham.ac.uk /lectures-and-events/the-victorians-empire-and-race.

13. Alex Haley and Malcolm X, *The Autobiography of Malcolm X* (London, 1965).

14. Corsan, *For Poulton and England*, 127.

15. Cited in Burton, *At the Heart of Empire*, 130.

16. Chris Wrigley, *A. J. P. Taylor, Radical Historian of Europe* (London, 2006), 107.

17. Peter Fryer, *Staying Power: The History of Black People in Britain* (London, 1984), 301.

18. Jacqueline Jenkinson, "Black Sailors on Red Clydeside: Rioting, Reactionary Trade Unionism, and Conflicting Notions of 'Britishness' following the First World War," *Twentieth Century British History* 19, no. 1 (2008): 29–60.

19. "Negro Hatred in England."

20. Jenkinson, "Black Sailors on Red Clydeside."

21. "Coloured Riots at Liverpool: Discharged Soldiers Petition Removal," *Manchester Guardian,* June 7, 1919, 11.

22. Fryer, *Staying Power,* 302.

23. Barbara Bush, *Imperialism, Race and Resistance: Africa and Britain, 1919–1945* (London, 1999), 207.

24. Leonard Harris, "Cosmopolitanism and the African Renaissance: Pixley I. Seme and Alain L. Locke," *International Journal of African Renaissance Studies* 4, no. 2 (2009): 181–92; Christopher Saunders, "Seme, Pixley ka Isaka (1882–1951)," *Oxford Dictionary of National Biography,* www.oxforddnb.com/view/article/92369.

25. Quoted in Fryer, *Staying Power,* 438.

26. Saunders, "Seme."

27. Harris, "Cosmopolitanism and the African Renaissance," 183.

28. Phillip Waller, "The Letters of Kuruvila Zachariah," in *Treasures of Merton College,* ed. S. Gunn (London, 2013), 120–24.

29. Pixley ka Isaka Seme, "The Regeneration of Africa" (speech), April 5, 1906, available at *South African History Online,* www.sahistory .org.za/archive/regeneration-africa-speech-pixley-seme-5-april-1906.

30. Alain Locke, "Oxford: By a Negro Student" (1909), in *The Works of Alain Locke,* ed. Charles Molesworth (Oxford, 2012), 427.

31. "Activities Abroad (1897–1906)," *Indian Rebels,* http://rebelsindia .com/ViewArticle.aspx?ai=190.

32. Quoted in Fryer, *Staying Power,* 268.

33. www.open.ac.uk/researchprojects/makingbritain/content/lala -har-dayal.

34. Quoted in Philip Sherlock, *Norman Manley* (London, 1980), 61.

35. Eric Eustace Williams, *Inward Hunger: The Education of a Prime Minister* (London, 1969), 47.

36. Ibid., 43.

37. As he explained "'as a colonial' to the examiner at his viva, I could not see the value of study unless there was that connection with the environment" (ibid.).

38. Ibid., 46.

39. Ibid.

40. "Methodists' World Conference: Opened at Oxford," *Chicago Defender,* August 29, 1951, 2.

41. Minutes, World Methodist Conference, 1951, 54, Wesley Historical Society Library, Oxford.

42. William J. Walls, *The African Methodist Episcopal Zion Church: Reality of the Black Church* (Charlotte, N.C., 1974), 480; *Jet,* November 1, 1951, 18.

43. Walls, *African Methodist Episcopal Zion Church,* 481.

44. Welfare Dept., Colonial Office, May 1946, "Colour Discrimination in the United Kingdom," Colonial Office Reports, 537/1224, National Archives, London.

45. "Racial Fights in Liverpool," *Manchester Guardian,* August 4, 1948, 6; "Liverpool Racial Disturbances," *Times,* August 4, 1948, 3.

46. "Policeman Laid about Him," *Manchester Guardian,* August 24, 1948, 3.

47. "100 London Cops Quell Race Riot," *Amsterdam News* (New York), July 23, 1949, 1.

48. "Welcome Home," *Evening Standard,* June 21, 1948, 1.

49. "Migration Plan in Caribbean," *Times,* November 3, 1948, 3.

50. Randall Hansen, "The Politics of Citizenship in 1940s Britain: The British Nationality Act," *Twentieth Century British History* 10, no. 1 (1999): 67–95.

51. "Second Report of the Working Party to Consider Certain Proposals to Restrict the Right of British Subjects from Overseas to Enter and Remain in the United Kingdom," October 22, 1954, DO 35/7990, National Archives, London.

52. Donald Hinds, *Journey to an Illusion: The West Indian in Britain* (London, 1966), 53.

53. Stephen Tuck, "Malcolm X's Visit to Oxford University: U.S. Civil Rights, Black Britain, and the Special Relationship on Race," *American Historical Review* 118 (2013): 82.

54. "'No Colour Bar,' Says Busmen's Union," *Oxford Mail,* April 13, 1956.

55. Alison Shaw, "Kinship and Continuity: Pakistani Families in Oxford," D.Phil. diss., University of Oxford, 1984, 42.

56. Ibid. Many of the immigrants' houses lacked hot water or indoor bathrooms. The only upside was that for men working long hours, sharing a house with many others kept rent down and allowed them to save money to send home.

57. Author interview with Judith Okley, August 21, 2013. Stereotypes of blacks as primitive were common. Vivian Witter in Leeds complained to one newspaper, "When my wife went to work she came home in hysterics because of jeers from her mates about grass skirts and mud huts," *Daily Herald,* September 2, 1958.

58. Shaw, "Kinship and Continuity."

59. Letter to Sir John Smyth, MP, from Mr. S. Tyson, 76 Kellett Rd., Brixton, July 19, 1959, passed to Miss P. Hornsby Smith, MP, Home Office, July 21, CO 1031/2543, National Archives, London.

60. "We are well aware of the causes of irritation to which you referred in your letter and the efforts of the Migrant Services Division

are directed continually to eliminating them. Indeed, that constitutes one of the important assignments of our Community Development Officers" (G.H. Gordon, Commissioner in UK for W.I., British Guiana, and British Honduras, to F. Kennedy, Colonial Office, October 8, 1959, CO 1031/2543, Public Records Office). See also reports in DO files for black London in this period, National Archives.

61. "Probe on Colonials," *Afro-West Indian Clarion,* June-July 1957, IRR.

62. Randall Hansen, *Citizenship and Immigration in Postwar Britain* (New York, 2004), 4.

63. Telegram to Commonwealth Relations Office, Delhi, August 16, 1958, DO 35/7990, Public Records Office.

64. Edward Scobie, "Unmask Hypocrisy of Britain's No Color Bar," *Chicago Defender,* March 19, 1955, 4.

65. George Barner, "Sex Seen at Bottom of London Riots," *Amsterdam News* (New York), September 6, 1958, 1.

66. George Lamming, "Journey to an Expectation" (1960), in *Writing Black Britain, 1948–1998,* ed. James Procter (Manchester, 2000), 57–58.

67. KC, docket order issued May 26, to London Corps Society, 451 Harrow Road, W10. "Inquisition," 8.7.59/5.8.59, Coroner, Gavin L.B., Thurston, London Metropolitan Archives, COR/LW/1959. See also MEPO Records, National Archives, London. The only police action of note, as one commander later admitted (July 9, 1959), was to tip off the local press with details of the case before those who knew the perpetrators could be questioned. Commander "C": "I think there can be no doubt at all that the information was supplied by a police officer closely connected with the enquiry, and therefore a C.I.D. officer" (MEPO 9883).

68. "W.I. Riled by London Murder," *Amsterdam News* (New York), May 30, 1959, 1.

69. David Killingray, "'To Do Something for the Race': Harold Moody and the League of Coloured Peoples," in *West Indian Intellectuals in Britain,* ed. Bill Schwarz (Manchester, 2003), 51–70.

70. See A. Sivanandan, "From Resistance to Rebellion: Asian and Afro-Caribbean Struggles in Britain," *Race and Class* 23, nos. 2–3 (1981):

111–52; Penny M. Von Eschen, *Race against Empire: Black Americans and Anticolonialism, 1937–1957* (Ithaca, N.Y., 1997); and Susan D. Pennybacker, *From Scottsboro to Munich: Race and Political Culture in 1930s Britain* (Princeton, 2009).

71. Order of Service, Funeral Service for Kelso Benjamin Cochrane, St. Michael and All Angels Church, Ladbroke Grove, London W10. Hymn Thy Kingdom Come; Service Rev. J. H. Goodman (Vic.); Lesson read by Rt. Rv. Bishop of Kensington; Hymn How Sweet the Name of Jesus Sounds. Kensal Green Cemetery, committal by Rev Ronald Campbell, Chaplain to W.I. migrants, June 6, 1959, folder 01/04/04/01/04/02/01-14, IRR.

72. Flyer, "Coloured People's Progressive Assocn, 14 Tavistock Crescent, London. Mass demon, Sun 21st Sept, 1958, orgnsd by MCF, 'This fight is your fight,'" folder 01/04/04/01/04/02/01-14, IRR. For a biography of Claudia Jones, see Carole Boyce Davies, *Left of Karl Marx: The Political Life of Black Communist Claudia Jones* (Durham, N.C., 2007).

73. "Black v. White," *Daily Mirror,* September 3, 1958.

74. MCF flyer, "No Colour Bar Against Commonwealth Immigrants," Folder 01/04/04/01/04/02/01-14, IRR.

75. "W.I. Immigrants Committee held in C.O.," 19.12.1961, CO 1031/3931, Public Records Office.

76. Telegram from CRO to various Commonwealth countries, August 1, 1962, CO 1031/3931, Public Records Office.

77. Nicholas Deakin, *Colour, Citizenship, and British Society: Based on the Institute of Race Relations Report* (London, 1970), 48.

78. "Central Ordnance Depot, Didcot (Closure)," *HC Deb (Hansard),* February 13, 1961, available at http://hansard.millbanksystems.com /commons/1961/feb/13/central-ordnance-depot-didcot-closure.

79. Shaw, "Kinship and Continuity," 46.

80. "Pakistani Jobless Cause Concern," *Oxford Mail,* May 19, 1962.

81. Caryl Phillips, "Stuart Hall," *Bomb* 58 (Winter 1997).

82. Zoe Williams, "The Saturday Interview: Stuart Hall," *Guardian,* February 10, 2012. "I came to England as a Jamaican," Hall said, but after meeting other Caribbean students for the first time "it was in Oxford that I really became a West Indian" (Kuan-Hsing Chen,

"Stuart Hall," in *Trajectories: Inter-Asia Cultural Studies,* ed. Kuan-Hsing Chen [London, 1998], 362).

83. Stuart Hall, "Life and Times of the First New Left," *New Left Review* 61 (January–February 2010): 179; Kwesi Owusu, *Black British Culture and Society* (London: Routledge, 2000), 446. Hall "met African students for the first time" and Caribbean students from other islands while at Oxford. As Hall later recalled, "We followed the expulsion of the French from Indochina with a massive celebration dinner" (ibid.).

84. Chen, "Stuart Hall," 327.

85. Author interview with Revan Tranter, February 13, 2014, Berkeley.

86. This minority culture included some outspoken communist students who were mostly (and ironically, given its history) to be found in Balliol, clustered around the celebrated historian of Civil War England, Christopher Hill. As a postgraduate, Hall would lodge with one such student, Raphael Samuel, a first-class historian, in a house in the central Jericho district that Hall described as a "sort of left-wing refuge from official Oxford." Samuel would go on to help pioneer the writing of the history of working-class lives, or "history from below." See Stuart Hall, "Life and Times of the First New Left," *New Left Review* 61 (January–February 2010): 179.

87. Elizabeth Pears, "Stuart Hall: The Man Who Helped the Country Understand Itself," *Voice,* September 8, 2013.

88. Chen, "Stuart Hall," 327.

89. The students were disproportionately from Africa, whereas the majority of immigrants were from the Caribbean and the Indian subcontinent. Some students stayed on in Britain to work after completing their degrees.

90. *Picture Post,* July 2, 1949, 257.

91. Tuck, "Malcolm X's Visit to Oxford University," 90.

92. "City to Tackle Big Problem," *Oxford Mail,* May 3, 1960.

93. Letter from Secretary, Delegacy of Lodgings, to B. W. Greaves, Tanganyika, May 26, 1960; see also Letter from Secretary, Delegacy of Lodgings, to Dr. S. Ganguly, Calcutta, March 11, 1960, and "Lodg-

ing House Delegacy, Minute Book, 1960–1970," LHD/M/2/8 and LHD SF/11/3, Duke Humfrey's Library, Bodleian Library.

94. Letter from Rosalind Hayward, October 9, 1962, LHD/C/7/1, Duke Humfrey's Library.

95. Clarence Senior, "Race Relations and Labor Supply in Great Britain," paper presented to the American Sociological Society, September 8, 1955, Detroit, 7, MSS292/805.7/2, Trade Union Congress Archives, University of Warwick Library.

96. Kenneth Little, "Research Report," *Sociological Review* 8, no. 2 (December 1960): 255–66.

97. Peter Searle, "Bristol—After the Bus Dispute," *IRR Newsletter,* July 13–16, 1963.

98. *IRR Newsletter,* September 1961, 7–8.

99. Roi Ottley, *No Green Pastures: The Negro in Europe Today* (London, 1951), 28.

100. "Colour-Barred: A Nigerian in Yorkshire," *Labour Monthly* 37, no. 1 (1955): 36.

101. A reporter for the glossy American *Picture Post* observed in 1949, "The British color bar . . . is invisible but . . . it is hard and real to the touch. Many colored people say that they would honestly prefer an official color bar, such as that which exists in America or South Africa" (July 2, 1949).

102. John Martinco, "Negroes Not Alone in 'Sting' of Race Bias," *Chicago Daily Defender,* May 5, 1964, 9.

103. "The Reasons Why at Notting Hill," *Observer,* September 7, 1958.

104. See, e.g., Thomas Sugrue, *The Origins of the Urban Crisis: Race and Inequality in Postwar Detroit* (Princeton, 2005).

105. John Davis, "Rents and Race in 1960s London," *Twentieth Century British History* 12, no. 1 (2001): 69–92, 78; Anthony McCowan, *Coloured Peoples in Britain,* Bow Group Pamphlet Series (London, 1952), 9.

106. Henri Tajfel and John L. Dawson, eds., *Disappointed Guests: Essays by African, Asian, and West Indian Students* (London, 1964), 149. This was not simply a case of landladies charging nonwhite lodgers more,

but of landladies in cheaper areas refusing to take in nonwhite lodgers, thus limiting the housing supply to more expensive parts of town.

107. Author interview with Anthony Smith, May 5, 2004; P.S. Copping to Senior Proctor, 3.18.60, file JACARI, 1959–61, Duke Humfrey's Library.

108. In the meantime, the NUS asked delegates in London to launch an "investigation into extent of landladies colour-bar in Britain" (*West Indian Gazette* 3, no. 4 [December 1960]).

109. "Lodgings Appeal for Overseas Students," *Oxford Mail*, May 10, 1960, 5. In turn, the Oxford branch of the Institute of Race Relations tried to "to compile a list of landladies who are willing to welcome the students from overseas." See *Racial Unity Bulletin* (formerly *Le Play House Bulletin—Racial Relations Section*), no. 114 (October 1953), 6, 01/04/03/02/133, IRR.

110. *Oxford Mail*, July 6, 1962; "Coffee Club," *Oxford Mail*, October 26, 1961.

111. *Racial Unity Bulletin*, no. 114 (October 1953), 6.

112. "British Students May Launch Boycott on Colour-Bar 'Digs,'" *West Indian Gazette* 3, no. 4 (December 1960): 1. Other stories in that issue included the exclusion by the union of a skilled Anglo-Indian fitter at a Sheffield transport department (though he had paid union dues for two years) and racist attacks on civil rights activists in Louisiana.

113. Ottley, *No Green Pastures*, 32.

114. Ibid., 32–33.

115. Tajfel and Dawson (eds.), *Disappointed Guests*, 1.

116. Ibid., 146 (epilogue).

117. Mervyn Morris, "Feeling, Affection, Respect," in Tajfel and Dawson (eds.), *Disappointed Guests*, 11, 13, 18.

118. Ibid., 19–20.

119. Ibid., 7.

120. Ibid., 22.

121. Ibid., 11.

122. Ibid., 25.

123. Ibid., 16.

124. Ibid., 26.

125. Patricia Madoo, "The Transition from 'Light Skinned' to 'Coloured,'" in Tajfel and Dawson (eds.), *Disappointed Guests, 56.*

126. Ibid., 58.

127. "The English have at last rendered him a service" (ibid., 62).

128. Carol Sicherman, "The Leeds-Makerere Connection and Ngugi's Intellectual Development," *Ufahamu: A Journal of African Studies* 23, no. 1 (1995): 3–20.

129. Hugh Trevor-Roper, *The Rise of Christian Europe* (New York, 1965), 1.

130. Malcolm X, *Autobiography.* (Trevor-Roper seemed to be channeling the leading historian of the early Victorian era, Thomas Babington Macaulay, who had argued over a century before that "a single shelf of a good European library was worth the whole native literature of India and Arabia" ["Minute on Indian Education" (1835), available at www.wwnorton.com/college/english/nael/victorian/topic_4/macaulay.htm].)

131. Ime Ikiddeh, foreword to Ngugi wa Thiong'o, *Homecoming: Essays on African and Carribean Literature, Culture, and Politics* (London, 1972), xiii.

132. On Ngugi's concern with language, see http://torch.ox.ac.uk/NgugiwaThiongo-video. His 1963 novel about repression, *Weep Not, Child,* was the first novel by an East African to be published in English.

133. Adil Jussawalla, "Indifference," in Tajfel and Dawson (eds.), *Disappointed Guests,* 135.

134. Sicherman, "Leeds-Makerere Connection," 4.

CHAPTER 3

1. Eric A. Abrahams to H. L. Wynter, March 29, 1961, Eric Abrahams, St. Peter's College student file (hereafter referred to as Abrahams file).

2. "Preparing Students for Leadership Roles," November 8, 2010, www.guardian.co.tt/archives/features/life/2010/11/07/preparing-students-leadership-roles#sthash.j9q37jM6.dpuf.

3. Hilary McD. Beckles, *The Development of West Indies Cricket,* Vol. 2: *The Age of Nationalism* (London, 1999), 76.

4. H.D. Huggins, Dean of Social Sciences Faculty, to H.L. Wynter, June 12, 1961, Abrahams file.

5. Eric. A. Abrahams to H.L. Wynter, March 29, 1961, Abrahams file.

6. Author interview with Hope Abrahams, July 16, 2013.

7. Rhodes Scholarship Application, Abrahams file.

8. H.D. Huggins, to H.L. Wynter, June 12, 1961, Abrahams file.

9. Master, St. Peter's College, to Warden, Rhodes House, March 2, 1962, Abrahams file.

10. Master, St. Peter's College, to Eric Abrahams, March 8, 1962, Abrahams file.

11. Master, St. Peter's College, to Warden, Rhodes House, November 13, 1962, Abrahams file.

12. Christopher Hollis, *The Oxford Union* (London, 1965), 220.

13. Hope Abrahams interview.

14. "Union Report," *Oxford Magazine,* February 6, 1964, 185.

15. Tariq Ali, *Street Fighting Years: An Autobiography of the Sixties* (London, 2005), 76.

16. Ibid., 77.

17. Ibid., 88.

18. Ibid., 92.

19. "Jonathan Aitken," *Independent,* October 27, 1999.

20. Quoted in Jan R. Carew, *Ghosts in Our Blood: With Malcolm X in Africa, England, and the Caribbean* (New York, 1994), 72.

21. Author interview with Louis Nthenda, February 25, 2014.

22. Carew, *Ghosts in Our Blood,* 40.

23. For more information on the proctorial system, see J.I. Catto, ed., *The History of the University of Oxford: The Early Oxford Schools* (Oxford, 1984), 82–84.

24. Senior Proctor to Vice Chancellor, October 19, 1956, File 1956–59, JACARI files, Duke Humfrey's Library, Bodleian Library.

25. "History of JACARI," http://jacari.blahwaffleblah.com/history /index.html.

26. "Students from Abroad, 1963–64," LHD/C/7/1, Duke Humfrey's Library.

27. Joseph A. Soares, *The Decline of Privilege: The Modernization of Oxford University* (Stanford, Calif., 1999), 36.

28. On the Labour Party, see "Another Monster Petition," *Cherwell*, November 1, 1955, 1; Anthony Howard, "The Labour Club through Thirty-Five Years," *Oxford Clarion*, Michaelmas 1954, 6–9; and "Undergraduates Busy in Slum and Palace," *Cherwell*, May 1, 1956.

29. Author interview with Hannan Rose, July 20, 2013.

30. Ali, *Street Fighting Years.*

31. Email from David Griffiths, September 2013.

32. Email from Tym Marsh, September 2013.

33. Letter from Patrick McAuslan, JACARI chair, to "all Freshers," October 1959, JACARI files.

34. "History of JACARI."

35. Passport issues delayed Mei's arrival by three years, which shook the morale of JACARI leaders and saw membership decline. He arrived in 1959.

36. P. S. Copping (Wadham), "Jacari Protest Letter to MCC," *Cherwell*, May 14, 1960, 1.

37. Clipping, *Oxford Mail*, February 23, 1962, 1: "S.A. Arms Protest by Six Oxford Students," File 1961–64, JACARI files.

38. "MP Tells JACARI Immigrants Bill Not Colour Bar," *Oxford Mail*, December 8, 1961, 11.

39. Flyer, "Protest March against the Commonwealth Immigrants Bill, Sunday, February 4th at 2.30 pm," JACARI files; "March Banned Protest Continues," *Cherwell*, February 3, 1962, 3.

40. Flyer, File 1961–64, JACARI files.

41. Hilary Termcard [academic calendar] 1959, JACARI, John Johnson Collection of Printed Ephemera, Bodleian Library, University of Oxford (hereafter John Johnson Collection).

42. P. S. Copping to Senior Proctor, March 18, 1960; reply, March 25, 1960; Copping's subsequent reply, April 4, 1960, JACARI files.

43. Michaelmas Termcard 1963, JACARI, John Johnson Collection.

44. Email from John Wright, September 2013.

45. Ali, *Street Fighting Years*, 104.

46. Wright email.

47. "JACARI Support," *Oxford Mail*, October 15, 1963, 4.

48. Kenneth Leech, *Race: Changing Society and the Churches* (London, 2005), x.

49. Carew, *Ghosts in Our Blood*, 76.

50. John Corbin, *An American at Oxford* (Boston, 1902), 64.

51. W. E. B. Du Bois, "Race Student," *Phylon* 4, no. 1 (1943): 83.

52. A brief biography of Solomon West Ridgeway Dias Bandaranaike (1899–1959) can be found at www.oxforddnb.com/templates/olddnb.jsp?articleid=30571.

53. Sumita Mukherjee, *Nationalism, Education, and Migrant Identities: The England-Returned* (London, 2009), 75.

54. "Oxford Union," Open University, www.open.ac.uk/research projects/makingbritain/content/oxford-union.

55. "Indian Student Protests Color Bar at Oxford," *Baltimore Afro-American*, March 31, 1934, 20.

56. *Oxford Mail*, March 9, 1934.

57. D. F. Karaka, "The Colour Bar in Britain," *Spectator*, March 30, 1934, 8.

58. Quoted in Carew, *Ghosts in Our Blood*, 41.

59. Rudolph Dunbar, "Fair Treatment of Individuals Who Prove Capabilities," *Chicago Defender*, September 12, 1942, 7.

60. *Pittsburgh Courier*, July 11, 1942, 18.

61. Du Bois, "Race Student," 83.

62. David Griffiths and John Wright, emails to author, September 2013.

63. Ali, *Street Fighting Years*.

64. "Oxford Union Votes against Blackball: Rule Not Used since 1840," *Guardian*, February 15, 1963, 4.

65. "Move to End Blackballing," *Guardian*, February 13, 1963, 18.

66. *Daily Mail*, February 12, 1963, 2; "The End of a Story: Women in the Union," *Oxford Mail*, February 19, 1963, 1.

67. See Oxford Union termcards, 1962–64, Union Archives, Oxfordshire County Records Office.

68. "Oxford Union Speaker Dies," *Times,* October 23, 1964, 17.

69. "Ceylon Leader Cheered," *Oxford Mail,* October 16, 1964.

70. "Demonstrations in Britain over Pretoria Sentences," *Times,* June 13, 1964, 9.

71. JACARI's intention was to pressure the British government to take a stand. The society's president that term, Robert Serpell, was quoted in the London *Times* warning that the removal of the ANC leaders "from the political scene will mean that the likelihood of a peaceful solution to the present situation in South Africa will be greatly diminished" ("Demonstrations in Britain over Pretoria Sentences," *Times,* June 13, 1964, 9).

72. "A Letter from Oxford," *Spectator,* July 4, 1930, 16; "The Oxford Proctor," *New York Times,* October 1, 1880.

73. Proctors to Shaw, June 25, 1964, JACARI files.

74. Shaw to Proctors, July 2, 1964, JACARI files.

75. "Proctors Ban Antiracial Demonstration," *Guardian,* May 27, 1964.

76. University Marshal to Shaw, May 28, 1964, and Senior Proctor to Shaw, June 6, 1964, JACARI files.

77. Trinity Termcard 1964, JACARI, John Johnson Collection.

78. *Oxford Mail,* June 9, 1964, 7.

79. Mary Proudfoot to Shaw, May 7, 1964, JACARI files.

80. Proudfoot to Shaw, June 7, 1964, JACARI files.

81. When I interviewed Shaw nearly fifty years after these events, he had forgotten about Proudfoot. When I reminded him, he fairly shuddered at the memory—and was appalled but not in the least surprised by the subterfuge.

82. Proudfoot to Mr. Bond, n.d., JACARI files.

83. Shaw to Senior Proctor, June 10, 1964, JACARI files.

84. "Mr. de Wet's Visit Off—'To Avoid Damage,'" *Oxford Mail,* June 13, 1964, 5.

85. University Marshall note to Senior Proctor, File 1961–64, JACARI files.

86. Hannan Rose to Junior Proctor, June 10, 1964, JACARI files.

87. "Students Form Joint Committee," *Guardian,* June 15, 1964.

88. Proudfoot to Senior Proctor, June 16, 1964, JACARI files.

89. "Four Arrested as Crowd Hustles Dr. de Wet," *Oxford Mail,* June 18, 1964, 7.

90. "Police Protect Ambassador in Riot," *Times,* June 18, 1964, 14.

91. "Protest on Apartheid," *Oxford Mail,* June 12, 1964.

92. "The Anti-Apartheid Demonstration," *ISIS,* October 10, 1964, 12.

93. "Crowd Riots as S. Africa Envoy Leaves Hall," *Times,* June 18, 1964, 14.

94. Ibid.; "Protests at de Wet Visit Rowdyism," *Oxford Mail,* June 18, 1964, 1.

95. *Oxford Times,* July 3, 1964, 12.

96. "Oxford to Gate Next Union President," *Telegraph,* June 20, 1964, 9; *Daily Express,* June 20, 1964, 1.

97. "MPs Hit at Oxford Ban on Politics," *Daily Herald,* June 24, 1964, 9.

98. "Students Were Too Severely Punished," *Oxford Mail,* June 26, 1964, 11.

99. "Dons in Protest over Students' Penalties," *Oxford Mail,* June 23, 1964, 3; "Proctorial Power," *Oxford Times,* June 28, 16.

100. "MPs Hit at Oxford Ban on Politics," 9; "Union Debates 'Standstill' Fear," *Daily Telegraph,* June 20, 1964, 9.

101. "Lights Out in Union Uproar," *Oxford Mail,* June 19, 1964, 3.

102. The ninth debate of TT 1964, Rough Minute Book, 1963–66, Union Archives, Oxfordshire County Records Office.

103. Minutes of Meeting of Standing Committee, June 24, 1964, Private Minute Book of Oxford Union Society Committee, 1964–68, Union Standing Committee, Michaelmas Term 1964, Union Archives, Oxfordshire County Records Office.

104. Vice Chancellor to Proctors, June 22, 1964, cc'ed to Master, St. Peter's College, Abrahams file.

105. Vice Master, St. Peter's College, to the Students' Officer, Office of the High Commissioner, Jamaica, July 17, 1964, Abrahams file.

106. "The Proctors—A Reply," *ISIS,* October 17, 1964, 4.

107. "Proctors Relent on Rustication," *Oxford Times,* July 3, 1964, 12. In the end, a group of JACARI students, including Michael Pinto-

Duschinsky, went to Mississippi after all to support the voter registration campaigns. Pinto-Duschinsky was arrested. My thanks to Michael Pinto-Duschinsky for this information (email, November 2012).

108. The committee was set up under the auspices of Oxford's Hebdomadal Council (the university's main council, so called because it met strictly once a week).

109. "Oxford Proctor Rules to Be Reviewed," *Daily Telegraph,* October 9, 1964.

110. "A Thankless Task," *Oxford Magazine,* October 22, 1964, 23.

111. "The Proctors—A Reply," 4.

112. The first debate of Michaelmas Term 1964 (October 15), Union Minutes, Union files. No record remains of who the dissenter was.

113. "Students Send Criticisms to Proctors," *Guardian,* October 13, 1964, 8.

114. "Letter from Abrahams," *Cherwell,* October 7, 1964, 2.

115. "Proctors at It Again," *Cherwell,* October 28, 1964, 4.

116. Ali, *Street Fighting Years,* 103.

117. "Really," *Cherwell,* October 14, 1964.

118. Michaelmas Termcard 1964, JACARI, John Johnson Collection.

119. M. Hartley-Brewer, "Smethwick," in *Colour and the British Electorate: Six Case Studies,* ed. N. Deakin (London, 1965), 84.

120. http://hansard.millbanksystems.com/commons/1964/nov/10/debate-on-the-address-sixth-day. See, too, Joe Street, "Malcolm X, Smethwick, and the Influence of the African American Freedom Struggle on British Race Relations in the 1960s," *Journal of Black Studies* 38, no. 6 (2008): 932–50.

121. *Times,* November 4, 1964, 4.

122. Muhammad Anwar, *Race and Politics: Ethnic Minorities and the British Political System* (Dorset U.K., 1986).

123. Grant Kamenju, Review of Henri Tajfel and John Dawson (eds.), *Disappointed Guests, Journal of Modern African Studies* 4, no. 1 (May 1966): 131–33.

124. Hannan Rose, "Lessons for the Future," *ISIS,* November 21, 1964.

125. Quoted ibid., 24.

126. Quoted ibid.

127. Ibid.

128. "Tories Smuggle Guest into Meeting," *Oxford Mail,* November 25, 1964.

129. For the full report, see JACARI, *Survey on Oxford Lodgings* (Oxford, 1964); or for a concise version, see Robert Serpell and Clive Sneddon, "Colour Prejudice and Oxford Landladies," *Race* 6, no. 4 (1965): 322–33.

130. Miss M. Eagle to Secretary of the Delegacy of Lodgings; Mrs. Lord to Secretary; and Anonymous to Secretary, all November 26, 1964, Overseas Students Files, Duke Humfrey's Library, Bodleian Library (hereafter referred to as Overseas Student Files).

131. "Oxford Claims Prejudice by Landladies," *Guardian,* November 26, 1964, 5; email from Clive Sneddon, November 11, 2012.

132. Miss M. Eagle to Secretary, Delegacy of Lodgings, November 26, 1964, Overseas Student Files.

133. Minutes, Delegacy of Lodgings, November 26, 1964, Overseas Student Files.

134. Edward Murrain, "Malcolm X Arrives, Sounds Off, and Then He's Off to Oxford," *New York Courier,* December 5, 1964, 1.

135. OAAU Homecoming Rally, Harlem, November 29, 1964, in *Malcolm X: Collected Speeches, Debates, and Interviews (1960–1965),* ed. Sandeep S. Atwal, PDF document.

136. FBI files, Malcolm X Little, Part 13 of 24, BUFILE 100-399321, http://vault.fbi.gov/Malcolm%20X/Malcolm%20X%20Part%2018%20of%2038.

137. Ibid.

138. Ibid.

139. Ibid.

140. OAAU Homecoming Rally, Harlem, November 29, 1964.

141. Eric Abrahams to Malcolm X, November 27, 1964, International Correspondence England, 1964, MXC.

142. Email from Tony Abrahams, July 30, 2010.

143. Carew, *Ghosts in Our Blood,* 77.

144. Lebert Bethune, "Malcolm X in Europe," in *Malcolm X: The*

Man and His Times, ed. John Henrik Clarke (New York, 1969), 232. In fact, Ali's term was the one after that of Abrahams's successor.

145. Telegram, Ebrahimsa to Malcolm X, November 28, 1964, International Correspondence England, 1964, box 3, folder 15, MXC.

146. Carew, *Ghosts in Our Blood,* 77.

147. Interview with Judith Okley, August 21, 2013.

148. Walter Partington, "Savage Simbas Hit Back," *Daily Express,* December 3, 1964, 2.

149. E.g., "At the Audubon Ballroom," December 13, 1964, in Atwal (ed.), *Malcolm X: Collected Speeches . . . (1960–1965).*

150. Okley interview.

151. Alex Haley and Malcolm X, *The Autobiography of Malcolm X* (London, 1965).

152. Okley interview. Also in his speech Malcolm X refers to a white woman he had spent time with the previous day.

CHAPTER 4

1. All quotations from the speeches are taken from recordings, available at the Union Archives.

2. Lebert Bethune, "Malcolm X in Europe," in *Malcolm X: The Man and His Times,* ed. John Henrik Clarke (New York, 1969), 232–33.

3. Jan R. Carew, *Ghosts in Our Blood: With Malcolm X in Africa, England, and the Caribbean* (New York, 1994), 74.

4. OAAU Homecoming Rally, November 29, 1964, in *Malcolm X: Collected Speeches, Debates, and Interviews (1960–1965),* ed. Sandeep S. Atwal, PDF document.

5. Ibid.

6. Malcolm X, "In Cairo," Speeches, box 9, folder 6, MXC.

7. Letter to the *Egyptian Gazette,* August 25, 1964.

8. "Islam in America," speech notes, MXC.

9. Carew, *Ghosts in Our Blood,* 45.

10. Ibid., 64.

11. Ibid., 138.

12. In his famous "Message to the Grassroots" speech, delivered to

militant black activists in a Christian church in Detroit on November 10, 1963, shortly before he left the Nation, Malcolm X didn't mention Islam at all.

13. "The Ballot or the Bullet," in Atwal (ed.), *Malcolm X: Collected Speeches . . . (1960–1965)*.

14. Ibid.

15. Malcolm X to Betty Shabazz, August 4, 1964, in Correspondence, Shabazz, Betty, 1960–1964, box 3, folder 2, MXC.

16. OAAU Founding Rally, Harlem, June 28, 1964, in Atwal (ed.), *Malcolm X: Collected Speeches . . . (1960–1965)*.

17. OAAU Homecoming Rally, Harlem, November 29, 1964. See, too, Paris rally, a week before Oxford: "Since the topic of this lecture" is political, he explained there, "I feel that I should speak in my capacity as chairman of the OAAU rather than in my religious capacity."

18. Rev. Albert Cleage, Friday Night Socialist Forum, Detroit, February 24, 1967, in *International Socialist Review* 28, no. 5 (September–October 1967): 33.

19. OAAU Homecoming Rally, Harlem, November 29, 1964.

20. Columbia University speech, November 20, 1963, in Atwal (ed.), *Malcolm X: Collected Speeches . . . (1960–1965)*.

21. "Millions of Britons See Malcolm X in Broadcast of Debate at Oxford," *Voice,* January 2, 1965; Carew, *Ghosts in Our Blood,* 77.

22. OAAU Homecoming Ralley, Harlem, November 29, 1964.

23. "U.S. Congo Policy," *Chicago Daily Defender,* December 7, 1964, 13.

24. "The Massacre," *Chicago Defender,* November 30, 1964, 13.

25. "African Disunity," *Chicago Defender,* December 21, 1964, 17.

26. OAAU Homecoming Rally, Harlem, November 29, 1964.

27. "Malcolm X In, Out to London," *Amsterdam News* (New York), December 5, 1964, 4.

28. "Nun Tells of Savage Beatings by Rebels in Congo: Recalls Wishing for Death as She Was Forced to Parade Naked through Street," *New York Times,* November 27, 1964, 12.

29. C.L. Sulzberger, "Foreign Affairs: The Witches' Cauldron Bubbles," *New York Times,* December 2, 1964, 46.

30. "Actors in Congo's Tragedy," *New York Times,* December 6, 1964, SM32.

31. OAAU Homecoming Rally, Harlem, November 29, 1964.

32. Malcolm X used the Hamlet argument again on his return to the United States, at the Harvard Law School Forum, December 16, 1964.

33. The eighth debate of MT 1964, Rough Minute Book, 1963–66, Union Archives, Oxfordshire County Records Office.

CHAPTER 5

1. Telegram, Ebrahimsa to Malcolm X, November 28, 1964, International Correspondence England, 1964, box 3, folder 15, MXC; "Row Feared over Malcolm X Visit," *Sheffield Star,* December 1, 1964, 9; Marika Sherwood, *Malcolm X: Visits Abroad* (Oare, Kent, 2012).

2. Sherwood, *Malcolm X,* 122.

3. "Malcolm X Row," *Yorkshire Post,* December 2, 1964, 5.

4. "Malcolm X to Visit Sheffied," *Sheffield Telegraph,* December 2, 1964.

5. "Malcolm X to Meet Colour Row Students," *Sun,* December 2, 1964.

6. Sherwood, *Malcolm X,* 128.

7. "Malcolm X, Statement by the Students' Union," *Sheffield Telegraph,* n.d., International Correspondence England, MXC.

8. The CAO's president, Kojo Amoo-Gottfried, followed up with an invitation in February (Gottfried to Malcolm X, January 17, 1964, International Correspondence England, MXC). He built up his media contacts, too. See, e.g., Lillian Lang to Malcolm X, December 15, 1964, International Correspondence England, MXC.

9. See Stephen Tuck, "Malcolm X's Visit to Oxford University: U.S. Civil Rights, Black Britain, and the Special Relationship on Race," *American Historical Review* 118 (2013).

10. Kojo Amoo-Gottfried to Malcolm X, December 22, 1964, International Correspondence England, MXC. See *Magnet: The*

Voice of the Afro-Asian Caribbean Peoples, February 27–March 12, 1965, 1, 01/04/03/02/110, IRR.

11. Joe Street, "Malcolm X, Smethwick, and the Influence of the African American Freedom Struggle on British Race Relations in the 1960s," *Journal of Black Studies* 38, no. 6 (2008): 939.

12. "Aid to Malcolm X by BBC Assailed: TV Aides Rebuked for Tour of Race-Friction Area," *New York Times,* February 14, 1965, 24; "Malcolm X Pays Smethwick Call," *Washington Post,* February 14, 1965, K1.

13. HC Deb 18 February 1965 vol. 706 c 264W, 81 and 82, *Hansard,* accessed via www.hansard.millbanksystems.com.

14. "Washington D.C. Centre of World Imperialism—Malcolm X," *West Indian Gazette,* February 1965, 4. See, too, influence on black militants: *Black Ram,* December 15, 1968, 01/04/03/02/046, 1, IRR.

15. "London Letter," *Guardian,* December 7, 1964, 10.

16. Tuck, "Malcolm X's Visit to Oxford University."

17. In Paris, he headed straight for a café on Rue St. André des Arts, which was a favorite meeting place of African students. See Lebert Bethune, "Malcolm X in Europe," in *Malcolm X: The Man and His Times,* ed. John Henrik Clarke (New York, 1969), 229.

18. Street, "Malcolm X," 939.

19. Malcolm X to Miss Sandra Devoto, University of Sheffield Union, December 15, 1964, box 3, folder 4, MXC.

20. Yale University speech, October 20, 1962, in *Malcolm X: Collected Speeches, Debates, and Interviews (1960–1965),* ed. Sandeep S. Atwal, PDF document. "The white man in Great Britain could once boast that his control extended over so much of the black man's land that the sun never set on the British Empire."

21. "God's Judgment of White America," December 4, 1963, in Atwal (ed.), *Malcolm X: Collected Speeches . . . (1960–1965).* On the focus on Africa and Asia and absence of Europe, see, for example, "African-Asian Unity Bazaar," Speechnotes, box 10, folder 1, MXC.

22. Street, "Malcolm X in Smethwick," 940.

23. Notes for London School of Economics (LSE) speech [1964], Travel Diary, MXC.

24. Speech at the Audubon Ballroom, December 20, 1964, in Atwal (ed.), *Malcolm X: Collected Speeches ... (1960–1965)*.

25. Transcript of telephone conversation with Lebert Bethune and a gathering in Paris, February 6, 1965, Series: Intellectual Works/Published Interview, 1964–1965, box 6, Carlos Moore Collection, Ralph J. Bunche Center for African American Studies, University of California, Los Angeles.

26. "After the Firebombing," Detroit, February 14, 1965, in Atwal (ed.), *Malcolm X: Collected Speeches ... (1960–1965)*.

27. Ibid.

28. OAAU Homecoming Rally, Harlem, November 29, 1964, in Atwal (ed.), *Malcolm X: Collected Speeches ... (1960–1965)*.

29. "Not Just an American Problem, but a World Problem," in Atwal (ed.), *Malcolm X: Collected Speeches ... (1960–1965)*; "After the Firebombing."

30. "After the Firebombing."

31. Ibid.

32. "Not Just an American Problem, but a World Problem."

33. Jan R. Carew, *Ghosts in Our Blood: With Malcolm X in Africa, England, and the Caribbean* (New York, 1994), 30.

34. Quoted in W. W. Daniel, *Racial Discrimination in England* (Harmondsworth, U.K., 1968), 48.

35. Carew, *Ghosts in Our Blood,* 30.

36. Notes for LSE speech, MXC; "There's a Worldwide Revolution Going On," February 15, 1965, in Atwal (ed.), *Malcolm X: Collected Speeches ... (1960–1965)*.

37. "Nobel Lecture by the Reverend Dr. Martin Luther King, Jr., Recipient of the 1964 Nobel Peace Prize, Oslo, Norway, December 11, 1964," available at www.nobelprize.org/nobel_prizes/peace/laureates/1964/king-lecture.html.

38. Author interview with Clarence Jones, January 18, 2011.

39. "London Program for Dr. Martin Luther King," *Washington Post,* December 7, 1964, 1; "Dr. King Preaches Negro Restraint," *New York Times,* December 7, 1964, 1.

40. Jones interview.

41. "London Programme for Dr. Martin Luther King, December 1964," Dr. Martin Luther King Nobel Peace Prize 1964, Bayard Rustin Papers, Schomburg Center for Research in Black Culture, New York Public Library.

42. "Dr. King Preaches Negro Restraint." *New York Times*, December 7, 1964, 1.

43. Wyatt Tee Walker to Canon Collins (on behalf of Dr. King), January 24, 1962, Records of the Southern Christian Leadership Conference, 1954–1970 [microfilm], Part 2: Records of the Executive Director and Treasurer, reel 14, box 51:12, frame no. 0359. Christian Action of London gave $561.25 (Payment Order, January 5, 1962; ibid.).

44. "Rough Notes," Bayard Rustin Papers, reel 3, no. 0258, Schomburg Center.

45. "Dr King's Racial Warning to Britain," *Times,* December 7, 1964, 6.

46. Brian Ward, "A King in Newcastle: Martin Luther King and British Race Relations, 1967–68," *Georgia Historical Quarterly* 79, no. 3 (1995): 622.

47. "A Negro Assays on the Negro Mood," *New York Times,* March 12, 1961.

48. On Black Power's salience during the early civil rights movement, see Timothy B. Tyson, *Radio Free Dixie: Robert F. Williams and the Roots of Black Power* (Chapel Hill, N.C., 1999). The United States was not the only one watching the British unrest from afar. Colonial nations were especially interested. See, for example, angry reactions in: Telegram to Secretary of State for the Colonies (Mr. Garnett Gordon), from the West Indies (from the Rt. Hon. Lord Hailes), September 25, 1959, "Racial Disturbance: Notting Hill Activities," PRO, HO 325/9; "Draft report to cabinet, BFM Samuel, Sec. Working Party to report on the social and economic problems arising from the growing influx into the United Kingdom of coloured workers from other Commonwealth countries," December 1, 1959, and telegram to CRO, Delhi, August 16, 1958, PRO, Dominions Office Records, DO 35/7990. On British awareness of international criticism, see Labour Party statement, "Racial Discrimination," 1958, 1, Labour Party Collection, Nuffield College, Oxford.

49. "Aid to Malcolm X by B.B.C. Assailed," *New York Times,* Febru-

ary 14, 1965, 24. See, too, transcripts of Malcolm X's telephone call to Paris, Carlos Moore Collection. Malcolm X sent a telegram to the U.S. secretary of state to demand an investigation: Telegram to Dean Rusk, February 18, 1965, box 3, folder 4, MXC.

50. "Malcolm X: 'Part of Global Disaster,'" *Oxford Mail*, February 24, 1965, 3.

51. Stokely Carmichael, *Ready for Revolution: The Life and Struggles of Stokely Carmichael (Kwame Ture)* (New York, 2003), 572.

52. Stokely Carmichael, *Stokely Speaks: From Black Power to Pan-Africanism* (Chicago, 2007), 79. See also *Black Panther Miscellany: Stokely Carmichael in London, 1967,* dir. Peter Davis (DVD, Villonfilms, 1967).

53. Malcom X, personal notebook, Notes, Outlines for Speeches, 1946–65, box 9, folder 8, MXC. See also "The Fight against Racism from South Africa to Australia to the U.S.A.," interview with the *Johannesburg Sunday Express,* February 12, 1965, in Malcolm X, *February 1965: The Final Speeches* (1992; repr. New York, 2010), 68–77 (quote 76).

54. The *Defender* called it the "Little Rock anti-negro epidemic" ("The London Riots," September 11, 1958, 11).

55. "Don't Laugh Too Soon," *Pittsburgh Courier,* September 20, 1958, 6. Similarly, the *Guardian* complained that "most Americans think [the two color problems] cancel each other out: mention segregation and they will mention the Notting Hill riot (they seem to think it occurs every weekend), as if our problem matched theirs" (W.J. Weatherby, "Alma Mater," *Guardian,* March 18, 1963, 7).

56. *News Chronicle,* September 9, 1958, Clippings File, Modern Records Centre, Warwick; "Jump on It," *London Observer,* September 14, 1958; Fenner Brockway, "Racial Discrimination," *Labour Monthly* 39, no. 2 (1957): 61–64; see, too, Edward Pilkington, *Beyond the Mother Country: West Indians and the Notting Hill White Riots* (London, 1988), 135. For broader discussions of southern segregationists' interaction with global racial politics, see Alfred O. Hero Jr., *The Southerner and World Affairs* (Baton Rouge, La., 1965); and Thomas Noer, "Segregationists and the World: The Foreign Policy of White Resistance," in *Window on Freedom: Race, Civil Rights, and Foreign Affairs, 1945–1988,* ed. Brenda Gayle Plummer (Chapel Hill, N.C., 2003), 141–62.

57. "Editorially Speaking: Mr James Crow, Esq.," *West Indies Observer* 1, no. 16 (March 23, 1963): 4.

58. Carew, *Ghosts in Our Blood*, 100.

59. See John L. Williams, *Michael X: A Life in Black and White* (London, 2008).

60. These individuals included Commonwealth leaders such as Norman Manley. See "Coloured Audience Shouts Down M.P.," *Guardian*, September 8, 1958.

61. The term was coined by Swedish sociologist Gunnar Myrdal in his 1944 book *An American Dilemma: The Negro Problem and Modern Democracy* (New York).

62. In 1947, fewer than 15,000 Britons had a television license; within a decade, 4.5 million did (and twice that number had a radio license). See Asa Briggs and Peter Burke, *A Social History of the Media: From Gutenberg to the Internet* (Cambridge, 2005), 191–95.

63. See, e.g., Joshua Bruce Guild, "You Can't Go Home Again: Migration, Citizenship, and Black Community in Postwar New York and London," Ph.D. diss., Yale University, 2007; and Kennetta Perry, "Black Migrants, Citizenship, and the Transnational Politics of Race in Postwar Britain," Ph.D. diss., Michigan State University, 2007.

64. Cutting from *AfraAmerican News Service*, January 3, 1968, Subgroup B (New York Office, 1960–1969), Series II (International Affairs Commission), 19, SNCC papers on microfilm, Cambridge University. There were numerous other influential visitors too, including Roy Wilkins, Ralph Bunche, and Bayard Rustin.

65. Author interview with Paul Stephenson, July 30, 1913.

66. John Ross, "Operation Guinness," *Flamingo*, February 1965, 9–11; letter to the editor, *Flamingo*, April 1965, 2. See also "West Indians Stage an American Style Sit-In," *Chicago Defender*, July 9, 1963, 4; "Strikers Protest Firing," *Chicago Defender*, July 16, 1963, 16; "Shabby Protest," *Chicago Defender*, June 22, 1963, 14; "Watch to Be Kept on Colour Bar Premises," *Irish Times*, April 9, 1965, 10.

67. Rosalind Eleanor Wild, "'Black Was the Colour of Our Fight': Black Power in Britain, 1955–1976," Ph.D. diss., University of Sheffield, 2008; Anne-Marie Angelo, "The Black Panthers in London, 1967–1972:

A Diasporic Struggle Navigates the Black Atlantic," *Radical History Review* 103 (Winter 2009): 17–35; and R. E. R. Bunce and Paul Field, "Obi B. Egbuna, C. L. R. James, and the Birth of Black Power in Britain: Black Radicalism in Britain, 1967–72," *Twentieth Century British History* 22, no. 3 (2011): 391–414. There was also a Black Eagles black power group; clipping from Black Eagles, n.d., folder 01/04/04/01/04/01/01–05, IRR.

68. "The Lunatic Fringe," *Flamingo*, September 1961, 41; W. J. Weatherby, "A Guest of the Ku-Klux-Klan," *Guardian*, December 3, 1960, 6.

69. Author interview with Godfrey Hodgson, May 20, 2010; "The Archbishop of Canterbury Talks with the Temptations," *Chicago Defender*, February 3, 1970, 11; "The Archbishop of Canterbury Receives Motown's Temptations," *Philadelphia Tribune*, February 3, 1970, 18. See also Mark Bonham Carter, "Measures against Discrimination: The North American Scene," *Race* 9, no. 1 (1967): 5; and Anthony Lester, *Justice in the American South* (London, 1964).

70. Calvin Trillin, "A Reporter at Large: Color in the Mother Country," *New Yorker*, December 4, 1965, 115–65.

71. Lionel Morrison, "Planning for Britain's Black Community," *Race Today* 1, no. 8 (December 1969): 246; Williams, *Michael X*.

72. See Wild, "'Black Was the Colour of Our Fight.'"

73. "Ku Klux Klan," *Flamingo*, September 1961, 41.

74. *IRR Newsletter*, July 1965, 5–6.

75. See Angelo, "The Black Panthers in London." British Black Power, notably, included South Asians; see editorial reply to letters in *Flamingo*, December 1963, 1; and Daniel, *Racial Discrimination in England*, 48.

76. Bill Patterson, "Alabama Window," *Flamingo*, December 1964, 9–12. The public support for African Americans but not black Britons echoed an observation made by the African American journalist Roi Ottley a decade before: "The English, who regard themselves as above the turbulence of racialism, actually are the most cruelly prejudiced people abroad—a profound fact because of the many black millions who come under the British flag" (Ottley, *No Green Pastures: The Negro in Europe Today* [London, 1952], 8).

77. "Busmen Heckle Marchers," *Bristol Evening Post*, May 2, 1963, 12. On complaints that racism was worse in Britain, see Inder Jit, "Brit-

ain's Coloured Outlaws," *Hindustan Times,* September 7, 1951, 7; Edward Scobie, "Black Englishman," *Flamingo,* November 1962, 32; letters to the editor, *The Guardian,* December 8, 1960, 10; Weatherby, "Alma Mater," 7; Peter Searle, "Bristol—After the Bus Dispute," *IRR Newsletter,* July 1963, 13–16; and "A President Decides," *West Indies Observer,* May 18, 1963, 1. See also Poppy Cannon White, "Another Birmingham," *Amsterdam News* (New York), May 27, 1965, 19.

78. Obi Egbuna, *Destroy This Temple: The Voice of Black Power in Britain* (London, 1971), 21.

79. *Black Dwarf* 13, no. 4 (August 14, 1968), 01/04/03/02/032, IRR.

80. Keith Hindell, "The Genesis of the Race Relations Bill," *Political Quarterly* 36, no. 4 (1965): 390–405. The chairman of the new Race Relations Board, Mark Bonham Carter, went to the United States in 1967 to learn "lessons [from the] American experience," the main lesson being "the necessity for a positive policy on the part of the central government." The revised British Race Relations Act of 1968 duly included more enforcement powers. See Carter, "Measures against Discrimination," 5. For details of the legislation, see www.parliament.uk/documents/commons/lib/research/rp2000/rp00-027.pdf.

81. Andrew Roth, *Enoch Powell: Tory Tribune* (London, 1971), 357.

82. Weatherby, "Guest of the Ku-Klux-Klan," 6.

83. "Topless Fails to Appear," *Oxford Mail,* December 5, 1964, 5.

84. "Governor Wallace May Visit Oxford," *Oxford Times,* April 22, 1965, 6.

85. "President 'Gave Nazi Salute'—Police," *Oxford Mail,* April 9, 1965.

86. "Sunday Morning with Mandrake: A Face to Follow," *Sunday Telegraph,* April 25, 1965, St. Peter's College Clippings File.

87. Darrell. M. Newton, "'How Can We Help You?' Hugh Greene and the BBC Coloured Conferences," *Ethnicity and Race in a Changing World: A Review Journal* 3, no. 2 (2012): 8–10.

88. Conversation with, and email from, Clive Sneddon, June 11, 2010.

89. Mrs. E. M. Talbert to Miss Davies, February 4, 1965, Delegacy

of Lodging Houses (DLH), Overseas Students File, Duke Humfrey's Library, Bodleian Library.

90. "Minutes of the Meeting on 27 November 1964," DLH, Minutes and Meeting Papers, 1868–1970, Minutes and Papers of the Delegates, 1960–70, LHD/M/2/8, Duke Humfrey's Library.

91. "The position in Black and White," *Guardian,* May 10 1965, 5; "Minutes of the Meeting on 11 June 1965," DLH, LHD/M/2/8, Duke Humfrey's Library.

92. SCORE newsletter, October 10, 1965, 01/04/03/02/139, IRR.

93. "College Faces Race Problem," *Cherwell,* March 2, 1966.

94. "Race Relations in Oxford," *Cherwell,* May 18, 1966.

95. "Colour Bar by Landladies," *Guardian,* June 4, 1966, 3.

96. "JACARI Launch New 'Friendship' Plan," *Cherwell,* June 8, 1966.

97. SCORE newsletter, October 25, 1965, 01/04/03/02/139, IRR.

98. *New Independent,* February 2–15, 1967, 4.

99. SCORE newsletter, January 14, 1966, 2–3, IRR.

100. "Student Demonstration in Bid to Save Gypsy Homes," *Cherwell,* February 15, 1967, 1.

101. "39 Held in Oxford Sit-Down," *Times,* June 8, 1968.

102. Michael Hill and Ruth Isaacharoff, *Community Action and Race Relations: A Study of Community Relations Committees in Britain* (London, 1971), 12–15, 273.

103. My thanks to Jed Fazakarley for sharing his knowledge of OCRI.

104. Hill and Isaacharoff, *Community Action and Race Relations,* 31.

105. "Where One Child in 10 Is an Immigrant," *Times,* September 12, 1967, 2.

106. *Commercial Motor Archive,* October 27, 1967.

107. HC Deb 20 February 1968 vol 759 cc238–42238, *Hansard,* accessed at http://hansard.millbanksystems.com/commons/1968/feb/20/mr-gupta

108. *Crossbar* (OCRI newsletter), July 1972, Oxford City Libraries.

109. Alison Shaw, "Kinship and Continuity: Pakistani Families in Oxford," Ph.D. diss., University of Oxford, 1984, 44.

110. For a short summary of Dummett's life, see www.theguardian.com/law/2012/feb/24/ann-dummett.

111. Ann Dummett, *A Portrait of English Racism* (London, 1984), 63.

112. Ibid., 56.

113. *ISIS,* June 28, 1965, St. Peter's College Clippings File.

114. Hannan Rose, "A Tactical Retreat," *ISIS,* October 27, 1965, 4.

115. "Vietnam Protests: Proctors Say No," *Oxford Mail,* April 27, 1967.

116. "Cherwell Ban: Students Hand in Ultimatum," *Daily Express,* October 18, 1967, 4; "Students on Parade" *Sketch,* October 21, 1967, 7; "Protest Meeting and March," October 1967, folder PR1/23/26/1, Duke Humfrey's Library.

EPILOGUE

1. http://literature.britishcouncil.org/linton-kwesi-johnson, accessed June 2014; Linton Kwesi Johnson, interview by Anne-Marie Angelo, London, August 2, 2011 (courtesy of Anne-Marie Angelo).

2. Obi Egbuna, *Destroy This Temple: The Voice of Black Power in Britain* (London, 1971), 16.

3. Tony Soares, interview by Anne-Marie Angelo, London, July 22, 2011, courtesy of Anne-Marie Angelo.

4. Robin Bunce and Paul Field, *Darcus Howe: A Political Biography* (London, 2013), 25.

5. Darcus Howe, "This Month We Have Been Celebrating the History of Black Social Achievement in Britain. In Contrast to the States, Little Social Change Has Been Effected, and Never by Mass Action," *New Statesman,* October 25, 1996, 9. See, too, Anne-Marie Angelo, "The Black Panthers in London, 1968–1972: A Diasporic Struggle Navigates the Black Atlantic," *Radical History Review* 103 (2009): 17–35.

6. Steve Bradley, "New Plaque Marks the Day Malcolm X Visited Smethwick," *Birmingham Mail,* February 22, 2012; Sitala Peek, "Smethwick Malcolm X Plaque 'Timely Reminder' Post Riots," *BBC News,* February 21, 2012 (available at www.bbc.com/news/uk-england -birmingham-17112209).

7. Oxford University Student Union (OUSU), "The 2014 Student Race Survey: Statistical Findings," March 2014, 4.

8. Darcus Howe, interview with Fiona Armstrong, BBC television, August 9, 2011.

9. See Robin Kelley, "Introduction," *The Other Special Relationship* (Basingstoke: forthcoming).

10. Bradley, "New Plaque"; Peek, "Smethwick Malcolm X Plaque."

11. Campaign for Racial Awareness and Equality (CRAE), "The 100 Voices Campaign 2: Black and Minority Ethnic Students of Oxford Speak Out," 2012; author interview with Brian Kwoba, May 15, 2014.

12. OUSU, "2014 Student Race Survey"; CRAE, "100 Voices Campaign 2"; CRAE Race Equality Summit, Note of final plenary summary, March 10, 2014 (copy in author's possession); author interviews with Michael Joseph and Shakina Chinedu, April 10, 2014.

13. Joseph interview.

14. See, e.g., "Rev Jesse Jackson Hits Out at Oxford-Cambridge Admissions," *BBC News Oxford,* December 3, 2013, available at www.bbc.com/news/uk-england-oxfordshire-25205251.

15. Author interview with student (anonymous), April 4, 2014.

INDEX

Abrahams, Eric Anthony
  (Tony), 115, 132, *photo section*;
  appointments and positions
  held by, 93, 95, 114–15, 189, 195;
  arrival at Oxford University,
  96; background, xi, 94–96;
  BBC and, xi, 100, 189;
  characterizations of, 96–97;
  as debater, 115; educational
  achievement, 96–97; elected
  president of Oxford Union,
  93, 97–99, 115; gender equality,
  women's liberation, and, 113,
  114, 188; Humphrey Berkeley
  and, 143; introduction of
  speakers, 143, 154; JACARI
  and, 101; Jamaica and, xi, 94,
  96, 100, 112, 122, 189; James
  Douglas-Hamilton and, 126;
  Judith Okley and, 114, 140;
  leadership, 95; Louis Nthenda
  and, 100; on Malcolm X, 100,
  154; Malcolm X and, 115, 139, 140,
  163, 186, *photo section*; Malcolm
  X invited to Oxford Union by,

  xi, 93, 138, 139, 145, 183 (*see also
  under* Oxford Union debate[s]);
  Malcolm X on, 139; Malcolm
  X's Oxford Union speech and,
  138, 139, 142, 143, 145–47, 183;
  overview, xi, 95–97; Oxford
  student union and, 127; Oxford
  Union and, 95, 114–15 (*see also*
  Oxford Union: a Jamaican
  and the); Oxford University
  Conservative Association
  and, 123–25; personal goals,
  95, 97; personality, 125; police
  encounters, 122–24; proctors,
  protesting, and, 122–27, 132, 195;
  selection of speakers for Oxford
  Union debate, 99–100; Solomon
  Bandaranaike and, 115; speeches,
  97–98, 143–44; student demands
  for civil liberties and, 195;
  student sit-in movement and,
  95; Tariq Ali and, 98, 99; Union
  debates and, 97–98; University
  College of the West Indies and,
  94–95; views, 100, 120